Identity Matters

IDENTITY MATTERS

Ethnic and Sectarian Conflict

Edited by

James L. Peacock, Patricia M. Thornton,
and Patrick B. Inman

Berghahn Books
NEW YORK • OXFORD

Published in 2007 by
Berghahn Books

www.berghahnbooks.com

Library of Congress Cataloging-in-Publication Data

Identity matters : ethnic and sectarian conflict / edited by James L. Peacock, Patricia
M. Thornton, and Patrick B. Inman.
    p. cm.
    Includes bibliographical references and index.
    ISBN 1-84545-308-5 (hardcover : alk. paper) — ISBN 1-84545-311-5 (pbk. : alk.
paper)
        1. Group identity. 2. Social conflict. 3. Ethnic conflict. 4. Collective behav-
ior. I. Peacock, James L. II. Thornton, Patricia M. III. Inman, Patrick B.

HM753.I354 2007
305.8—dc22

2006100367

British Library Cataloguing in Publication Data

A catalogue record for this book is available from
the British Library.

Printed in the United States on acid-free paper

CONTENTS

ILLUSTRATIONS

Figures

Tables

ACKNOWLEDGMENTS

We are pleased to acknowledge the help of many parties. The Fulbright New Century Scholars Program brought us together in 2003 to discuss ethnic, sectarian, and cultural conflict under the chairmanship of Professor Edward Tiryakian of Duke University, and supported our individual fieldwork and survey research. We are most grateful to the staff of Fulbright, especially Micaela Iovine and Patti Peterson, to Ed, and to the other NCS Program participants for enlightening conversations on many of the topics included in this volume, to the United States Institute of Peace, which hosted a discussion of the results of our research, and to the public for their comments. In drawing together the materials, we were aided by the staffs of the University Center for International Studies and the Department of Anthropology at the University of North Carolina at Chapel Hill and the librarians of UNC-Chapel Hill and Duke University. The National Humanities Center, directed by Geoffrey Harpham and Kent Mullikan, provided an opportunity for writing and revision.

Vivian and Marion Berghahn were supportive from the moment we first discussed the project with them. Charles Tilly read the entire manuscript and provided extensive, helpful comments. Ruth Homrighaus's timely, reliable copyediting rescued us when the manuscript was first submitted. Adam Brill transformed the mathematical diagrams into publishable illustrations quickly and painstakingly. Melissa Spinelli and Michael Dempsey planned and managed the production process. Shawn Kendrick copyedited and typeset the entire book after revisions were complete, lending consistency to our use of English and clarity to our arguments. Elizabeth Martin drafted the index. Any errors that remain are, of course, our own.

Finally, we thank Belinda, Florence, and Thomas for their unstinting support and appreciation.

CONTRIBUTORS

Drs. Peacock and Thornton co-chaired the "Identity Matters" group of Fulbright New Century Scholars for 2002–2003. With the exception of Patrick Inman and Wee Teng Soh, all of the contributors to this volume are Fulbright 2002–2003 New Century Scholars. More information on our work together is available at the Fulbright Web site (http://www.cies.org/NCS/NCS_II.htm) and at the United States Institute of Peace Web site (http://www.usip.org/events/2003/1119_WKSethnic_conflict.html).

Badeng Nima is a Tibetan, a Professor at the Southwest University of China, and Professor and Dean of the Faculty of Education at Sichuan Normal University in China. He has been a visiting scholar at the University of Hong Kong, the University of Tromsø, the University of Oslo, the Institute of Education, University of London, and the University of Washington. His publications include *The Echo of Modernization: Ambo Tibet Development Study* (2005), *Civilization's Puzzle—the Way of Tibetan School Education* (2000), *Tibetan Education on the Basis of Their Culture* (1998), "The Poverty, Structure and Development in the Ethnic Areas of Sichuan of China" (1998), and "The Way Out for Tibetan Education" (1997).

David Brown is Associate Professor in Politics and International Studies at Murdoch University, Western Australia. He taught previously at the National University of Singapore, the University of Birmingham, UK, and Ahmadu Bello University in Nigeria. His publications include *Contemporary Nationalism: Civic, Ethnocultural and Multicultural Politics* (2000), and *The State and Ethnic Politics in Southeast Asia* (1994).

Kwanchewan Buadaeng is a researcher at the Social Research Institute of Chiang Mai University, Chiang Mai, Thailand, who has long worked in the area of research and development among the Karen and other highland ethnic groups of Northern Thailand. Her published works include *Buddhism, Christianity* *and the Ancestors: Religion and Pragmatism in a Skaw Karen Community of North Thailand* (2003), and "Khuba Movements and the Karen in Northern Thailand: Negotiating Sacred Space and Identity" (2002).

Patrick B. Inman is a freelance academic editor and independent historian. He did the bulk of the editing for this project, working with the contributors to shape their separate research projects into a cohesive study. With Dr. Peacock, he co-authored a draft consensus document for the "Identity Matters" group prior to its plenary discussions in November 2003. He and Dr. Peacock revised that essay to serve as the conclusion to this volume.

Karina V. Korostelina is an Associate Professor at the Institute for Conflict Analysis and Resolution, George Mason University, and a Fellow of the European Research Centre on Migration and Ethnic Relations (ERCOMER). She has received grants from more than twenty foundations and institutions in the United States and Europe. Her recent publications include *Identity, Morality and Threat*, edited with Daniel Rothbart (2006), "National Identity Formation and Conflict Intentions" (2006), "The Impact of National Identity on Conflict Behavior: Comparative Analysis of Two Ethnic Minorities in Crimea" (2004), and "The Multiethnic State-Building Dilemma" (2003).

James L. Peacock is Kenan Professor of Anthropology and Professor of Comparative Literature at the University of North Carolina at Chapel Hill. He is immediate past director of the University Center for International Studies and is co-director of the Rotary Center for International Studies in Peace and Conflict Resolution at UNC–Chapel Hill and Duke University. His fieldwork includes studies of proletarian culture in Surabaja, Indonesia, of Muslim fundamentalism in Southeast Asia, and of Primitive Baptists in Appalachia. He was President of the American Anthropological Association from 1993–1995. In 1995, he was inducted into the American Academy of Arts and Sciences. The American Anthropological Association awarded him the Boas Award in 2002. His publications include include *Grounded Globalism* (2007), *The Anthropological Lens* (1986, 2001), *Pilgrims of Paradox* (1989), and *Rites of Modernization* (1968, 1987).

Thomas F. Pettigrew is Research Professor of Social Psychology at the University of California, Santa Cruz. Specializing in intergroup relations throughout his career, he has conducted intergroup research in Australia, Europe, and South Africa, in addition to North America. He served as President of the Society for the Psychological Study of Social Issues from 1967 to 1968 and in 1987 received the Society's Gordon Allport Intergroup Research and Kurt Lewin Awards. In 1978, the American Sociological Association gave him the Sydney Spivack Award for Race Relations Research. In 2002, the Society for Experimental Social Psychology presented him with its Distinguished Scientist Award. His publications include hundreds of articles and books, including

"A Meta-Analytic Test of Intergroup Contact Theory" (2006), *How to Think Like a Social Scientist* (1996), *The Sociology of Race Relations* (1980), and *Racial Discrimination in the U.S.* (1975).

Wee Teng Soh is a doctoral candidate in anthropology at the University of North Carolina at Chapel Hill. Her previous research on Singapore looked at the cultural politics and poetics of everyday language and identity contestation between state and civil society. She is currently working on her PhD project on the political ecology of the organic agriculturalists' movement in Tamil Nadu, South India.

Hamadou Tidiane Sy is a freelance journalist based in Dakar, Senegal. He works for several international news organizations, including the BBC and the South Africa-based Media24 Group. From 1997 to 2004, he worked for the third-largest global news agency, Agence France Presse (AFP), in Dakar. He has a Higher Degree in Journalism (1992) from the School of Communications in Senegal (Centre d'Etudes des Sciences et Techniques de l'Information, CESTI), which has produced a number of the leading French-speaking journalists in Africa. He contributed to Transparency International's *Global Corruption Report 2001*.

Patricia M. Thornton is an Associate Professor of Political Science at Trinity College in Hartford, CT, where she has also served as Director of Asian Programs and Coordinator of the East Asian Studies Program. Her expertise is in Chinese politics, political corruption, and popular contention. She has been a Fulbright Fellow in Taiwan and a Post-doctoral Fellow at Harvard University's Fairbank Center for East Asian Research. Her recent publications include *Disciplining the State: Virtue, Violence, and State-Making in Modern China* (2007), "Syncretic Sects in Contemporary China: Old Wine in New Bottles?" (2nd ed., 2003), "Framing Dissent in Contemporary China: Irony, Ambiguity and Metonymy" (2002), "Insinuation, Insult and Invective: The Thresholds of Power and Protest in Modern China" (2002), and "Beneath the Banyan Tree: Bottom-Up Views of Local Taxation and the State during the Republican and Reform Eras" (1999).

Mohammad Waseem is Professor of Political Science at Lahore University of Management Sciences (LUMS). He formerly chaired the Department of International Relations of Quaid-i-Azam University in Islamabad. He held the Pakistan chair at St Anthony's College Oxford for four years and has served as the team leader of research projects sponsored by the Department for International Development, London, and the United Nations Development Programme, Islamabad. His recent publications include *Democratization in Pakistan* (2006), "Sectarian Conflict in Pakistan" (2001), and "Ethnic Conflict in Pakistan" (1999).

In memory of Rodney Needham, officer in the 1st Gurkha Rifles,
veteran of the 1944 Burma campaign, professor of social anthropology,
fellow of All Souls College, Oxford University,
esteemed friend and inspiration
1923–2006

INTRODUCTION
Identity Matters

Patricia M. Thornton

In February 2003, as news of American military operations in Afghanistan was giving way to speculation in the press about the looming invasion of Iraq, a multidisciplinary group of thirty-one scholars gathered in Pocantico, NY, to consider the continuing problem of sectarian, ethnic, and cultural conflict around the world. Brought together under the auspices of the Fulbright Foundation's recently inaugurated New Century Scholars Program, the participants were actively engaged in individual research projects pertaining to the larger theme of political conflict from a broad range of perspectives. During the course of the program year, the New Century Scholars came together as a group on three separate occasions to exchange ideas and information, to discuss and update one another on the progress of individual research projects, and to participate in collaborative activities in smaller working groups, each one addressing a particular theme within the larger field of conflict studies. This book represents one such effort, a partial record of what has been a long, complex, and open-ended conversation about the role of identity in creating, averting, and assuaging conflict.

Our working group originally formed at the Pocantico conference as a loose caucus of New Century Scholars with a particular interest in the issue of identity as it pertains to conflict. The participants included a Hungarian historian, a Senegalese journalist, a Tibetan educational scholar, social psychologists from Ukraine and the United States, Thai and American anthropologists, and political scientists from Australia, Latvia, Pakistan, and the US.[1] Our individual research projects not only spanned the globe but also were arrayed in degrees of discord, including cases in which long-term simmering conflicts had been successfully contained and even resolved; areas in which deadly riots, civil wars, and secessionist movements threatened to destroy the social fabric; and contexts in which widespread violence might have been expected to erupt yet failed to materialize. We also differed significantly in our methodological orientations, with some of us relying primarily upon survey data, some on texts housed in historical archives, and others almost solely on ethnographic interviews. Our hope was that these vast differences in experience, outlook, and training, when brought to bear on a single issue, would shed some new and helpful light on the problem of ethnic and sectarian violence.

Over the course of our program year, in face-to-face meetings and through electronic communication, we prodded, probed, and challenged one another to define and refine our ideas about the nature of identity and its relationship to social conflict. The chapters that follow can be read as a rough-hewn map of our collective intellectual journey, which originated with the shared agreement that the two main approaches commonly found in the literature on conflict and identity were wanting. These approaches are, first, that primordial group ties may give rise to conflicts that are intractable, irrational, and susceptible to being suppressed but never fully resolved; and, second, that while such conflicts may appear on the surface to be driven by ancestral religious or ethnic hatred, most internecine violence is fueled by economics. Primordialists posit that unlike class and interest group conflicts, cultural conflicts have a peculiarly intensive, affective, or emotional nature because they touch on a particular type of identity. As a result, primordialists frequently view the continuing violent "clash of civilizations" as inevitable.[2] "Instrumentalist" or "economic opportunity" models, by contrast, are predicated upon the notion that the interests of the self, rather than the identity of the self, are at the core of collective disputes (Berdal and Keen 1997; Keen 1998). The range of our cases—which include ethnic and sectarian identities with long and established collective histories, as well as groups that are only just beginning to emerge—pushed us beyond primordialist models that portray conflict as the result of age-old animosities. With respect to instrumentalist models, we agreed that while economic factors can certainly exacerbate pre-existing tensions, not all intercommunal conflicts are essentially rivalries for scarce resources that employ ethnic, sectarian, or cultural divisions as tools for the pursuit of underlying economic goals. Our individual research clearly demonstrated that identity—apart from interest—does matter, although not always in ways that are easily quantifiable and readily processed by statistical models designed to predict and control for a variety of outcomes.

The concept of "identity" is hotly contested, not only within contemporary politics, but within scholarly discourse as well. In a semantic history of the concept, Gleason (1983: 930–931) laments that within three decades of its introduction to the social-scientific vocabulary in the 1950s, the fact that "the term can be legitimately employed in an number of ways" invited its slapdash application by scholars, quickly transforming this "ubiquitous and elusive" term into "a cliché.... [I]ts meaning grew progressively more diffuse, thereby encouraging increasingly loose and irresponsible usage. The depressing result is that a good deal of what passes for discussion of identity is little more than portentous incoherence." More recently, Brubaker and Cooper (2000: 1) argue that the term "tends to mean too much (when understood in a strong sense), too little (when understood in a weak sense), or nothing at all (because of its sheer ambiguity)." Accordingly, they propose for the sake of conceptual clarity that the term be abandoned altogether in social analysis. While as a group we also encountered considerable difficulty with the concept in our collective deliberations and individual research projects, we agreed with Charles Tilly (2002: xiii; 2005: 209), who proposed instead "that we get identity right."[3]

We soon recognized that moving beyond this rudimentary consensus would require us to stake out some common ground capable of anchoring our collective deliberations. At our second face-to-face meeting in Belfast, we began by laying out a common framework upon which to build. Jim Peacock, the leader of our working group, put together a series of queries designed to elucidate areas of agreement between us, as well as key points of contention for our group as a whole. His questions focused on five issues fundamental to our collective research. First, we strove to clarify our individual working definitions of ethnic and sectarian identity in ways that seemed useful to both our individual research projects and our collective discussions. Second, we sifted through those concepts as a group in order to assess the conceptual strengths and weaknesses of our working definitions, highlighting the core characteristics of the terms in our common vocabulary. Third, we reflected on those circumstances under which multiple identities seemed to co-exist without violence, looking for common trends among those cases. Fourth, we also compared cases in which the tensions between identities seemed to fuel violence, again searching for patterns among them. Finally, we considered how such violence might be stopped: what types of intervention might have an impact, at which point(s) in the cycle, and to what end.

David Brown, a political scientist who has written extensively on the related problems of ethnic identity, conflict, and nationalism, bravely volunteered to draft a document that would reflect the majoritarian trends in our collected answers to these core questions. His initial draft, produced midway through our program year, served as a touchstone document for our working group members as we headed out to the field to pursue our individual research projects. From our various locations, as our research unfolded, we continued to challenge, embroider upon, and test the limits of his model, a fuller and more nuanced version of which appears in his chapter in this volume.

This early draft—which we collectively referred to as our "manifesto"—drew conceptual distinctions between various forms of nesting identities, proposing that while ethnic and religious identities rely upon myths of common kinship/ancestry and "cultural sameness," civic or political identities "rely instead upon visions of a common future." The document noted that the existence of multiple overlapping or intertwining identities inhibits collective violence and promotes social cohesion; however, particularly intense conflicts of interest pressure individuals with diverse, fluid identities to valorize their loyalty to one interactive community over another, prompting social fragmentation into mutually antagonistic identity-communities. The successful resolution of such conflicts, we theorized, ultimately rests not in elaborately crafted power-sharing arrangements, but rather in the depolarization and reintertwining of identities.

Yet even as our draft "manifesto" served to highlight common ground among us, it also revealed key differences between our projects and perspectives. First, it quickly became clear that our case studies were evenly divided into studies of identities currently in conflict, on the one hand, and those in which conflict had been kept at bay, on the other. Thus, our collective deliberations stretched to include, for example, the causes of separatist movements in southern Senegal and the Thai-Burmese border, as well as the relatively pacific polities of contemporary Germany and Singapore. Second, while ethnic and sectarian identities emerged in some of our cases primarily as elective systems of personal affiliation, in other contexts, highly politicized stereotypes or labels were coercively imposed on individuals and groups who might have sought to define themselves rather differently, if given the power to do so. This division had important implications, not only for our collective understanding of how social identities worked at the individual level, but also for the relations of power that enveloped them. Finally, whereas our original draft drew no firm distinction between ethnic and sectarian identities, those of us researching movements that were distinguished at least in part by their religious beliefs or spiritual practices argued that such cases were shaped by very different sets of dynamics. Much of our subsequent discussion centered on these divides and on coming to terms with the limits imposed by our "manifesto."

Many of the core elements that appear in this initial draft document are further elaborated and refined by David Brown in his contribution, the first chapter of this volume. In his own work, Brown proposes that while three distinct but intertwining types of national identity ("civic," "ethnocultural," and "multiculturalist") hold nation-states together, it is the "civic" conception of the nation-state as a moral community that performs the crucial role of the buffer between the other two, thereby mitigating the potential for ethnic conflict. These overlapping visions of national identity may become disentwined, he argues, when the disparate interactive communities that comprise the nation-state are disrupted by any number of factors and incumbent elites are no longer able to maintain their legitimacy. When such interactive communities begin to ideologize the source of such disruptions, Brown notes, overarching civic attachments may erode, raising the likelihood of overt ethnic conflict.

In his response to the group "manifesto," social psychologist Tom Pettigrew chose to focus on the meaning of ethnic identity at the individual level. Defining identity as "those aspects of the self-concept that derive from an individual's knowledge and feelings about the group memberships the person shares with others," he explores survey data on prejudice and discrimination against immigrants in the European Union, using rigorous statistical analysis. Like Brown, Pettigrew envisions social identity as potentially comprising several nested levels of affiliation: membership in a minority or majority group, citizenship in the nation-state, and an overarching identification as a citizen of the European Union. His research in chapter 2 correlates more inclusive identities with higher levels of tolerance and lower levels of overt violence, suggesting that more universalistic identities (like those described in Brown's chapter as "civic nationalism") serve to blunt the negative effects of narrower forms of nationalism. In chapter 5, Pettigrew reconciles the research of political scientists, which shows that as the threat posed by an out-group population to an in-group increases (presumably as its numbers increase), prejudice against the out-group increases, with the findings of social psychologists, which demonstrate that contact between groups (which also presumably increases with population) reduces prejudice. His research reminds us that much has been learned about the patterns of prejudice in the last half-century: some means of defusing intergroup distrust, such as integration in housing, the workplace, and everyday activities, are now known to be effective, notwithstanding apparent paradoxes.

Karina Korostelina, also a social psychologist and the author of chapter 3, offered the most voluntaristic definition of identity, arguing that it was both the "function and result of choice: in the world of different 'social offers' of political, ethnic, national, and sectarian identities, people can choose the most useful or attractive one." Combining a method similar to Pettigrew's with a conceptual framework that bears some resemblance to Brown's, she employs surveys to measure how the readiness to fight associated with a salient ethnic identity is affected by the ways in which members of two competing ethnic minorities in the Crimea understand Ukraine's national identity. She finds that Crimean Tartars, a relatively small minority whose historical collective experience is rooted in the multiethnic Ottoman Empire, are more accepting of the dominant position of other groups within the contemporary Ukrainian state. The more numerous and powerful ethnic Russians, by contrast, expect to maintain the level of ethnic dominance they historically exercised in both Crimea and Ukraine. Like Brown and Pettigrew, Korostelina concurs that the widespread adoption of a more inclusive, civic concept of group identity may reduce the potential for conflict in Crimea and Ukraine, but she also discusses two other ways of thinking about the nation, one which seems to increase the belligerence of powerful minorities and decrease the aggressiveness of weak minorities, and another associated with readiness for violence among weak groups and less inclination for conflict among stronger ones.

Kwanchewan Buadaeng's chapter traces the remarkably fluid identity of a single ethnic group that spans an international border. Her research illustrates how the historical processes of colonization and modernization in Burma and Thailand produced very different identities among the speakers of Karenic languages and their descendants in the two states. In Thailand, 440,000 Karen are but one of several "hill tribes" who subsist in relatively simple and isolated rural communities. By contrast, the roughly four million Burmese Karen have mobilized a military force that has waged a secessionist war against the central state for about five decades. Buadaeng finds that the dissimilar manners in which Burmese and Thai state elites sought to construct unique Karen identities allowed the Karen different opportunities to contest national identity and jockey for higher collective status, and created different, new symbolic spaces within which Karen leaders have acted politically. Citing Appadurai's (2000: 162) observation that "nationalism and ethnicity ... feed each other, as nationalists construct ethnic categories that in turn drive others to construct counterethnicities, and then in times of political crisis these others demand counterstates based on newfound counternationalisms," she shows how, over time, the ethnic identity of the Karen has interacted with and reacted to the respective nation-building processes of Burma and Thailand.

Buadaeng's chapter marks a shift in our collective research to address the question of ethnic and sectarian identities that are at least partially constructed by a dominant group and then imposed upon another. This theme is developed more fully in chapter 6, written by Badeng Nima, who conducted a series of interviews among Tibetans living in western China. The responses he received to a range of questions regarding the current social, economic, and political situation of the Tibetan people revealed considerable collective concern about the manner in which the Chinese educational system has undermined the Tibetans' status as an ethnic minority within the People's Republic of China (PRC). Economic opportunities are generally afforded to those ethnic Tibetans who complete mandatory schooling, but the existing curriculum structurally recognizes only the interests and beliefs of the majority Han Chinese. Badeng describes some of the more recent educational innovations that have attempted to make space in the curriculum for traditional Tibetan cultural beliefs. He concludes, however, that such practices remain the exception in the PRC rather than the rule, and that current policies continue to exert serious social and political strain on traditional Tibetan communities.

By contrast, the Singaporean state has been more successful at negotiating the delicate balance required to craft public policy that is multicultural by design. In chapter 7, Jim Peacock and Wee Teng Soh observe that although Singapore's governing People's Action Party has attempted to standardize both ethnicity and religion—essentializing their qualities into something measurable, manageable, and therefore less frightening than the threat posed by Singapore's majority Muslim, majority Malay, poorer neighbors to its richer economy and its very mixed but majority Confucian, Buddhist, and ethnic Chinese population—harmony may be more the result of organic interaction than of social engineering. Like patches of crabgrass (though perhaps a better analogy would be wildflowers) disrupting a manicured lawn, ethnic mixes, religious movements, and art projects flourish in a society famed for its regularity and conformity.

Whereas the case of Singapore represents social harmony by (or, Peacock and Soh suggest, despite) bureaucratic design, Hamadou Tidiane Sy, a Senegalese journalist, explores the evolution of a separatist movement in his country through the interweaving of cultural, ethnic, and economic interests. Despite extensive field research among the rebel groups of the Casamance region, the cause of the insurrection, even the moment that the conflict started, is unclear. In chapter 8, Sy traces several possibilities and discusses how Senegalese came to speak of the region—and of one of its many ethnic groups, the Diola—as rebellious by nature. While there are differences, as well as a history of discrimination, the question remains, why did this group but not another develop a distinct collective identity and begin a decades-long armed struggle against the central Senegalese state? Sy finds that in the midst of ongoing secessionist conflict, the Diola identity that emerged can be described neither as "primordial" nor "constructed," but rather as the ideologized, politicized result of a process he refers to as "identitism." Identity, once set in motion, can take on a life of its own, and war in particular can deepen divisions between people who were once neighbors.

In chapter 9, my research on *qigong* sects in contemporary China raises similar issues about the creation of sectarian identities that are imposed by central-state officials who seek to control and eliminate social practices deemed undesirable. While the quasi-spiritual practice of *qigong* enjoyed unprecedented popularity in the PRC during the 1990s, once groups of practitioners began to press for political recognition, Chinese authorities reacted by branding such groups "evil heretical sects" and marginalizing their members. As the crackdown widened and intensified in 1999, the process of violent repression served to craft new sectarian identities among those who continued to practice Chinese *qigong*. The group commonly known as Falun Gong responded to such pressures by retreating to the Internet, where they managed to construct a viable community of faith in virtual reality. From their base in cyberspace, Falun Gong practitioners continue their struggle to maintain and reshape their own collective identity, contesting official representations of the group as inherently subversive. In this case, a sectarian identity created by central-state officials and coercively imposed upon a target population has spurred a transnational social movement—under the guise of what I refer to as "cybersectarianism"—that actively seeks to undermine state authority.[4]

A rather different transnational sectarian effort is described in the final case study. In chapter 10, Mohammad Waseem contends that Western nations have invoked a discourse of difference that has reified Islam as utterly alien by emphasizing classical Islamic religious texts over the contemporary social context, by conflating religion and politics, and by assuming that religious identity is inherently primordial, never instrumental. His research on Pakistan demonstrates that it is the modern ruling elite in that country that has engaged, mobilized, promoted, co-opted, and strengthened the religious establishment so as to exclude mainstream liberal forces from political power. In Pakistan,

Waseem argues, religious identities are balanced by other types of identity, some of which are rooted in exchange networks, the mutual recognition of common law and property rights, and even dissent against authority. He proposes that the adoption of specific policies would broaden the participation of heretofore silenced groups and reinvigorate a constitutional tradition inherited from Britain.

In the conclusion, Pat Inman and Jim Peacock return to an issue debated by the group at length: how do religious identities differ? Their response, based on the insights of Max Weber and the social philosopher Charles Taylor, moves in a very different direction from that of Brown, whose opening chapter suggests that winner-take-all ethnocentrism, divide-the-spoils multiculturalism, and principled civic nationalism compete for the loyalties of citizens and control of the state. Inman and Peacock begin by asking, what is identity? They answer, with Taylor, that it is at root an orientation to good, a moral framework that is acquired like language in childhood, requires dialogue with others to persist, and defines communities much as do languages or other markers of culture. Asserting that the core problem is to facilitate communication between identity groups, they propose that ethnic and sectarian identities—instead of being set aside as marginal to the modern world, as irrational primordial remnants to be superceded by civic virtue—can function as Weberian ideal types. These types provide a basis for the analytical comparison of the aspirations and horizons of identity-based groups and serve as a heuristic device to direct our attention to important clues concerning the ways in which collective violence may be triggered or intergroup accommodation may be reached.

I should say a word about a chapter that is missing from this book. Balázs Szelényi was a key participant in our group's discussions. An essay he shared with us on the historical dimensions of ethnic identity among three German minority groups in the Austro-Hungarian Empire—the Saxons, the Zipsers, and the Schwabs—helped us all think about the mixture of choice and destiny that gives birth to identity (Szelényi forthcoming). He traced the respective passages of these groups through German democratization in the late nineteenth century and their reactions to the rise of National Socialism. The Saxons, he demonstrated, strove to maintain a distinct cultural and sectarian identity within the empire; the Zipsers, by contrast, voluntarily abandoned their native dialect to become better citizens of the Magyar polity; and the linguistic diversity among the Schwabs frustrated the emergence of a unique collective identity until the founding of the German state. These rather different conceptions of belonging presented Nazi authorities with a wide range of issues as they sought to incorporate these three distinct ethnic experiences under the umbrella of National Socialism. Szelényi found that while the "triangular configuration" for each of these ethnic groups had an impact on their collective responses to Nazification, it was the socioeconomic status of each group within the host country that was most decisive.[5] His discussion of this case influenced the development of several essays in this book, and his efforts as the Webmaster of our group's discussion board allowed us to work together in spite of being spread across four continents.

Despite the complex differences that divided the members of our working group, it is worth noting that some broad patterns of agreement emerge in our case studies. Three possible relationships between collective identity and conflict are reflected in our research. First, some of our cases explore sub- or transnational ethnic and sectarian divides that undermine national and civic identities, leading to the breakdown of national unities. This pattern is first described in general terms in Brown's chapter. In such cases, we found that the evolution of particularistic ethnic or sectarian affiliations can fuel regional or civil wars that pull nations apart from the inside, but often involve agents or forces operating largely from beyond national borders. Similar dynamics are noted by Sy in his chapter on the Casamance conflict in southern Senegal, as well as by Waseem in his study on the emergence of radical Islam in Pakistan.

A second pattern finds that nation-states can and do construct and impose identities from above. Buadaeng, for example, explores how Burmese and Thai elites applied very different understandings of group identity to the Karen peoples that inhabit their shared border region, setting in motion a process by which the Karen have redefined themselves rather differently in each state. In some of our case studies, authorities use identity markers to selectively mobilize state forces against their own subject populations, defining target groups from within their midst in an attempt to control, subdue, or even eliminate specific types of people. As reported in my chapter on *qigong* sect members in contemporary China, I found that state officials selectively labeled certain practices and beliefs as "feudal superstition" and then as "evil heretical sects," finally outlawing certain groups and targeting their members for punitive treatment. In such cases, while group identities may undermine national unities, the nation-state emerges less as a victim of separatist impulses and more as the primary instigator of social violence.

Finally, it is important to stress that our collective research finds evidence that not all ethnic, sectarian, and political memberships cause conflict. A third pattern that emerges in our collective work demonstrates that some collective identities can actually reduce conflicts instead of triggering them. For example, Pettigrew's survey research, conducted in Germany, finds that a strong personal identification as a citizen of the European Union correlates with lower levels of prejudice against out-group members. Karina Korostelina finds similar connections between the prevalence of multiple, nested identities and low levels of intergroup conflict in Crimea.

The case studies assembled in this volume impart two lessons for those interested in understanding how and why collective violence emerges from ethnic, sectarian, and cultural divides. First, as a group we were struck at how deeply imbricated the processes of social violence and social identity often are, as well as how multifaceted the connections may be. While some identities may indeed reduce conflict, others clearly incite, foster, and sustain protracted conflicts in ways that merit further exploration. We conclude, therefore, that there is no single, simple, modular connection between identity and violence. It is perhaps only by close observation on the ground, carried out by researchers deeply situated in the linguistic, cultural, and geographic contexts of violent and potentially violent situations, that the contours of a broader understanding can begin to emerge. And when it does, we believe that a careful attention to shifting identity issues in context can uncover markers of escalating or declining levels of political violence that may suggest potential avenues and opportunities for intervention.

Second, our collective research is driven by the shared conviction that while economic, political, and geographic factors certainly play contributing roles in violent conflicts, identity is not wholly reducible to any one factor, or any set combination of factors, and is therefore worthy of consideration in its own right. A bottom-up grassroots examination of violent and potentially conflict-ridden situations shows that, indeed, identity matters—and that it matters profoundly to those most immediately affected by social violence. Whereas much of the literature on the subject of ethnic, sectarian, and cultural conflict is predicated upon the notion that violent conflict represents an aberration in social and political life, we propose that conflict is not extraordinary but instead grows out of the more quotidian practices and ordinary behaviors that characterize everyday life. As Duffield (1998) noted: "If we wish to examine conflict we must begin by analyzing what is normal. Or at least, those long-term and embedded social processes that define the conditions of everyday life. The purpose and reasons for conflict are located in these processes. From this perspective, political violence is not different, apart or irrational in relation to the way we live: it is an expression of its inner logic." Likewise, we also propose that the seeds of the successful resolution or avoidance of intergroup conflict grow directly from the often mundane conditions of everyday life and the lived experience of individuals inhabiting several interactive communities.

As recent international developments have shown, political action and intervention in conflict situations are most successful when policymakers are able to track back and forth between a broad-based understanding of the few shared themes and patterns present in a variety of cases, while at the same time remaining attentive to the "distinctive" and even "idiosyncratic" features of a particular context in which action or intervention may be required. The totalizing and "world-making" capacities of violence defy any straightforward attempts to reduce them to quantifiable variables in the quest for prediction and control. The inherent flexibility of such a two-pronged approach, while admittedly not easy to codify into a single set of standard operating procedures or action agendas, nonetheless holds more promise for the creation of effective and positive responses tailored to fit the needs of complex and evolving situations.

What we take away from our work together, and what we hope the reader comes to share, is an appreciation for the usefulness of several different approaches to the study of identity and of intergroup violence. Our essays make use of a wide range of disciplinary approaches and methodological tools to explore more fully the complex linkages between conflict and identity. We recommend to policymakers and the citizens and denizens of divided societies alike a similar eclectic, heuristic approach to understanding cultural differences. As our concluding essay argues: "Ethnic and sectarian conflict challenges everyone involved—minorities, majorities, those who control the state and the institutions of civil society. To find ways to resolve such conflicts, it is necessary for all to react creatively, to understand what is at stake for each identity, and to create new identities that bridge yet respect the old, lest mutual distance fuel prejudice and violence."

Notes

1. Our Latvian and Hungarian colleagues are the only group members who did not contribute an essay to this volume. We are grateful to Mihails Rodins for his contributions to our discussions, which deepened our understanding of the sense of identity as defined by social psychology. Balázs Szelényi's contribution is addressed later in this introduction.

2. Clifford Geertz (1973: 259) defined the primordial attachment as "one that stems from the 'givens' ... of social existence: immediate contiguity and kin connection mainly, but beyond them the givenness that stems from being born into a particular religious community, speaking a particular language, or even a dialect of a language, and following particular social practices. These congruities of blood, speech, custom and so on, are seen to have an ineffable, and at times overpowering, coerciveness in and of themselves. One is bound to one's kinsman, one's neighbor, one's fellow believer, ipso facto; as the result not merely of personal affection, practical necessity, common interest, or incurred obligation, but at least in great part by virtue of some unaccountable absolute import attributed to the very tie itself." More recently, Horowitz (2002) has used the term "primordialism" to denote arguments that posit that ethnic bonds are ineffable, explained by a myth of common ancestry—part and parcel of the collective memory of a particular group.

3. Tilly's recent work (2002, 2005) proposes that group identities are best understood by studying their interactions. In the approach he recommends (2002: 72), the focus is on "connections that concatenate, aggregate, and disaggregate readily, form[ing] organizational structures at the same time as they shape individual behavior. Relational analysts follow flows of communication, patron-client chains, employment networks, conversational connections, and power relations from the small scale to the large and back." He suggests that we not "treat identities as characteristics of individual consciousness" but instead define them as a set of relationships and study them in terms of "four components" (2005: 7–9, 209):

    1. a boundary separating me from you or us from them
    2. a set of relations within the boundary
    3. a set of relations *across* the boundary
    4. a set of stories about the boundary and the relations

This method requires a degree of detachment that in most cases was not appropriate to the goals of this book. Our intention was to demonstrate that identity as experienced by Europeans, Tibetans, Singaporeans, Karen, Pakistanis, and others can be a trigger for violence or a bulwark against it, and to suggest means of studying and analyzing those experiences.

This does not mean that relational analysis is unimportant. Both Buadaeng and Thornton make use of it in their case studies. Part and parcel of the scientific study of prejudice from Allport forward, relational analysis is at the heart of several of the nomological approaches to identity that Inman and Peacock discuss in the conclusion. It is also central to their analysis of cultural conflict in terms of ethnic and sectarian ideal types of group identity. If they do not consider any objective approach to the study of cultural conflict sufficient, however, it is because some means of promoting conversation and intersubjectivity that cuts across the boundaries of identities is also required. Their contention on that point mirrors our group's experience of working across the boundaries between disciplines.

4. The Internet has provided both threatened and resurgent identities with symbolic space. For the former, see, for example, the Karen nationalist Web sites cited by Buadaeng. For the latter, and a particularly cogent reflection on how the Internet and human rights discourse interact to alter once-isolated groups, see Niezen (2005).

5. According to Rogers Brubaker (1996), an ethnic minority's position in a given society is largely defined by three interrelated factors: the ethnic minority's relationship to its host country, whether the minority has a home state to defend its interest and the relationship of that group to its home state, and, finally, the relationship between the home state and the host state.

References

Appadurai, Arjun. 2000. *Modernity at Large*. Minnesota: University of Minnesota Press.

Berdal, Mats, and David Keen. 1997. "Violence and Economic Agendas in Civil Wars." *Millennium* 26, no. 3: 804–805.

Brubaker, Rogers. 1996. *Nationalism Reframed: Nationhood and the National Question in the New Europe*. Cambridge: Cambridge University Press.

Brubaker, Rogers, and Frederick Cooper. 2000. "Beyond 'Identity.'" *Theory and Society* 29: 1–47.

Duffield, Mark. 1998. "Post-modern Conflict: Warlords, Post-adjustment States and Private Protection." *Civil Wars* 1, no. 1: 65–102.

Geertz, Clifford. 1973. "The Integrative Revolution: Primordial Sentiments and Civil Politics in the New States." In Geertz, *The Interpretation of Cultures*, 255–310. New York: Basic Books.

Gleason, Philip. 1983. "Identifying Identity: A Semantic History." *Journal of American History* 69, no. 4: 910–931.

Horowitz, Donald L. 2002. "The Primordialists." In *Ethnonationalism in the Contemporary World: Walker Connor and the Study of Nationalism*, ed. Daniele Conversi, 72–82. London: Routledge.

Keen, David. 1998. *The Economic Functions of Violence in Civil Wars*. Adelphi Paper #320. London: Oxford University Press for the International Institute for Strategic Studies.

Niezen, Ronald. 2005. "Digital Identity: The Construction of Virtual Selfhood in the Indigenous Peoples' Movement." *Comparative Studies in Society and History* 47, no. 3: 532–551.

Szelényi, Balázs. Forthcoming. "The German Diaspora of Hungary, Slovakia, and Romania." *Past and Present.*

Tilly, Charles. 2002. *Stories, Identities and Political Change.* Lanham, MD: Rowman and Littlefield.

_____. 2005. *Identities, Boundaries, and Social Ties.* Boulder, CO: Paradigm Publishers.

1

ETHNIC CONFLICT AND CIVIC NATIONALISM
A Model

David Brown

It has frequently been suggested that the appeal of ethnicity and nationalism derives from the sense of security they offer to people experiencing social upheaval. This was at the core of several "modernist" explanations for the rise of nation-states, including the influential arguments of Karl Deutsch and Ernest Gellner. Deutsch (1966: 105) explained how the uprooting and mobilization of traditional societies could engender the transformation "from tribe to nation." Gellner (1983: 63) argued that the shift from agrarian to industrial society meant the "dissipation" of rigid social structures, leaving "very little in the way of an effective, binding organization at any level between the individual and the total community." Individuals are thereby exposed to the stress and "perpetual humiliation" of modern life (Gellner 1996: 626). They thus seek identity in the nation "linked ... both to the state and to the cultural boundary" (Gellner 1983: 63).

A similar anomie argument has also been a frequent theme in the literature on the rise of contemporary ethnic nationalisms, as in Eric Hobsbawm's (1990: 171) argument that "what fuels such defensive reactions, whether against real or imaginary threats, is a combination of internal population movements with the ultra-rapid, fundamental, and unprecedented socio-economic transformations so characteristic of the third quarter of our century." In Anthony Smith's (1981: chap. 5) explanation, concerning both the rise of nation-states and the subsequent ethnonational revival, the significance of the dislocations of community brought about by modernization was to create crises of legitimacy for intellectuals seeking to regenerate these communities—crises that were resolved by nationalisms built on "ethnic historicism." The formulations vary, but the core idea is that the disruption of the interactive communities within which individuals had hitherto found security and moral certainty leads them to seek a reimagined *Gemeinschaft*.

The purpose of this chapter is to revisit this line of argument in order to examine its relevance for an understanding of contemporary ethnic conflicts, and to discuss the relative merits of civic nationalism and ethnic nationalism as candidates for the *Gemeinschaft* role. Ethnic and national consciousnesses have frequently been theorized in "instrumentalist" terms as collective identities employed by groups of individuals to defend their material and power interests against perceived threats. But this view has been supplemented and modified by recent "constructivist" approaches, which depict the *ethnie* and the nation as "moral communities," constructed in the course of social and political interactions in which the moral identity of the Us and the Other is repeatedly redefined (Yeros 1999). Two images emerge from the constructivist literature: the first is of ethnic and national identities in flux and intertwining, as they are repeatedly renegotiated; the second is of ethnic and national identities that become "sticky" and "sedimented over time," acting as ideological blinkers that inhibit the flexibility of identity (Norval 1999: 84).

This essay suggests that such "sticky" ideologization of ethnic and national consciousnesses occurs when interactive communities and their authority structures are disrupted, with the result that displaced or aspiring elites and dislocated masses both become amenable to simplistic moralistic formulas offering absolutist diagnoses to otherwise disorientating changes. The question as to whether this process of nationalistic ideologization leads to ethnic conflict is then seen to depend crucially on the relationships between civic and ethnic nationalisms. The first section outlines a model of the nation-state as built on the intertwining of civic, ethnocultural, and multiculturalist national identities. The second section describes the disentwining of the nation-state so as to trigger conflict between contending ideologies of ethnic nationalism. The third section indicates the potentiality for the resolution of ethnic conflict through a strengthening of the civic "buffer."

Ethnic and Civic National Identities

Individuals tend to identify with the multiple interactive communities that they inhabit and within which their interests are invested. These collective identities, constructed in the course of social interactions, thus refer to various levels of interaction (from local to global) and to differing areas of interaction (e.g., occupational or religious). The tendency to develop multiple identifications with overlapping interactive networks has an instrumental or a functional basis, but is also fostered both by psychological tendencies toward conformism and by the socializing impact of group activities (Tajfel 1981).

The concern here is with those particular types of collective identity that involve attachment to interactive communities clustered around perceived commonalities of religion, race, language, or territorial homeland. The conventional designations for such collective identities need to be initially summarized. The ethnic community is constructed around perceptions of cultural sameness that are assumed, by its members, to derive from a common ancestry. This means that not all linguistic groups comprise ethnic (ethnolinguistic) identity communities, and not all religious groups comprise ethnic (ethnoreligious) identity communities. The terms "race," "religion," "language," and "territory" each refer to potentially observable social attributes (albeit in gradations), while the term "ethnicity" indicates a form of collective consciousness that employs those attributes as the symbolic markers for bounded communities of assumed common ancestry, thereby attributing to them moral significance. Though sometimes claimed as genetic fact, this myth of common ancestry is often accepted as allegory—as a kinship bond assumed to derive from a long history of interactions or, in the case of ethnoreligious communities, from subscription to the idea of a spiritual family founded by some father/mother figures. The significance of the ethnic myth is that it counterposes the relevant racial, religious, linguistic, or territorial collectivity as one ancestral community demarcated from other communities.

The term "nation" is sometimes used simply to substantiate the claim made by an ethnic community that it has the right to autonomous control over its own affairs. But the term is also applied to a state-territorial community (or a putative state) whose members may have diverse racial, religious, and linguistic attributes and places of birth, but who have developed an overarching attachment to the public institutions and the common way of life associated with the territorial state they inhabit, and who have therefore now come to develop significant nonethnic cultural affinities. This second variant of community is the civic community, perceived as built on nonethnic ties such as shared patriotism, similarities of lifestyle, and access to a common media and intelligentsia—and on a shared vision of equal citizenship in the territorial and political residential homeland. It should be noted that there is no assumption here that an attachment to the state will necessarily engender a civic national identity, merely that it might do so. It is quite feasible that loyalty to a state might derive from a perception of the state as the agency of an ethnic nation, but it is equally feasible that national identities can develop in the absence of any ethnic referent.

This distinction between the ethnic nation and the civic nation has sometimes been employed to compare nation-states in terms of their differing social structures (ethnically mixed or ethnically pure) and the differing norms influencing government policies (ethnic-blindness or ethnic bias in favor of the ethnic core). But the ethnic-civic distinction as a basis for descriptive categories is problematical in various ways (Kuzio 2002; Kymlicka 2001; Yack 1999),[1] and it is employed here rather to refer to ideal-type elements in the construction of the national identities of citizens.

There is a rational basis for the moral ideals (ethnically blind equality or the cultural sameness arising from ethnic assimilation) that attach to national identity, in that the rational concern to maximize the interest-benefits of involvement in an interactive community is promoted by the employment of ideals that can be used by citizens as the criteria for evaluating the community's functioning with regard to the pursuit of their interests. Instrumental attachments thus have a normative dimension. This normative aspect to the social construction of ethnic and civic identities can provide the basis for an insightful model of the integrated nation-state (and of its potential disintegration). But this needs an initial modification of the classic civic-ethnic distinction.

It is widely recognized that ethnic majorities have frequently employed the apparatus of nation-states to promote their dominance over ethnic minorities (Connor 1994; Smith 1995). Ethnic conflict has consequently been seen as arising from the state oppression of ethnic minorities and the latter's reactive assertions of autonomy. It has therefore seemed to follow, for many observers, that the resolution or amelioration of ethnic conflict is to be found in the multiculturalist restructuring of existing nation-states, rectifying the bias in favor of the ethnic core by accommodating variously formulated ethnic minority rights (Kymlicka 1995). But this contemporary focus on the ethnic character of the nation-state— as the agency for either ethnic majority domination or for progress toward interethnic justice—constitutes a significant shift from the well-established literature, which sees the nation-state as an agency for the construction of a civic national identity, distinct from both ethnic majority and ethnic minority identities (Deutsch 1966; Gellner 1983; Greenfeld 1992; Miller 1995).

The implication is that the classic distinction between civic and ethnic national identities needs to be refined into a three-fold distinction between the civic, ethnocultural, and multiculturalist ideals of national identity. Thus, civic identity involves the perception of the nation as being built on a distinctive nonethnic national culture into which all citizens ought to be integrating. Ethnocultural national identity involves the perception by citizens that their nation-state is built around an ethnic core community and that ethnic minorities should assimilate into this ethnic core or remain marginalized.[2] Multiculturalist national identity is the perception by citizens that their nation-state is a coalition of ethnic communities held together by a shared vision of progress toward the just allocation (based on agreed-upon ethnic-arithmetic formulae) of power, resources, and rights to its diverse ethnic segments.[3]

The terms "civic," "ethnocultural," and "multiculturalist" are thus used here to denote differing ideals of national identity rather than different types of nation-state.[4] But it would seem reasonable to expect that in the modern world citizens within each nation-state vary in their beliefs as to the normative character of their national community and the collective ideals toward which they consider public policies should be oriented, with some favoring civic integration, others ethnic assimilation, and others interethnic accommodation. Indeed, individuals may well hold all three views concurrently or may hold differing views regarding different aspects of public policy, for example, favoring multiculturalist ideals for policies on religion, civic ideals for civil and criminal law, and ethnocultural ideals for state education.

Moreover, it cannot be assumed that all members of ethnic minority communities will favor the multiculturalist vision, while all members of ethnic majority communities will favor the ethnocultural vision. It seems to be something of a hallmark of many contemporary nation-states that their citizens (from ethnic core and ethnic minority backgrounds alike) are presently in a state of some confusion as to whether to espouse ideals of ethnic blindness, ethnic assimilation, or interethnic accommodation.[5]

But the co-existence of these diverse ideas of national identity within each nation-state does not necessarily generate disunity and conflict. Rather, it might be this very co-existence that promotes the cohesion of the nation-state.[6] Modernization theorists used to employ an ideal-type model of the nation-state as characterized by normative consensus; in this view, the nation-state was one community whose political cohesion arose from a shared national identity. But normative consensus is not necessary. All that is needed, as John Rawls (1993) indicated, is an "overlapping consensus." Rawls used this phrase to refer to a minimal agreement by all parties in an ethnically diverse society on some basic "rules of the game." However, it might also be modified to refer to the overlapping and interweaving of divergent visions of national identity. Individuals frequently proclaim that they hold ideals of ethnic-blindness, interethnic accommodation, and assimilation without any seeming awareness of tensions among these diverse goals. The intertwining of these three ideas is facilitated when they are each articulated in similar language and symbolism. Thus, adherents to each vision may appeal to norms of equality and justice, so long as these norms are ambiguously defined. Claims that the nation is inherited from "the ancestors" can be supported by all, as long as the question of whether this refers to the constitutional founders of the civic nation, to the claim to one common ethnic lineage, or to the diverse ancestries claimed by each ethnic segment remains of low political salience. Similarly, the language of "homeland" can be used by all citizens, so long as its usage repeatedly alternates between referring to the residential territory of the state, the birthplace of the common ancestor, or the diverse birthplaces of each ethnic segment. The same symbols and myths of nationhood can be variously interpreted so that the distinction between the different views of the nation remains inchoate and indistinct, thus inhibiting political tensions.

In this revised heuristic model, it is precisely such intertwining of the different ideas of nationhood that promotes and sustains the cohesion of the nation. The ideal-type nation is reconceptualized as one in which three visions of national identity are interwoven in the symbolism and policies of the state and in the minds of its citizens: the civic vision of ethnically blind citizenship, the ethnocultural vision of assimilation into an ethnic core, and the multiculturalist vision of the just accommodation of ethnic diversity. Nations remain united and strong to the extent that the distinctions between these differing ideas of national identity remain fudged and out of the limelight of public political discourse.

In practice, such a depoliticization of the potential tensions between divergent national identities is often achieved merely by authoritarian means. But even in those democratic nation-states where the national-identity strategies of the state and the language and symbolism of political discourse do promote the ambiguous entwining of the three ideas of national identity, the general salience of nationalism in the late twentieth century and thereafter seems likely to have generated some consciousness of the distinction between civic, ethnocultural, and multiculturalist visions of community. Even if the nation is the unit that is taken for granted by many people as the arena within which much of politics occurs, it nevertheless comes under the spotlight for scrutiny whenever such key issues as immigration, social justice, or interstate relations are debated. It seems likely, in other words, that at least a partial disentwining of the three ideas is widespread.

In such circumstances, confrontation between the three ideas may nevertheless be inhibited so long as the civic vision of national community has sufficient resonance in the society to act as a kind of buffer between the ethnocultural and multiculturalist visions. Since the ethnocultural vision of the nation-state asserts the higher status of those who have inherited or assimilated the attributes and values of the ethnic core, whereas the multiculturalist vision seeks to protect the ethnic minorities from assimilation into or marginalization by this ethnic core, the two ideas clearly have the capacity to confront each other and thence to become the basis for political contention. But if the civic idea of national identity is strongly articulated in the strategies and policies of state elites and has widespread resonance in the society, then it can serve partially to defuse both the ethnocultural and the multiculturalist visions, and also to direct their fire toward itself rather than against each other. Proponents of the ethnocultural idea can seek to employ policies of civic integration as a means toward the advancement of ethnocultural assimilation. At the same time, proponents of the multiculturalist idea can seek to adapt the civic ideal of equal citizenship toward their goal of interethnic social justice. Both can direct their political energies into reforming ethnically blind civic institutions of the state and civil society in the direction of their ethnically focused goals. The civic vision, in other words, can be expanded to incorporate elements of "soft" assimilation and "soft" multiculturalism. Proponents of the ethnocultural and multiculturalist visions may indeed seek goals that are distinct from each other and from the ethnically blind civic idea of national identity. But so long as they all feel that there is mileage in adopting and adapting civic values and civic institutions, direct conflict between proponents of ethnocultural and multiculturalist ideas is inhibited. Thus, for example, proposals for democratic decentralization might accord with the liberal civic ideal, but they can also be supported by multiculturalists as a first step toward ethnic federal power-sharing, or by ethnoculturalists as a move by the ethnic core to co-opt and tame ethnic minority elites.

This is the virtue of the civic ideal of the nation-state. It does not necessarily offer a more liberal polity than that offered by ethnic ideals (it can be just as collectivist-authoritarian); rather, it can offer a middle ground between advocates of ethnoculturalism and multiculturalism if they each believe, however misguidedly, that civic integration can provide a cover for their own divergent goals of ethnic assimilation and multiculturalist accommodation.

The first proposition, therefore, is that the cohesion of the nation-state depends on the intertwining of the three ideas of community and on the capacity of the civic idea to perform a "buffer" role. This generates the core argument that it is the disentwining of the three ideas of national identity—arising particularly from the erosion of faith in the state's ability to promote the civic ideal—that provides the necessary conditions for ethnic conflict.

Ethnic Conflict

The question arises as to how the disruptive impact of the diverse processes denoted by the terms "modernization" and "globalization" might generate such a disentwining and thus weaken the civic buffer. It is argued here that instrumental national identities give way to ideological nationalisms when the established authority structures of interactive communities are dislocated. These ideological nationalisms offer simplistic and morally absolutist formulas with which to diagnose and resolve complex contemporary problems, but the potential power of the civic-nationalist ideology is frequently vitiated by the perception that it is state elites who bear the blame for these problems. Such a weakening of the civic buffer leaves radicalized ideologies of ethnocultural nationalism and multiculturalist nationalism to confront each other, a political contention that manifests itself in the various forms of contemporary ethnic conflict.

The Disruption of Interactive Communities

Rational choice theories, including their "class" and "internal colonialism" variants, have offered the argument that ethnic conflict derives from resource grievances generated by economic disparities between interactive communities (Hechter 1986; Wolpe 1986). But as Horowitz (2001: 39) has noted in his recent discussion of ethnic riots, there appears to be "a considerable disjunction between objective conditions and the occurrence of violence, which can scarcely support any version of relative deprivation theory." An alternative, then, is to suggest that economic, political, and cultural changes might generate ethnic conflict to the extent that they disrupt status and power relationships *within* an interactive community rather than *between* such communities. Instead of leading toward an assumption that ethnic conflict reflects a rational (i.e., externally validated) tension between rival communities, the "internal disruption" approach indicates that the development of absolutist nationalist ideologies should be regarded as a retreat from the realities of disrupted interactions into myths of collectivist certitude. Thus, even when political disputes commence as clashes of interest between distinct interactive communities, these cases translate into ethnic conflicts when disagreements of interest change into confrontations between collectivist moral certainties.

The sources of social disruption vary enormously. They might include global and local factors and may relate, for example, to the rate of economic development or decline, the extractive activities of the state, or the social dislocations accompanying migration. The suggestion is that it is those groups who have been most subjected to sociopsychological stress, through the disruption of their interactive communities and their authority structures, who are the most likely to be mobilized by nationalist visions of communal harmony located either in the past (articulated in myths of a lost social cohesion to be restored) or in the future (articulated in myths of a prospective utopia).

This general proposition can be stated more specifically.[7] First, the disruption of the interactive communities within which individuals invest their material interests, at locality level or beyond, needs to be sufficiently intense and widespread to generate a reservoir of mass anomie and fear that can be resolved by ideological myths of certainty, which provide a simplistic diagnosis of contemporary disruptions. Nationalism offers one such diagnosis.[8] The disrupted society is imagined as the historical or potential nation that has been contaminated by the Other, whose removal is therefore imperative.

Second, the disruption is such that incumbent and/or aspiring elites within the interactive community are no longer able to legitimate their claims to leadership by appealing either to their previous positions of patronage in the interactive networks or to their prior positions of authority. Such displaced elites seek not only a simplistic explanation of their displacement and the disruption of their community, but also new ideological bases for establishing legitimate authority. Nationalism supplies one such legitimation. Collective memories and aspirations are reinterpreted by elites as either ethnic myths or civic visions, so as to justify the claim that they themselves are the sole articulators of the national will.[9]

Third, when the disruption occurs in the context of disillusionment with the benefits accruing from development, such that faith in progress toward a future utopia is weaker than faith in the possibility of return to a nostalgic, lost idyll, those seeking the resolution of contemporary disruptions are more likely to locate them in ethnic myths of an idealized past. But when disruption is accompanied by a perception that the alien and disruptive Other is on the verge of collapse or defeat, so that hopes of developmental progress begin to revive, then resolution can be imagined in civic myths of an idealized future.

Fourth, relative deprivations relating to economic and power disparities can contribute to nationalism in two ways. Firstly, such disparities are frequently linked to social disruptions within an interactive community, due to their association with such potentially dislocating processes as migration, rapid economic change, and the escalation of state restrictions on autonomy. It is not the disparity between communities per se that generates the nationalist reaction; it is the consequent dislocation within the Us community. Secondly, relative deprivation situations provide a useful means for ideological demonization in the form of the simplistic argument that the existence of material disparities between two political collectivities constitutes, in itself, proof of intentional discrimination or exploitation of the one by the other.

Nevertheless, it is clear that disruptive social change does not always engender a retreat into ideological certitudes. One possibility is that the dislocation of interactive communities and authority structures will turn out to be temporary, and that those who begin to feel disorientated by disruptive social change will quickly gain access to new interactive networks within which they can invest their interests. In particular, when established patrons are displaced, new patrons might become available, particularly in those instances where the state machinery functions on a patrimonial basis. In such cases, when there is the possibility of rebuilding patronage interactions through which interests can be pursued, the extent of ideologization is limited. Disorientated individuals and groups can seek refuge in clientelistic dependence. But the extent to which patrimonialism offers an alternative to ideologization is crucially influenced by the extent to which that patrimonialism itself functions on an ethnic basis. Where state patronage is perceived as biased in favor of the ethnic core, its availability to those on the ethnic peripheries declines, and the potentiality for their ideologization therefore increases.[10]

It is thus when access to new patronage networks is unavailable that the dislocation of authority structures leads displaced and aspiring elites to begin searching for new ideological bases for legitimacy in their societies. It also induces followers experiencing social disruption to search for new myths of communal harmony and new forms and figures of authority capable of resolving the social disharmony they are experiencing.

Ideologization

Nationalist ideologies claim to offer descriptive expressions of national identity, but when an ideology professes to describe reality, it is for prescriptive purposes: to advocate the reconstruction of society toward new moral ends.[11] As John Breuilly notes, nationalism begins by treating social changes as upsetting a state of equilibrium: "Deviations from that natural state are, of course, unnatural, and what is unnatural is bad" (1982: 341). Thus, "Nationalist ideology is neither an expression of national identity (at least there is no rational way of showing that to be the case) nor the arbitrary invention of nationalists for political purposes. It arises out of the need to make sense of complex social and political arrangements.... To work effectively as a popular political ideology it needs simplification.... Simplification involves above all the construction of stereotypes" (ibid.: 343–344).

Nationalism, in its ethnic or civic form, offers an ideological formula that employs the myths and visions of national identity in order to construct a "goodies" versus "baddies" explanation of contemporary social disruptions. In this conception, the pure and just nation is disrupted or contaminated by the demonized Other. Once conflicts of interest are reimagined as moral confrontations between the virtuous Us and the diabolical Other, their resolution is inhibited. Moreover, such nationalist ideologization of political conflict potentially changes the structure of confrontation. Instrumental conflict occurs when one party perceives that the threat to its interests comes from another party, which is therefore portrayed as the enemy. Ideological conflict, on the other hand, arises when members of a dislocated community are unable rationally to make sense of the complex social forces that have brought about the dislocation. The search for ideological formulas begins when the objective causes of social disruption are not easily identified by those subjected to the stress of that disruption. Unable to make rational calculations of political interest, societies then turn to nonrational diagnoses for social dislocation and to dramatic prescriptions for their resolution. Ideological nationalism tends therefore to identify enemies selected on the basis of collective stereotyping rather than because of their objective guilt.[12]

Such a shift from instrumental ethnic and national identities to ideological ethnic and civic nationalisms is not an inevitable or evolutionary one. Whether or not it occurs depends on the extent of the social disruption, the degree of the resultant psychological stress, the availability of displaced or aspiring elites, the ways in which these elites seek to employ available repertoires of myths and symbols for mobilization and legitimation purposes, and the resonance of such myths and symbols in the wider society. The argument, therefore, is that instrumental ethnic and civic attachments to interactive communities have the capacity to change into ideological ethnic or civic nationalisms when those interactive communities are disrupted, with the result that displaced elites seek legitimatory myths and dislocated masses seek myths of communal harmony.

The Disentwining of the Nation-State

This ideologization of national identities into nationalisms has immediate implications for the nation-state. It means that the eclectic national identities of nation-states come to be regarded as incoherent. Instead of the tensions between the civic, ethnocultural, and multiculturalist bases for nationhood being either suppressed by authoritarian means or hidden by their ambiguous interweaving in the language and symbolism of national identity and nationalist discourse, they become the focal point for politics. Each vision of the nation comes to be asserted or attacked as an independent claim to nationhood. Civic national identity becomes articulated as the claim (by "patriots") that the territorial integrity and collective unity of the existing state is under threat from liberals within, or enemies without, and must be defended. Ethnocultural national identity becomes articulated as the claim (by majoritarian populists) that the culture of the ethnic majority within the state is under threat and must be defended. Multiculturalist national identity becomes articulated as the claim (by minority-rights activists) that the rights of ethnic minority communities within the state are under threat and must be defended.

Such disentwining of the different ideals of national identity into contending nationalist ideologies is inhibited from developing into overt ethnic conflict as long as it is tripolar rather than bipolar. But the very conditions of social disruption that generate the ideologization of ethnic and civic national identities can also contribute to the erosion of civic nationalism, thus removing the buffer that inhibits overt conflict between the majoritarian claims of ethnocultural nationalism and the minority-rights claims of multiculturalist nationalism.

The Potential Erosion of Civic Nationalism

Civic nationalism rests on a "developmental optimism"—a faith in progress toward an idealized future state. Ethnic nationalism, on the other hand, offers a vision of a return to an idealized past, and thus tends to flourish where disillusionment with progress has become widespread. This means that the weakening of civic nationalism is particularly likely under two conditions: first, when the experience of social disruption is accompanied by the perception that socioeconomic development is giving way to socioeconomic decline, to the point that pessimistic nostalgia begins to replace developmental optimism; and, second, when the state is seen as the agency of both the disruption and the perceived decline.

Aspiring elites experiencing the disentwining of nationalist ideologies can respond by seeking to restructure the state according to civic ideals, characteristically advocating a liberal-pluralist version of civic nationalism in contrast to a "failed" authoritarian-collectivist civic nationalism. This was the case with the Indonesian students who overthrew Suharto, and with Anwar Ibrahim's challenge to Mahathir's regime in Malaysia. Moreover, the ideals of civic nationalism may be espoused by some citizens if they can locate an alternative agency for its attainment, in either a regionalist secessionism or an appeal to the international community. However, each of these responses relies on an optimism that is often in short supply among those communities that have experienced the most severe and disruptive impacts of social change. The implication is that where social dislocation occurs in the context of widespread pessimism related to state-focused development, the appeal of civic nationalism at mass level will tend to weaken. Insufficient civic integration, difficulties in accessing legal equality and social rights, or incidents of economic injustice and ethnic discrimination need not, of themselves, inhibit the civic vision of the nation. If it is widely believed that these shortcomings are being tackled by some state elites and will reduce over time, the vision of the attainment of the civic ideal still has mobilizing power. But where state elites come to be perceived as the agents of disruption and decline, faith in the civic potential of the nation-state is directly eroded. Meanwhile, ethnic nationalism can flourish on the nostalgia that is prevalent in times of widespread disillusionment.

While the actual sources of disruption and socioeconomic decline may vary, and the extent of state control over "the forces of globalization" may in some cases be minimal, belief in state sovereignty nevertheless remains sufficiently widespread for state elites to be frequently portrayed and perceived as culpable. This is particularly so in those countries where the very formation of the state was legitimated by the promise of developmental progress. When governing elites in such "developmental states" fail to keep these promises—because of arbitrary, extractive, and corrupt rule, or because of limited governmental capacities—some citizens begin to lose faith that their state has the capacity to move in the direction of their nationalist ideal.

The potentiality for an erosion of faith in civic nationalism is exacerbated by its inherent volatility. The extent of this faith varies not just with fluctuations in national economic performance but also with variations in the ideological skills of state elites in mobilizing civic nationalism in response to external enemies and internal threats. This means that ethnic tensions can intensify or ameliorate in response to variations in popular perceptions of the developmental or social-justice capacities of an incumbent regime or even an individual leader.

The erosion of the civic-nationalist vision becomes evident when ethnic minorities begin to suspect that civic rhetoric has been used as a cover for ethnic majority claims, and when ethnic majorities begin to suspect that civic norms have been subverted by concessions to ethnic minority claims. The more the civic vision comes to be regarded as simply a camouflage for ethnic bias, the less it can act as an effective buffer between the ethnocultural and multiculturalist visions of national identity.

As civic nationalism loses its mobilizing power, adherents of ethnocultural nationalism begin to see the state elites as having betrayed the ethnocultural ideals of promoting the status of the ethic core, and thus launch populist majoritarian movements to put pressure on the state to change its policies back in the right direction (Betz and Immerfall 1998). Similarly, adherents of multiculturalist nationalism come to see the state as having betrayed the ideals of interethnic justice, and seek recourse in demands for some degree of autonomy from the state. Both ethnocultural populism and multiculturalist separatism face real political problems in promoting their goals, but the adherents of civic nationalism face a problem that is in a sense more fundamental. Whereas a perceived weakening of the state can serve to promote ethnic nationalisms, it can only erode civic nationalism.

The Radicalization of Ethnocultural and Multiculturalist National Identities

The tendency to blame the state for social disruptions applies to the proponents of ethnocultural and multiculturalist nationalisms, just as it does to the civic nationalists. For ethnocultural and multicultural nationalists, however, the culprit is not the state per se, but rather the ethnic communities that are perceived as influencing the state elites. Ethnocultural nationalists explain the state's failure to effectively promote and protect the ethnic core by blaming the influence of ethnic minorities pursuing multiculturalist nationalism. For their part, the ethnic minorities blame the failure of the state to foster interethnic justice on the disproportionate influence exercised by an ethnic core preaching ethnocultural nationalism. Once such ethnic-nationalist formulas of Us versus Them have taken hold, each vision becomes modified and radicalized. The ethnocultural goal of ethnic assimilation is replaced by that of defending the ethnic core against ethnic minority contamination, while the multiculturalist ideal of interethnic accommodation is discarded in favor of the ideal of ethnic minority separatism. Instead of being advocated as guiding principles for the nation-state, and potentially being moderated by their interweaving with the civic vision, ethnic nationalisms are now espoused as radical antistate ideologies, employed by nonstate elites seeking to mobilize and legitimate support among disrupted and disaffected populations.

If faith in the capacities of the state to promote the civic-nationalist vision is weak, there is little to buffer the resultant contention as radicalized ethnocultural and multicultural nationalists each accuse the state of a failure to defend them against the other. With nothing to act as a buffer, their confrontation engenders an ideological confrontation that manifests itself in the various forms and intensities of ethnic conflict.

But it needs to be recognized at the outset that such ideological polarization is never complete. The disruption of interactive communities and the displacement of authority structures eventually give way to the revival of interactions of everyday life. In those cases where the state is deeply involved in patrimonial activities, the search for instrumental clientelist networks and for ideological certitude produce countervailing tendencies. On the one hand, those who have developed ethnocultural or multiculturalist preconceptions are likely to reject state-focused patronage as a trick by the ethnic Other. On the other hand, those who have rebuilt their patron-client linkages with the state are likely to reject ideological ethnic nationalisms, which inhibit their instrumental search for material advantage. This tension between instrumental and ideological behavior helps to explain why conflicts between ethnic ideologies tend to be characterized as much by divisions within as by confrontations between ethnic communities.

Strengthening the Civic Buffer

The argument that it is the disruption of interactive communities and their authority structures that generates the development of disentwined and potentially counterposed nationalist ideologies is a reformulation of one of the core themes in the modernization literature on ethnicity and nationalism. It might therefore seem to be vulnerable to one of the key criticisms leveled at the modernization school—that it posits a linear direction to social change, though in this case one of inevitable decline into ethnic conflict rather than one of progress toward cohesive nations. If it is disruptions of interactive communities and disillusionment with the capacities of existing states to promote the civic vision that lie at the heart of ethnic conflict, then are we not back in the realm of a "globalization inevitably weakens the nation-state" form of argument?

At one level, the rebuttal of this charge involves merely the reminder that nationalist ideology is but one of numerous responses to social disruption, and that social disruption is but one of many impacts of multifaceted globalization. But more fundamentally, it implies the need for a closer examination of the role of the state. Even if societal disruptions do promote the ideologization of national identities, and thence their disentwining, it still remains the case that the strength or weakness of civic nationalism depends primarily upon whether state strategies and policies have tended toward promoting civic integration, favoring the ethnic core, or advancing ethnic minority group rights.

The dominant diagnosis of ethnic conflict—that it originates in the capture of states by their ethnic cores—points to the conclusion that the bias toward ethnocultural nationalism is to be corrected by a shift toward multicultural-ist nationalism. But the implication of this discussion has been to revise this diagnosis and prescription. If it is the weakness of faith in the civic vision of nation-state identity that generates confrontation between proponents of ethnocultural and multiculturalist visions, then it is the strengthening of the civic vision that is crucial to ameliorating and ending ethnic conflicts. It is faith in progress toward a civic polity that turns a zero-sum ethnic confrontation into a positive-sum process of "reintwining" a political community, so that advocates of civic, ethnocultural, and multiculturalist ideals of nationhood can all see scope for investment. As has been noted, the civic vision of equal citizenship is indeed prone to being hijacked, on the one hand, by proponents of ethnocultural nationalism, eager to invest the civic culture with ethnocul-tural norms, and, on the other, by supporters of multiculturalist nationalism, keen to modify the civic vision of equal citizenship by promoting group-spe-cific rights. But this does not mean that the civic vision is doomed to be torn asunder by the contending ethnocultural and multiculturalist forces. Rather, as Habermas (2000: 145) has highlighted, the emotive power of the civic vision (to which Habermas's "constitutional patriotism" is closely related) is best pro-moted when it is perceived by all parties as "a process of inclusion."

Michael Walzer (1999: 212) has reminded us that there is no "quick theoretical fix" to the politics of contending "tribalisms": "We have to work slowly and experimentally to find arrangements that satisfy the members (not the militants) of this or that minority." But it should be noted that this practical messiness does not imply any corresponding conceptual messiness, as long as the pragmatic acceptances of ethnic claims are seen as concessions to facilitate the processes of civic integration. Thus, even while Walzer is urging the construction of "protected spaces ... to match the needs of different tribes," he is nevertheless advocating the construction of a new sense of collective identity beyond the tribe, based on "adherence to some new community of interest" (ibid.: 213). "The primary function of the state, and of politics generally, is to do justice to individuals, and in a pluralist society, ethnicity is merely one of the background conditions of this effort. Ethnic identification gives meaning to the lives of many men and women, but it has nothing to do with their standing as citizens" (Walzer 1995: 153–154).

State policies and strategies clearly play a crucial role in influencing the strength of the civic vision. In the case of Indonesia, for example, it is evident that faith in a civic Indonesia was crucially weakened by the corruption, nepotism, and arbitrary coerciveness of the Suharto regime (Anderson 1999). When the removal of Suharto finally opened the door to democratization, visions of diverse Islamic majority rights and ethnic minority separatist rights set the political agenda, rather than any faith in the capacity of the state to move toward a liberal, pluralist civic nation.[13] On the other hand, Suharto's contemporaries in Southeast Asia—Mahathir in Malaysia and Lee Kuan Yew in Singapore—both responded to the ethnic conflicts of the 1960s by embarking on state strategies that promoted the civic vision of the nation-state, thus inhibiting tensions between ethnic majorities and minorities.[14]

Nevertheless, it is quite clear why efforts to end violent ethnic conflicts have frequently sought ethnic power-sharing solutions, rather than seeking ways of promoting ethnically neutral governance (Darby and McGinty 2003). Where both sides have come to see the state as ethnically biased against them, and neither side trusts the state to be ethnically neutral, there seems no alternative but to seek resolution in measures of affirmative action, consociationalism, or ethnic federalism, with various agencies of the international community acting as guarantors that the formulas will be fair to both sides. However, the danger of such arrangements is clearly that they institutionalize and therefore reinforce the ethnic-nationalist mindsets that structured the conflicts.

In a recent discussion of "stateless nationalisms" Michael Keating (2001: 169) has noted that the EU provides "supra-state fragments," which disputants within the component nation-states can employ in the hope of gaining support of various kinds. He suggests that "[t]his Europe, as shorthand for an emerging normative order, may ... provide new ways to manage a plurinational space.... Europe is an essentially contested project, and this contestation is not a transitional phase to a new, integrated state, but its essence. It is a place where, within a common value set and through evolving institutions, the question of state and nation can continually be debated, in the search for positive-sum outcomes."

This formulation of the EU has immediate implications for the present discussion. It has been suggested here that civic national identities could inhibit zero-sum confrontations between proponents of ethnocultural and multiculturalist visions of community by persuading both sides that it is possible for them to "bend" civic norms to accommodate their aims. In the past, the vision of a civic "world of nations" offered a contested normative project that potentially inhibited ethnic conflict. But now that globalization has disaggregated the functions of the state, so that some of these roles are being performed by various sub- and suprastate "fragments," the hope for a shift from contemporary zero-sum confrontations toward positive-sum outcomes lies in the building of suprastate structures that can be appealed to by each side in ethnic conflicts in the hope that these structures will favor their cause.

Instead of ethnic majorities trying to capture the state, and ethnic minorities trying to secede from it, both sides can begin to see an advantage in manipulating suprastate fragments to their advantage. But this is feasible only if such fragments are sufficiently eclectic and ambiguous so that all contending parties see potential success in manipulating them to their own ends. Thus, in the case of the EU, some members of ethnic minority communities can perceive its structures as offering a vision of a "Europe of the regions" that is favorable to ethnic and ethnoregional minorities. At the same time, others can look to the EU for the protection of a pan-European core of Christians and Caucasians against Islamic and other minorities. It is the ambiguities of the diverse EU structures that have the capability to reintwine presently counterposed ethnic majorities and minorities. Based on predominantly civic values of ethnic neutrality, most of these structures are nevertheless variously perceived as offering resources and legitimations for ethnocultural and multiculturalist, as well as civic, goals.

The aim of external interventions, then, is not to offer definitively "fair" solutions for ethnic conflicts or to give unequivocal support to one side over another, but rather to shift the focus from zero-sum conflict through violence to the search for positive-sum outcomes through political negotiations. No matter how "messy," these negotiations begin the process of reintwining ethnocultural and multiculturalist visions of community around civic norms, so that the three visions of community become, once more, ambiguously interwoven in the consciousness of citizens.

Notes

1. It has frequently been claimed (notably by theorists sometimes designated as "primordialists") that the ethnic bond has greater emotional power than the civic bond, leading to the criticism that there are no real civic nations, and that those portrayed as such by naive academics merely employ civic rhetoric to camouflage favoritism of the ethnic core. The claim that there are no pure civic nations might presumably be accompanied by the recognition that there are no pure ethnic nations—that is, nations whose national societies are ethnically homogeneous or nations whose public policies and norms prioritize the ethnic core in the allocation of all rights and resources. Regarding the claim that loyalties to organic ethnic nations are necessarily stronger than those to civic nations, note the findings of social psychology that preferential in-group attachments frequently attach even to arbitrary groupings (Tajfel 1981). For an example of ethnic attachments proving weaker than civic attachments, see the examination of the relative strengths of Ewe nationalism and of Togolese and Ghanaian nationalisms in Nugent (2002).

2. The term "ethnic nation" is often interpreted narrowly to mean the coinciding of ethnic and state boundaries. In order to refer to the idea that a nation-state might be built around perceptions of an ethnic core but might also contain communities depicted as ethnic minorities (to be marginalized or assimilated), the term "ethnocultural nation" is employed here.

3. The term "multiculturalism" is sometimes used, in its "soft" sense, to refer to the argument that the state ought to grant special resources to ethnic minorities in order to facilitate their civic integration. Here the term is used to refer to the belief that minority ethnic communities within a nation-state ought to be granted those individual and group rights appropriate to the retention and development of their ethnic autonomy within the national polity.

4. For an initial elaboration of this argument, see Brown (2000).

5. For dramatic examples of politically salient confusion, note the recent contention in France concerning the issue of religious symbolism in the secular state and the clashes in New Zealand concerning the articulation of the ethnic-blindness norm in reaction to the various affirmative actions for Maori rights.

6. Anthony Smith (1998: 213) stresses the ethnic core of nation-states and the ethnocultural tendencies of governments, but he nevertheless recognizes "how closely intertwined all three conceptions of the nation tend in practice to be."

7. The following four points are adapted from Brown (2004b: 284–285).

8. But nationalism is not the only concept to provide a diagnosis. Today, its main competitor is religious fundamentalism; in the recent past, it was communism.

9. Whereas instrumentalism depicts nationalist elites as Machiavellians who cynically employ nationalist myths in pursuit of their elite self-interests, this constructivist formulation implies that elites subscribe to these nationalist myths because the ideologies offer comprehensible explanations of, and resolutions to, the erosion of their authority.

10. For a discussion of the relationship between patrimonialism and ethnic conflict in the case of Indonesia, see Brown (2004b).

11. As Kenneth Minogue (1967: 154) sees it, this is a case of "the political tails trying to wag the dogs."

12. Horowitz (2001: 150), in his study of ethnic riots, argues that "cumulation"—the rational basis for the selection of ethnic targets on the basis of accumulated grievances—is supplemented by "displacement," whereby grievances against superior class, caste, or ethnic groups are converted into attacks on parallel ethnic communities. He notes a

pattern in which resentments against superior groups can be displaced onto parallel status groups, but suggests that there is no consistent "scapegoat" pattern in which the target ethnic group is selected simply because it is the most vulnerable. Rather, he argues that targets of ethnic violence are chosen because they are "strong," but are attacked "at a time of momentary weakness or at a time when retribution is improbable."

13. Norms of civic nationalism were articulated by the Indonesian students who launched the initial rebellion against Suharto, but these norms played a noticeably smaller role in the subsequent politics of mass mobilization between 1998 and 2003 (Brown 2004a).

14. On Mahathir's success in shifting from the ethnocultural nationalist position, which he inherited and initially espoused, toward a more civic direction, see Cheah (2002). On the state's role in building civic national identity in Singapore, see Hill and Lian (1995).

References

Anderson, Benedict R. O'G. 1999. "Indonesian Nationalism Today and in the Future." *Indonesia* 67: 1–11.

Betz, Hans-Georg, and Stefan Immerfall, eds. 1998. *The New Politics of the Right: Neo-Populist Parties and Movements in Established Democracies*. London: Macmillan.

Breuilly, John. 1982. *Nationalism and the State*. Manchester: Manchester University Press.

Brown, David. 2000. *Contemporary Nationalism: Civic, Ethnocultural and Multicultural Politics*. London: Routledge.

_____. 2004a. "The Democratization of National Identity." In *Democratization and Identity: Regimes and Ethnicity in East and Southeast Asia*, ed. S. J. Henders, 43–46. Lanham, MD: Lexington Books.

_____. 2004b. "Why Independence? The Instrumental and Ideological Dimensions of Nationalism." *International Journal of Comparative Sociology* 45, no. 3–4: 277–296.

Cheah, Boon Kheng. 2002. *Malaysia: The Making of a Nation*. Singapore: Institute of Southeast Asian Studies.

Connor, Walker. 1994. *Ethnonationalism: The Quest for Understanding*. Princeton, NJ: Princeton University Press.

Darby, John, and Roger McGinty, eds. 2003. *Contemporary Peacemaking: Conflict, Violence and Peace Processes*. Basingstoke: Palgrave Macmillan.

Deutsch, Karl W. 1966. *Nationalism and Social Communication: An Inquiry into the Foundations of Nationality*. 2nd ed. Cambridge, MA: MIT Press.

Gellner, Ernest. 1983. *Nations and Nationalism*. Oxford: Blackwell.

_____. 1996. "Reply to Critics." In *The Social Philosophy of Ernest Gellner*, ed. John A. Hall and Ian Jarvie, 625–687. Amsterdam: Rodopi.

Greenfeld, Liah. 1992. *Nationalism: Five Roads to Modernity*. Cambridge, MA: Harvard University Press.

Habermas Jürgen. 2000. *The Inclusion of the Other: Studies in Political Theory*. Cambridge, MA: MIT Press.

Hechter, Michael. 1986. "Rational Choice Theory and the Study of Race and Ethnic Relations." In *Theories of Race and Ethnic Relations*, ed. John Rex and David Mason, 264–279. Cambridge: Cambridge University Press.

Hill, Michael, and Kuen Fee Lian. 1995. *The Politics of Nation Building and Citizenship in Singapore*. London: Routledge.

Hobsbawm, Eric J. 1990. *Nations and Nationalism since 1780*. Cambridge: Cambridge University Press.

Horowitz, Donald L. 2001. *The Deadly Ethnic Riot*. Berkeley: University of California Press.

Keating, Michael. 2001. *Plurinational Democracy: Stateless Nations in a Post-Sovereignty Era*. Oxford: Oxford University Press.

Kuzio, Taras. 2002. "The Myth of the Civic State: A Critical Survey of Hans Kohn's Framework for Understanding Nationalism." *Ethnic and Racial Studies* 25, no. 1: 20–39.

Kymlicka, Will. 1995. *Multicultural Citizenship: A Liberal Theory of Minority Rights*. Oxford: Clarendon Press.

_____. 2001. "Western Political Theory and Ethnic Relations in Eastern Europe." In *Can Liberal Pluralism Be Exported? Western Political Theory and Ethnic Relations in Eastern Europe*, ed. M. Opalski and W. Kymlicka, 13–106. New York: Oxford University Press.

Miller, David. 1995. *On Nationality*. Oxford: Clarendon Press.

Minogue, Kenneth R. 1967. *Nationalism*. London: Batsford.

Norval, Aletta J. 1999. "Rethinking Ethnicity: Identification, Hybridity and Democracy." In *Ethnicity and Nationalism in Africa: Constructivist Reflections and Contemporary Politics*, ed. Paris Yeros, 61–88. London: Macmillan.

Nugent, Paul. 2002. *Smugglers, Secessionists and Loyal Citizens on the Ghana-Togo Frontier*. Athens: Ohio University Press.

Rawls, John. 1993. *Political Liberalism*. New York: Columbia University Press.

Smith, Anthony D. 1981. *The Ethnic Revival*. Cambridge: Cambridge University Press.

_____. 1995. *Nations and Nationalism in a Global Era*. Cambridge: Polity Press.

_____. 1998. *Nationalism and Modernism*. London: Routledge.

Tajfel, Henri. 1981. *Human Groups and Social Categories*. Cambridge: Cambridge University Press.

Walzer, Michael. 1995. "Pluralism: A Political Perspective." In *The Rights of Minority Cultures*, ed. Will Kymlicka, 139–154. Oxford: Oxford University Press.

_____. 1999. "The New Tribalism: Notes on a Difficult Problem." In *Theorizing Nationalism*, ed. Ronald Beiner, 229–253. Albany: State University of New York Press

Wolpe, Howard. 1986. "Class Concepts, Class Struggle and Racism." In *Theories of Race and Ethnic Relations*, ed. John Rex and David Mason, 110–130. Cambridge: Cambridge University Press.

Yack, Bernard. 1999. "The Myth of the Civic Nation." In *Theorizing Nationalism*, ed. Ronald Beiner, 103–117. Albany: State University of New York Press.

Yeros, Paris. 1999. "Towards a Normative Theory of Ethnicity: Reflections on the Politics of Constructivism." In *Ethnicity and Nationalism in Africa: Constructivist Reflections and Contemporary Politics*, ed. Paris Yeros, 119–138. London: Macmillan.

2

Social Identity Matters
Predicting Prejudice and Violence in Western Europe

Thomas F. Pettigrew

The extensive use of the concept of social identity throughout the social sciences and humanities attests to its fundamental importance. However, one social science discipline—social psychology—uses the concept as a central tool for much of its work. As the social science that explicitly sets out to study individuals within their social contexts, social psychology has shaped social identity into one of its most important concepts linking individual human beings with their groups and societies.

Social identity has many functions, both cognitive and emotional. Its primary cognitive function involves social location. Identity helps to answer the important question for every human: "Who am I?" Early in life, gender identity forms. Before five years of age, national and racial identities begin to form. When asked to describe who we are, we often use these subidentities as initial responses: "I am a female African American." Indeed, when asked to describe who they are, American college students typically list their membership groups more than their personal characteristics (Kuhn and McPartland 1954).

Social psychologists think of social identity as the group component of the self-concept—the collective "we" as opposed to the internal "I." As such, it directly influences self-esteem and many other aspects of self-identity. We typically identify with our membership "in-groups" and contrast ourselves with rival, nonmembership "out-groups." Moreover, our self-esteem is lowered or raised partly by how well our membership groups perform and are regarded. Sports fans "bask in the reflected glory" of victories by athletic teams with

---

Notes for this chapter begin on page 45.

which they identify (Cialdini et al. 1976). And some members of subordinated, lowly regarded groups come to think of themselves as less worthy than members of dominant groups.

Strong emotions also are obviously involved with social identity. We are "proud" to be a citizen of our nation or to be a union member or to proclaim any other membership tie that we have saliently incorporated into our extended view of ourselves. We "feel" happy and rewarded when our favorite teams, with which we identify, win.

Thus, social psychologists define social identity as those aspects of the self-concept that derive from an individual's knowledge and feelings about the group memberships that the person shares with others. Following from this definition, the discipline typically measures social identity by asking respondents how "proud" they are of their membership group, how much they "feel" like a member of the group, and "how close" they regard themselves to be to the group. A Norwegian who is quite proud of Norway, who feels like a Norwegian, and who regards herself close to Norway and its people appears highly identified with Norway. Although this view of social identity is narrowed to allow direct quantitative measurement, it is closely related to what writers in other social sciences and the humanities mean by the term.

Using this social-psychological approach, we will explore the links between social identities, prejudice, and the potential for group violence. We will analyze two surveys that measured these variables with large probability samples of Western Europeans. The European Union sponsored the first survey (labeled Euro88), which was conducted face to face in 1988 in France, Great Britain, the Netherlands, and West Germany. The second survey is more recent. Sponsored by the Volkswagen Foundation, this 2002 phone survey (labeled GMF02) focused solely on Germany.

Study 1: National Pride and Prejudice

First, we employ the extensive data provided by the European Union's 1988 Eurobarometer 30 survey—Euro88 (Pettigrew and Meertens 1995; Reif and Melich 1991). This survey is one of the largest international studies of prejudice using probability samples ever conducted. Among other data, it drew seven independent national samples from Western Europe. The survey asked 3,796 adult, majority group respondents in France, Great Britain, the Netherlands, and West Germany an array of prejudice-related questions and the following social identity questions: "Would you say you are very proud, quite proud, not very proud, not at all proud to be (British, Dutch, French, or German)?" This item serves as our measure of national identity (NID). "Does the thought often, sometimes, or never occur to you that you are not only (British, Dutch, French, or German) but also European?" This item serves as our measure of European identity (EID).

In Euro88, two different measures of prejudice are employed. The Blatant Prejudice Scale boasts an alpha of .88, indicating a highly reliable measure. It consists of two components—one a threat-and-rejection factor (e.g., "West Indians have jobs the British should have"), the other an intimacy factor (e.g., "I would not mind if a Turk who had a similar economic background as mine joined my close family by marriage"). Blatant prejudice is the more traditional form—close, hot, and direct.

By contrast, subtle prejudice is the modern form—distant, cool, and indirect. This new form has been widely studied and validated throughout the Western world (Arcuri and Boca 1996, 1999; Dovidio, Mann, and Gaertner 1989; Gaertner and McLaughlin 1983; Hamberger and Hewstone 1997; Hightower 1997; Katz and Hass 1988; Kinder and Sanders 1996; McConahay 1983; Meertens and Pettigrew 1997; Pedersen and Walker 1997; Pettigrew 1997, 1998; Pettigrew and Meertens 1995; Pettigrew et al. 1998; Rattazzi and Volpato 2000, 2001; Rise et al. 2000; Rueda and Navas 1996; Sears 1988; Sears, Sidanius, and Bobo 2000; Sisbane, Rimè, and Azzi 2000; Six and Wolfradt 2000; Vala, Brito, and Lopes 1999; Villano 1999; Volpato and Rattazzi 2000; Wagner and Zick 1995; Zick et al. 2001).

The Subtle Prejudice Scale used in the Euro88 survey attains an alpha of .78. It has three components that share an ostensibly nonracial focus. The first consists of a traditional values factor (e.g., "Asians living here teach their children values and skills different from those required to be successful in France"). The second component concerns views of the out-group as extremely different culturally from the in-group. The final component involves the denial of sympathy and admiration for the out-group. Note that this component tests for the denial of positive emotions rather than the expression of negative emotions—fear, envy, hatred—that are associated with blatant prejudice.

Researchers have successfully employed these two scales and their adaptations in a variety of intergroup situations and a number of nations, including Australia, Belgium, France, Germany, Great Britain, Italy, the Netherlands, Norway, Portugal, Spain, and the United States (Arcuri and Boca 1996, 1999; Hamberger and Hewstone 1997; Hightower 1997; Pedersen and Walker 1997; Pettigrew 1997; Pettigrew et al. 1998; Rattazzi and Volpato 2000, 2001; Rise et al. 2000; Rueda and Navas 1996; Sisbane, Rimè, and Azzi 2000; Six and Wolfradt 2000; Vala, Brito, and Lopes 1999; Villano 1999; Volpato and Rattazzi 2000; Wagner and Zick 1995; Zick et al. 2001).

Table 2.1 shows first-order correlations (r)[1] between our two identity items and blatant prejudice and the traditional values component of subtle prejudice for the seven Western European samples and the total sample. The findings are strikingly consistent in direction. In all seven samples from four different nations and six diverse out-group targets, strong national identity is linked to greater prejudice on both measures, while European identity is linked to reduced prejudice on both measures. And though not large in magnitude, all of these correlations are statistically significant, given the large sample sizes.

TABLE 2.1 Identity and Prejudice, 1988

	N	National Identity		European Identity	
		Blatant prejudice	Trad. values prejudice	Blatant prejudice	Trad. values prejudice
British on Asians	481	+.263	+.334	-.332	-.268
British on blacks	470	+.214	+.246	-.218	-.254
Dutch on Surinamers	461	+.122	+.104	-.105	-.017
Dutch on Turks	474	+.143	+.146	-.166	-.041
French on Asians	473	+.154	+.197	-.226	-.186
French on North Africans	455	+.267	+.245	-.159	-.103
Germans on Turks	984	+.272	+.197	-.337	-.164
Total Sample	3,798	+.177	+.212	-.269	-.146

Note: Traditional values prejudice is a sub-scale of the Eurobarometer Subtle Prejudice Scale.
Source: Data from Eurobarometer 30 (Reif and Melich 1991).

Interestingly, the two identity measures are uncorrelated in the total sample. Indeed, a third of the respondents are both proud of their nation and at least sometimes think of themselves as European. It is at the extremes of these two identity continua that we locate the links with prejudice (i.e., there is an interaction between the two variables: p<.02). Thus, by far the greatest prejudice is found among those who are "very proud" of their nation and "never" think of themselves as European. Likewise, the most tolerant respondents are "not at all proud" of their nation and "often" think of themselves as Europeans.

Europeans who are highly identified with their nation tend to be older, more politically conservative, and somewhat less educated than the general population. By contrast, those who identify more broadly with Europe tend to be better educated than the general population. Figure 2.1 indicates these relations in a diagram of a simple structural equation model that predicts the Blatant Prejudice Scale against foreigners. The advantage of such a model is to see the key variables as an explanatory system rather than just viewing the specific relationships between variables as in table 2.1.

Note that the two identity variables act as mediators for prior predictors of prejudice. Education, political conservatism, and national identity mediate age. That is, a large part of why increasing age is related to greater prejudice against foreigners is because older respondents tend to be less educated and more politically conservative and nationally identified. Similarly, national identity mediates the effects of political conservatism on prejudice. Conservatives are more nationally identified, and this accounts in part for why conservatives are more prejudiced. Finally, education is mediated through both national and European identities. The highly educated are likely to be less identified with their nation and more with Europe, and both of these effects lead to reduced prejudice against foreigners. These results strongly suggest that the importance of social identities is their role as mediators of such basic phenomena as age, education, and political views.

FIGURE 2.1 Identities as Mediators

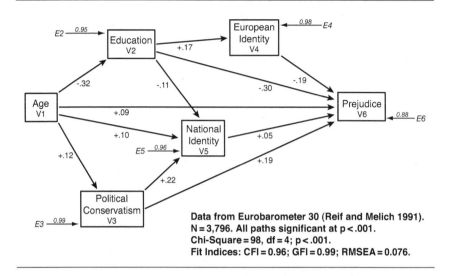

Data from Eurobarometer 30 (Reif and Melich 1991).
N = 3,796. All paths significant at p < .001.
Chi-Square = 98, df = 4; p < .001.
Fit Indices: CFI = 0.96; GFI = 0.99; RMSEA = 0.076.

Study 2: Social Identities, Prejudice, and the Potential for Intergroup Violence

We turn now to a more recent data set with more extensive measures of social identity. Here we employ a probability phone survey conducted in Germany (GMF02; cf. Heitmeyer 2002).[2] The survey contains data on 2,722 adult respondents without a migration background and includes a varied set of prejudice and social identity questions. Note the marked differences between our two data sets in terms of location, time, and items used to test social identity and prejudice. Such differences provide rigorously diverse tests for investigating the identity-prejudice link.

Shaped by the findings on identity in the Euro88 and other surveys, the GMF02 study provides more indicators of key concepts. In this rich data set, two items each measure three different types of social identity. German identity is indicated by the following questions: "How much do you feel like a German? (Very much, rather much, not much, not at all). And how much do you approve of this statement—I am proud to be a German (Fully correct, rather correct, not correct, not at all correct)?" The survey uses the same two indicators to tap European identity: feeling European and pride in being a European. A final identity measure resembles Habermas's (1996) "constitutional patriotism" concept. We shall label it "universalistic identity" to distinguish it from the more common particularistic nationalism measured by the "feel" and "pride" items. The survey measures this special type of identity with two questions concerning how proud the respondent is of German democracy and the German social security system.[3]

We will employ two scales to measure attitudes toward violence. One of these scales taps an acceptance of violence committed by others, while the other taps a personal readiness to commit violence. In addition to many other variables, the GMF02 questionnaire also has two prejudice scales we shall use—a two-item scale of anti-Semitism and a seven-item scale of antiforeigner prejudice (alpha = .87). Items in the latter measure possess a blatant quality, for example, "Foreigners have jobs that we Germans should have."

Unlike the 1988 data, the three identities are positively and significantly related to each other. Even more respondents on this second survey report both national and European identities. The two identities are highly associated with each other (r = +.41), while the universalistic identity is moderately related to the German (r = +.14) and European (r = +.17) identities. Yet in table 2.2, we note that they differ sharply in their associations with the four dependent variables. Looking first at just those correlations in table 2.2 that are *not* in brackets, we see that those high in German identity are more prejudiced against both foreigners and Jews and somewhat more favorable toward violence. By contrast, those universalistically identified—proud of Germany's democracy and social security system—are less prejudiced against foreigners and slightly less anti-Semitic and less favorable toward violence. Overall, although four of the correlations attain statistical significance, the links with the pro-violence scales are smaller than those with the prejudice variables. And unlike the Euro88 results, identification with Europe alone has little relation to the prejudice or violence measures.

Once again, however, we must dig deeper in the analysis. In brackets, table 2.2 also provides the correlations between the three identity measures and our

TABLE 2.2 Identity, Prejudice, and Violence, 2002

	N	German Identity	European Identity	Universalistic Identity
Prejudice against foreigners	2,660	+.364** [+.130**]	+.029 [−.120**]	−.245** [−.194**]
Anti-Semitism	2,664	+.214** [+.037]	+.040* [−.056**]	−.063** [−.028]
Acceptance of violence	2,640	+.131** [+.011]	−.004 [−.058**]	−.048* [−.006]
Readiness for violence	2,658	+.082** [+.029]	−.036 [−.068**]	−.075** [−.034]

Notes: * = p <.05; ** = p <.01. Correlations in brackets [ ] are partial correlations that control for the other two identification variables plus eight key predictor variables (age, education, political conservatism, social dominance, right-wing authoritarianism, negative and positive experiences with foreigners, and the intergroup opinions of the respondents' friends).

Source: Data from GFE Survey (Heitmeyer 2002).

four dependent variables of interest when eight other relevant predictors are controlled. This procedure represents a strong test of whether the identity variables really matter. Are the three identity variables independently contributing to a prediction of attitudes about out-groups and violence? Or are they merely reflecting the importance of other, more powerful predictors? The eight control variables are all major predictors of prejudice. In addition to age, education, and political conservatism, we control for the two major personality predictors of prejudice—right-wing authoritarianism and social-dominance orientation (Adorno et al. 1950; Altemeyer 1988, 1998; Sidanius and Pratto 1999). We also control for the positive and negative intergroup experiences reported by the respondent as well as the intergroup opinions of the respondents' friends—an indicator of an area's prejudice norms.

These controls greatly diminish the relationships between the violence and identity measures; they remain significant only for European identity. This result does not mean that identity plays no role in pro-violence attitudes. Separate analyses show that four of the largest predictors of the violence measures involve prejudice against foreigners, Jews, homosexuals, and people who have recently moved into the respondents' areas.[4] Thus, the identity variables play a role in enhancing the potential for violence due to their influence on prejudice.

This point is underlined by the fact that the identity variables remain important for prejudice despite the severity of our controlled test. Indeed, European identity now yields small but predicted relations similar to the first study; it *negatively* relates to all four of the prejudice and violence scales. And the prejudice correlations with the German and universalistic identity measures are smaller but retain the same signs. But note that these associations are now much stronger for prejudice against foreigners than against Jews. This difference suggests that the three identities relate to attitudes toward non-European, "distant" foreigners and much less so to attitudes toward Jews—a significant group within Germany and Europe for centuries.

Moreover, these data replicate the strong interaction between national and European identities that appeared in the first survey. Thus, those Germans highly identified with Europe but not with Germany are the least prejudiced and the least pro-violence of all respondents. This trend holds true for both measured prejudices and the acceptance of violence scale. In other words, European identity acts as a moderator of German identity effects. Thus, respondents who are highly identified with Germany may or may not be especially prejudiced, depending on their feelings about Europe. Those German identifiers who also identify with Europe are on average only moderately prejudiced against foreigners and Jews, whereas those who identify strongly with Germany but not with Europe tend to be especially prejudiced.

These 2002 German survey data also replicate the Euro88 survey finding that the identity variables act as important mediators of the effects of other important correlates of prejudice. Figure 2.2 displays this phenomenon with a structural equation model that is comparable to figure 2.1. Note how German

FIGURE 2.2 German Identity as Mediator

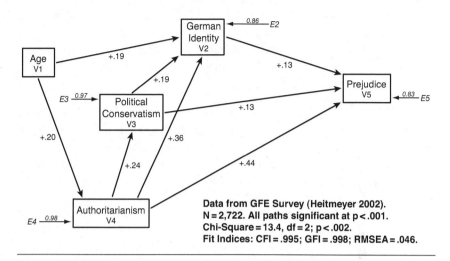

Data from GFE Survey (Heitmeyer 2002).
N = 2,722. All paths significant at p < .001.
Chi-Square = 13.4, df = 2; p < .002.
Fit Indices: CFI = .995; GFI = .998; RMSEA = .046.

identity mediates age, political conservatism, and authoritarianism. That is, German identity accounts for portions of the influence of these three predictors of antiforeigner prejudice. Older, conservative, and authoritarian respondents tend to possess stronger national identities, and this in turn contributes to their higher rejection of foreigners. Note also that there is no direct path from age to prejudice. This indicates that the full effect of older Germans revealing greater prejudice is explained by the fact that they are both more authoritarian and highly identified with their nation.

Discussion

These consistent results across the two diverse surveys demonstrate that identity does indeed matter for issues of intergroup prejudice and violence. Thus, these findings have methodological, theoretical, and practical policy significance. Consider each in turn.

Methodological Implications

When predicting intergroup prejudice at the individual level of analysis, identity matters. In both surveys, the five different measures of social identity all independently contribute to the predictions, even when other salient predictors are controlled.

But these relationships are complex. The more expansive European identity moderates the prejudicial and pro-violence effects of national identity. And often these identities serve as important mediators of the effects of other key predictors of prejudice. Thus, Western Europeans who are prone to prejudice and violence—such as the poorly educated—are more likely to reveal these effects if they also are highly identified with their nation and not at all with Europe. Thus, future research on intergroup prejudice and violence must be careful to check on these subtle but crucial moderating and mediating effects of identity measures.

Theoretical Implications

These results are relevant for numerous theories in the social sciences.[5] They are especially consistent with social identity theory in social psychology (Tajfel 1982; Turner and Reynolds 2001). They also carry particular relevance concerning a larger question that for a century has been a major focus of social-scientific theory on intergroup relations.

In his classic volume, *Folkways,* William Graham Sumner (1906) described ethnocentrism as a view by "which one's own group is the center of everything, and all others are scaled and rated in reference to it." Note that this conception has two components: one is an exaggeration of the in-group's position and cultural superiority, the other, a disparagement of all out-group cultures. Sumner held the two components—in-group aggrandizement and out-group denigration—to be two sides of the same coin. Indeed, he held this relationship to be universal. Thus, the Sumner hypothesis maintains that hostility toward out-groups is a direct reciprocal function of an in-group's sense of superiority and strong identification. Numerous other theories make the same prediction (Levine and Campbell 1972).

Since Sumner also believed that virtually all groups feel themselves to be superior, the hypothesis holds intergroup hostility and conflict to be natural and inevitable. Intergroup competition for scarce resources exacerbates the process. Such contentions were a critical part of Sumner's general position of Social Darwinism. A political reactionary, he agreed with Herbert Spenser that human society advanced by "the survival of the fittest." He viewed social reforms to be destructive of society's advances because they interfered with the natural selection process that led to superior human beings. Although ordained as an Anglican clergyman, he scoffed at "the absurd effort to make the world over."

Thus, Sumner viewed societies as evolving organisms as Darwin had posited for animal species. The greater the society's inequality, the more likely "the steady growth of civilization and advancement of society by and through its best members." He further believed conflict is inherent in such a process.

Sumner raised a key question for intergroup conflict, but research throughout social science shows that he overstated his case. His contention that in-group pride and conflict with out-groups are invariably and universally correlated positively is not correct. In developmental psychology, for example, Aboud (2003) conducted two investigations of Canadian children between the ages of three and seven, measuring both in-group favoritism and out-group prejudice. Aboud found that the two types of evaluations differed in important ways. For example, in-group favoritism formed earlier in life than out-group prejudice. She also found that the two measures were positively related only in the study in which the young white children had no contact with the black and native Indian people about whom they were questioned. But Aboud's second study took place in a racially mixed kindergarten, and here the two variables did not covary.

Why the difference between the two samples? Aboud suggests that the children in the all-white setting had no experience with the out-groups on which to base their out-group evaluations. So they used their in-group attachment as a referent comparison to evaluate the other groups. By contrast, the second sample did have direct experience with out-group children and based their out-group evaluations independent of their in-group attachments.

These developmental data with children indicate that the validity of the Sumnerian hypothesis is context dependent rather than universalistic, as Sumner assumed. Aboud's research suggests that favorable, face-to-face intergroup contact is one factor that moderates the hypothesized relationship between in-group favorability and out-group prejudice. With optimal intergroup contact, it is possible to possess positive attitudes toward both the in-group and out-groups.

Results from social-psychological experiments also question the Sumnerian hypothesis. In conflict with Sumner's assumptions, people who appear quite willing to favor their in-group are often reluctant to hurt out-groups blatantly (Brewer 1999; Mummendey and Otten 1998).

Turning to studies at the societal level of analysis, we find similar falsifications of the hypothesis. One study collected individual data from thirty different tribes in East Africa (Brewer and Campbell 1976). Averaging these data, the tendency to view their own in-group in a positive light was widespread across the groups. Hence, almost all of the tribes systematically considered themselves more trustworthy, obedient, friendly, and honest than other tribes. But this in-group bias did not correlate at all with their trait ratings of the other tribes or their willingness to interact with the other tribes.

Cashdan (2001) used the invaluable file of published codes on 186 preindustrial societies developed by Murdock and White (1969). Catastrophic food shortages, but not routine food shortages, were consistently associated with stronger in-group loyalties. External warfare also consistently related to greater in-group loyalty. This latter finding can be interpreted in several ways. Cashdan saw it as evidence that external warfare led to enhanced loyalty. But the causal paths could go in both directions. As Sumner held, greater loyalty could be contributing to the increased external warfare. There is a third possibility—namely, both causal paths could be operating to produce the association between external warfare and in-group loyalty.

Other tests, however, failed to support the universality of Sumner's hypothesis. Cashdan found that three out of four correlations between ratings of group loyalty and out-group hostility were in the opposite direction from that predicted by Sumner. Similarly, the degree of internal warfare was positively related with hostility toward out-groups—not negatively, as predicted by the hypothesis.

The identity results reported in this chapter are consistent with this wide-spread rejection of Sumner's contention. To be sure, Sumner was not all wrong: strong national identities are related throughout Western Europe with prejudice against foreigners. But this relationship partly reflects the mediating role of national identity for other predictors of prejudice. More importantly, we noted that national identity often combines with other important social identities—European and universalistic identities—that ameliorate Sumner's hypothesized link between in-group loyalty and out-group rejection. One can love and identify with one's nation without disparaging out-groups and supporting violence. This possibility is all the more likely when one also identities with larger entities (e.g., Europe) and takes pride in the nation's universalistic achievements (e.g., democracy and social security).

Social Policy Implications

National identification has obvious positive functions for any nation-state. It facilitates high morale, national cohesiveness, patriotism, pride, and loyalty. Such phenomena are especially valuable in times of war or other threats to the nation, when national identification invariably increases.

But there is a dark side to national identification. It can lead, as Sumner emphasized, to a sense of in-group superiority, and this belief can have negative consequences for others as well as for the nation itself. In addition to making harmonious intergroup relations with other groups more problematic, such a belief can foster arrogant inflexibility and blindness that prevent actions needed for the nation's welfare.

One obvious implication for social policy is that unbridled nationalism, especially if set in a context of out-group enemies and tinged with moral superiority, is a dangerous phenomenon. Even in the relatively tolerant Netherlands, annual remembrances in May of the end of the German occupation of World War II have served to preserve virulent anti-German prejudice across Dutch generations.

But the negative effects of national pride and identity are not inevitable. Following the insight of Habermas (1996), we have seen how tolerance flows from pride in a nation's universalistic achievements, such as democracy and social security for its people. In addition, we have seen that the more inclusive European identity relates to greater tolerance of even non-Europeans. This encouraging finding is consistent with a major social-psychological theory. Gaertner and Dovidio's (2000) common in-group identity model holds that identification with superordinate groups (such as "European") can reduce prejudice between two previously separate groups.

The European identity result contradicts in part a major fear that recent restrictions on immigration by the European Union constitute a narrow and bigoted conception of "Fortress Europa" (e.g., Castles 1984; Geddes 2000). These fears may be justified at the structural level, but at the individual level of analysis, a sense of being European is consistent with greater acceptance of outsiders in all the probability samples tested in this chapter. One can speculate that the increasing restrictions on immigration in Europe are fueled more by narrow nationalistic sentiments than by broader continental perspectives.

A Final Word

Identity matters. Social identities of many varieties are deeply implicated in intergroup prejudice and conflict; the Western European findings presented here offer repeated evidence for this claim. But the links between social identities and prejudice are considerably more complex than is generally appreciated. To be sure, narrow nationalistic identity is related to prejudice against a wide variety of out-groups across the nations of Western Europe. Part of this association is explained by the replicated finding that national identity serves as an important mediator for channeling prejudice-prone sectors of the population onto out-group targets.

But this well-known effect of narrow nationalism is only part of the story. The consistent links of both European and universalistic identities with greater tolerance and rejection of violence are not widely understood. Indeed, such identities blunt the negative effects of nationalism. These findings have important methodological, theoretical, and social policy implications.

Notes

1. For the reader unfamiliar with statistics, "r" is the Pearson product-moment coefficient that indicates how much two variables are interrelated. It varies in value between −1.00 (a completely negative correlation) and +1.00 (a completely positive correlation). Fractional values of "r" show how closely the variables are associated with each other.
2. The author wishes to express his appreciation to Professor Wilhelm Heitmeyer of Bielefeld University for permission to analyze these early data from the Institute for Interdisciplinary Research on Conflict and Violence project, "Group-Focused Enmity Syndrome—Longitudinal Empirical Observation of Attitudes of Enmity in the Population," a study begun in April 2002 and planned to continue through March 2012. For their unstinting help in organizing the data set and offering valuable ideas, I must also thank my Marburg University colleagues, Professor Ulrich Wagner, Dr. Jost Stellmacher, and Oliver Christ.
3. See Heyder and Schmidt (2002) for another analysis of these variables with these same data.

4. Four other predictors of pro-violence attitudes are important. Age is a strong negative correlate, with young people being considerably more prone to violence than older respondents. The other three predictors point to the possibility of psychopathological involvement: compulsiveness, "general socioemotional disintegration," and especially a sense of social isolation.

5. This section draws from an earlier discussion of ethnocentrism by the author (Pettigrew 2004).

References

Aboud, F. E. 2003. "The Formation of In-Group Favoritism and Out-Group Prejudice in Young Children: Are They Distinct Attitudes?" *Developmental Psychology* 39: 48–60.

Adorno, T. W., E. Frenkel-Brunswik, D. J. Levinson, and R. N. Sanford. 1950. *The Authoritarian Personality*. New York: Harper.

Altemeyer, B. 1988. *Enemies of Freedom: Understanding Right-Wing Authoritarianism*. San Francisco: Jossey-Bass.

_____. 1998. "The 'Other' Authoritarian." *Advances in Experimental Social Psychology* 30: 47–92.

Arcuri, L., and S. Boca. 1996. "Pregiudizid e affiliazione politica" [Prejudice and political affiliation]. In *Psicologia e politica*, ed. P. Legrenzi and V. Girotto. Milan: Raffaello Cortina Editure.

_____. 1999. "Posicionamentos politicos: Racismo subtil e racismo flagrante em Italia" [Political Positions: Subtle and Blatant Racism in Italy]. In *Novos Racismos: Perspectivas Comparativas*, ed. J. Vala. Oeiras, Portugal: Celta Editora.

Brewer, M. B. 1999. "The Psychology of Prejudice: Ingroup Love or Outgroup Hate?" *Journal of Social Issues* 55, no. 3: 429–444.

Brewer, M. B., and D. T. Campbell. 1976. *Ethnocentrism and Intergroup Attitudes: East African Evidence*. Beverley Hills, CA: Sage.

Cashdan, E. 2001. "Ethnocentrism and Xenophobia: A Cross-Cultural Study (1)." *Current Anthropology* 42: 760–765.

Castles, S. 1984. *Here for Good: Western Europe's New Ethnic Minorities*. London: Pluto.

Cialdini, R. B., R. J. Borden, A. Thorne, M. R. Walker, S. Freeman, and L. R. Sloan. 1976. "Basking in Reflected Glory: Three (Football) Field Studies." *Journal of Personality and Social Psychology* 34: 366–375.

Dovidio, J. F., J. Mann, and S. L. Gaertner. 1989. "Resistance to Affirmative Action: The Implications of Aversive Racism." In *Affirmative Action in Perspective,* ed. F. Blanchard and F. Crosby, 83–102. New York: Springer Verlag.

Gaertner, S. L., and J. F. Dovidio. 2000. *Reducing Intergroup Bias: The Common Ingroup Identity Model.* Philadelphia: Psychology Press.

Gaertner, S. L., and J. P. McLaughlin. 1983. "Racial Stereotypes: Associations and Ascriptions of Positive and Negative Characteristics." *Social Psychology Quarterly* 46: 23–30.

Geddes, A. 2000. *Immigration and European Integration: Towards Fortress Europe?* Manchester: Manchester University Press.

Habermas, J. 1996. *Between Facts and Norms: Contributions to a Discourse Theory of Law and Democracy.* Trans. W. Rehg. Cambridge, MA: MIT Press.

Hamberger, J., and M. Hewstone. 1997. "Interethnic Contact As a Predictor of Blatant and Subtle Prejudice: Tests of a Model in Four West European Nations." *British Journal of Social Psychology* 36: 173–190.

Heitmeyer, W., ed. 2002. *Deutsche Zustände* [The German Situation]. Part 1. Frankfurt am Main: Suhrkamp Verlag.

Heyder, A., and P. Schmidt. 2002. "Deutscher Stolz: Patriotismus ware besser" [German Pride: Patriotism Is Better]. In *Deutsche Zustände* [The German Situation], part 1, ed. W. Heitmeyer, 71–82. Frankfurt am Main: Suhrkamp Verlag.

Hightower, E. 1997. "Psychosocial Characteristics of Subtle and Blatant Racists As Compared to Tolerant Individuals." *Journal of Clinical Psychology* 53: 369–374.

Katz, I., and R. G. Hass. 1988. "Racial Ambivalence and Value Conflict: Correlational and Priming Studies of Dual Cognitive Structures." *Journal of Personality and Social Psychology* 55: 893–905.

Kinder, D. R., and L. M. Sanders. 1996. *Divided by Color: Racial Politics and American Ideals*. Chicago: University of Chicago Press.

Kuhn, M. H., and T. McPartland. 1954. "An Empirical Investigation of Self-Attitudes." *American Sociological Review* 19: 68–76.

Levine, R. A., and D. T. Campbell. 1972. *Ethnocentrism: Theories of Conflict, Ethnic Attitudes, and Group Behavior*. New York: Wiley.

McConahay, J. B. 1983. "Modern Racism and Modern Discrimination: The Effects of Race, Racial Attitudes, and Context on Simulated Hiring Decisions." *Personality and Social Psychology Bulletin* 9: 551–558.

Meertens, R. W., and T. F. Pettigrew. 1997. "Is Subtle Prejudice Really Prejudice?" *Public Opinion Quarterly* 61: 54–71.

Mummendey, A., and S. Otten. 1998. "Positive-Negative Asymmetry in Social Discrimination." *European Review of Social Psychology* 9: 107–143.

Murdoch, G. P., and D. R. White. 1969. "Standard Cross-Cultural Sample." *Ethnology* 8: 399–460.

Pedersen, A., and I. Walker. 1997. "Prejudice against Aborigines: Old-Fashioned and Modern Forms." *European Journal of Social Psychology* 25: 561–587.

Pettigrew, T. F. 1997. "Generalized Intergroup Contact Effects on Prejudice." *Personality and Social Psychology Bulletin* 23: 173–185.

———. 1998. "Responses to the New Minorities of Western Europe." *Annual Review of Sociology* 24: 77–103.

———. 2004. "Ethnocentrism." In *Encyclopedia of Social Measurement*. San Diego, CA: Academic Press.

Pettigrew, T. F., J. Jackson, J. Ben Brika, G. Lemain, R. W. Meertens, U. Wagner, and A. Zick. 1998. "Outgroup Prejudice in Western Europe." *European Review of Social Psychology* 8: 241–273.

Pettigrew, T. F., and R. W. Meertens. 1995. "Subtle and Blatant Prejudice in Western Europe." *European Journal of Social Psychology* 57: 57–75.

Rattazzi, A. M. M., and C. Volpato. 2000. "The Social Desirability of Subtle and Blatant Prejudice Scales." Unpublished paper submitted for publication, Department of General Psychology, University of Padua.

———. 2001. "Forme sottili e manifeste di pregiudizio verso gli immigrati" [Subtle and Blatant Forms of Prejudice against Immigrants]. *Giacuale Italiano di Psicologia* 28: 351–375.

Reif, K., and A. Melich. 1991. *Euro-Barometer 30: Immigrants and Out-Groups in Western Europe, October–November 1988*. ICPSR 9321. Ann Arbor, MI: Inter-university Consortium for Political and Social Research.

Rise, J., K. Haugen, E. Klinger, and G. Bierbrauer. 2000. "Subtle and Blatant Prejudice in a Norwegian Population." Unpublished manuscript, University of Oslo.

Rueda, J. F., and M. Navas. 1996. "Hacia una evaluacion de las nuevas formas del prejuicio racial: Las actitudes sutiles del racismo" [Toward an Evaluation of the New Forms of Racial Prejudice: The Subtle Attitudes of Racism]. *Revista de Psicologia Social* 11: 131–149.

Sears, D. O. 1988. "Symbolic Racism." In *Eliminating Racism: Profiles in Controversy*, ed. P. A. Katz and D. A. Taylor, 53–84. New York: Plenum Press.

Sears, D. O., J. Sidanius, and L. Bobo, eds. 2000. *Racialized Politics: The Debate about Racism in America*. Chicago: University of Chicago Press.

Sidanius, J., and F. Pratto. 1999. *Social Dominance: An Intergroup Theory of Social Hierarchy and Oppression*. New York: Cambridge University Press.

Sisbane, F., B. Rimè, and A. Azzi. 2000. "Dealing with Emotional Similarity in Intergroup Relations: Consequences for Prejudice Reduction." Paper presented at the 3rd Jena Workshop on Intergroup Processes, Schloss Kochberg, Germany, 1 July 2000.

Six, B., and U. Wolfradt. 2000. "Authoritarianism and Some More Social Psychological Traits: Structures and Contingencies." Paper presented at the International Congress of Psychology Conference, Stockholm, Sweden, 25 July 2000.

Sumner, W. G. 1906. *Folkways*. New York: Ginn.

Tajfel, H., ed. 1982. *Social Identity and Intergroup Relations*. Cambridge: Cambridge University Press.

Turner, J. C., and K. J. Reynolds. 2001. "The Social Identity Perspective in Intergroup Relations: Theories, Themes and Controversies." In *Blackwell Handbook of Social Psychology: Intergroup Processes*, ed. R. Brown and S. Gaertner, 89–111. Oxford: Blackwell.

Vala, J., R. Brito, and D. Lopes. 1999. "O racismo flagrante e o racismo subtil em Portugal" [Blatant and Subtle Racism in Portugal]. In *Novos Racismos: Perspectivas Comparativas*, ed. J. Vala. Oeiras, Portugal: Celta Editora.

Villano, P. 1999. "Anti-Semitic Prejudice in Adolescence: An Italian Study on Shared Beliefs." *Psychological Reports* 84: 1372–1378.

Volpato, C., and A. M. M. Rattazzi. 2000. "Pregiudizio e immigrazione: Effecti del contatto sulle relazioni interetniche" [Prejudice and Immigration: Effects of Contact upon Interethnic Relations]. *Ricerche di Psicologia* 24: 57–80.

Wagner, U., and A. Zick. 1995. "The Relation of Formal Education to Ethnic Prejudice: Its Reliability, Validity, Explanation." *European Journal of Social Psychology* 25: 41–56.

Zick, A., U. Wagner, R. van Dick, and T. Petzel. 2001. "Acculturation and Prejudice in Germany: Majority and Minority Perspectives." *Journal of Social Issues* 57: 541–557.

3

READINESS TO FIGHT IN CRIMEA
How It Interrelates with National and Ethnic Identities

Karina V. Korostelina

Theories have been developed to explain the social and psychological processes by which category membership influences identity and intergroup conflict (Gaertner et al. 2000; Tajfel and Turner 1986; Turner et al. 1987), but considerably less attention has been given to the interrelations between identities. Research on ethnic conflicts and violence reveals a set of factors that have a significant impact on conflict behavior and negative intentions toward out-groups. Numerous studies show that in weak states with sizable minorities, the presence of salient ethnic identity among those minorities strongly encourages ethnic violence (Berry et al. 1989; Brewer 1991, 1996; Conover 1988; Crocker and Luhtanen 1990; Gellner 1994; Kaiser 1994; Miller et al. 1981). As Brubaker (1996) has pointed out, ethnic identity politics and minority grievances create tensions, and the formation of a new, independent state often leads to conflicts initiated by national minorities. Yet the establishment of new states also encourages the development of a new national identity associated with economic independence, human dignity, and popular self-esteem (Kelman 1997). Such superordinate identity is sometimes more powerful than ethnic identity, encouraging the resolution of ethnic conflicts. Thus, national identity building, which is now taking place throughout the postcommunist world, has contributed in some cases to the escalation of ethnic conflicts and in other cases to their resolution.

The purpose of this chapter is to analyze the impact of the interrelation between national and ethnic identities on the readiness of ethnic minorities to initiate or participate in conflict with other ethnic groups. I argue that the salience and meaning of other social identities acts as a powerful moderator of the influence of a specific social identity on a person's attitudes and behavioral intentions. In particular, I investigate how both identity salience and concepts of national identity moderate the impact of ethnic identity on the readiness of representatives of ethnic minorities to clash with out-groups. I also explore how this moderation effect depends on the relative socioeconomic position and population proportion of a given ethnic minority in a particular region. I regard salient ethnic identity, which has been described as an indicator of ethnic conflicts, as an independent variable. Readiness for conflict with other ethnic groups is the dependent variable. I hypothesize that the effect of ethnic identity on conflict readiness or willingness to compromise would vary with the salience of national identity and with different meanings of national identity—ethnic, multicultural, and civic.

The System of Social Identities

Adler (1994), Crenshaw (1998), and King (1988) stress that an individual's system of identities is not simply a combination of that person's ethnic, multicultural, and civic identities, but rather a system in which identities have multiple effects. Some approaches to conceptualizing multiple social identities exist. According to Brewer's (2001) classification of identity theories, theories of person-based social identity (Cross 1991; Phinney 1990; Skevington and Baker 1989) suggest that one's self-concept consists of different stereotypes, attitudes, and values that one receives from membership in groups. Some of these particulars may be more salient than others, but they all serve as parts of a single representation of the individual self. Theories of relational social identity assume that the self is a set of discrete identities, each of which is differentiated from a person's other role identities. This system is organized and structured, and it determines which identity will be salient in a particular social context (Stryker 2000; Stryker and Serpe 1994). Theories of group-based social identities suggest that one's identity system depends on the social context (Turner et al. 1994) but that some social categories can be relatively stable across time and situations (Abrams 1999). The idea of the fluidity of identity in social categorization theory (Turner et al. 1987) grew out of research on situational identities in laboratory settings. Research into ethnic identity reveals, however, that it shows remarkable stability over time (Alwin, Cohen, and Newcomb 1992; Ethier and Deaux 1994; Sears and Henry 1999).

Applying the insights of this scholarship to the matter of identity formation, I define identity as a system that involves core identities, short-term identities, and situational identities. Core identities are fairly stable and dominant: they exist for a relatively long time and change only in situations of considerable social shifting. Some core identities persist throughout an individual's entire lifetime. Short-term identities are inconstant, and changes to them occur frequently. Situational identities are connected to concrete situations and depend on those situations. They are a "building material" for the creation of short-term and core identities.

All identities are interrelated, and correlations within the subsystem of core identities are the most strong and firm. One identity can influence the development process of another identity, increase or decrease its salience, and strengthen or weaken its impact on attitudes and behavior. In particular contexts of intergroup relations—for instance, when an individual is in a minority position, suffers from discrimination, or engages in conflict—different identities become strongly interconnected and reshape one another. Research has confirmed the existence of strong interrelations between identities. For example, when men, normally the members of the higher-status group, are in the minority, they are more likely to think of themselves in gender-stereotypic terms—and thus to identify with their gender—than are women, the members of a lower-status group (Swann and Wyer 1997).

The theory of social identity stresses that each identity is formed as a result of an individual's membership in an in-group and is in opposition or comparison to members of an out-group (Tajfel and Turner 1979, 1986). The existence of an out-group and the in-group's negative and conflict-ridden relations with it strengthen group identity (concerning the effect of simple social categorization, see, e.g., Allen and Wilder 1975; Billig and Tajfel 1973; Brewer and Miller 1984; Brewer and Silver 1978; Doise and Sinclair 1973). The position, achievements, and losses of the group as a whole are incorporated into the self and respond to personal outcomes (e.g., Hirt et al. 1992).

The results of this research and numerous other studies encourage us to understand social identity as an open, unstable system. The factor of asymmetry, the element of chance, and feedback play important roles in the development of such systems. The progressive development of an identity system is a contradictory process. The joining of new groups, the formation of new out-groups, and changes to the status and power of in-groups and out-groups all lead to the reorganization of identity systems, the formation of new identities, and the emergence of contradictions between different identities, which cause changes in a person's social behavior. The rise, development, and disappearance of any identity leads to modifications within the whole system. Such reconstruction affects the subsystem of short-term identities, but correlations within the identity system do not change fundamentally.

An identity system serves five psychological functions for group members: it increases self-esteem, increases social status, provides personal safety, provides support and protection from the group, and grants a sense of recognition by the group (Korostelina 2003b). A person's needs for personal security and social status can change, and these needs exert an influence on the structure of that person's identities. If a new identity begins to fulfill necessary functions, it can lead to the quick disappearance of old identities. If one of the identities ceases to fulfill its functions, it gradually loses its significance and vanishes.

Core identities can remain, however, even in the situation of the destruction and disappearance of their respective social groups: identity-related processes continue to be organized in the same way that they had been within the whole system in the past. Consider, for example, the Soviet identity of the populations of the newly independent states of the former Soviet Union. In spite of the disappearance of the common "Soviet people," Soviet identity still occupies a leading place as a core identity among middle-aged and elderly people. Carl Rogers (1961) has postulated that a sense of identity involves seeing ourselves as we really are—who we have been, who we are today, and who we will become. Thus, a sense of identity can be attained only when we discover and chart our own destinies in life. As Tajfel (1969) observed, situations of rapid social transformation involving changes in out-group and in-group relations play an important role in structuring people's visions of the future. When an identity system functions according to its "memory," without reference to the present or future, it leads to contradiction in the system of identities.

The development of an identity system is not based on the principle of "imposition"; instead, differentiation and integration are its main characteristics. It evolves by means of two basic processes: first, assimilation and accommodation, i.e., the restructuring of new components of the identity system; and, second, estimation, or the evaluation of the significance and value of new and old identities. One of the characteristic features of an identity system is the existence of mechanisms of competition between identities, which ends in the selection of the most stable identities, the rise of new identities, and the breaking of established patterns of behavior. The development mechanism of the identity system ensures the greatest possible initial variety of identities. Within this context, important and insignificant elements are revalued, and irrelevant identities are neglected. Some identities develop on the basis of others; contradictions between identities, mutual strengthening or weakening, and changes in the correlation between core and short-term identities can also arise. This process is most vigorous among adolescents, who "try on" many different identities before selecting core identities to organize the whole system (Phinney 1990). But the same processes, although in more latent forms, take place throughout a person's whole life, especially in periods of social change. When there is rapid social change and new information is introduced, people come to understand that their values, beliefs, and information are out of date. As a result, they do not know where to turn. They become alienated and unsure of how to resolve the problems associated with their identity.

Identity Salience

Stryker (1969) has argued that various identities exist in a hierarchy of salience and that one identity can be invoked over others not only because of its salience but also because of the person's level of commitment to that identity. If an identity has salience for a long period, it becomes a central identity and exerts a strong influence on behavior. The salience of an ethnic identity may have both stable and situational characteristics. Ting-Toomey et al. (2000) note that "for some individuals, ethnic identity only becomes salient when they are forced to confront interpersonal issues of 'being different' like stereotypes, prejudice, and discrimination." According to Oakes's (1987) functional approach to salience, the use of a particular identity category in a given context depends on the accessibility of the category and the fit between the category and reality. Huddy (2001) has argued that four factors influence the acquisition of identity: the valence of group membership, the defining social characteristics of typical group members, the core values associated with membership, and the characteristics of common out-groups that help to define what the in-group is not. Gerson (2001: 183) maintains that the development and salience of identity are influenced by practices—by "what people do and how they conceptualize or represent what they do as constituting membership in various groups." The salience of any particular identity also depends on its interconnections with other identities and their salience. Thus, research shows that the degree of a person's identification with different levels of identity categorization may be inferred from an examination of the interrelationships between the different categories (Huici et al. 1997).

I would maintain that identity salience is interconnected with the stability of identity systems. Like many unstable systems, the identity system tends to become stable. In various situations, different identities become salient, restoring the stability of the identity system. If any change occurs in the social situation or in the balance of power, then another identity becomes salient, leading to the restructuring of the system of identities. When one of the core identities becomes more salient than another, the changes to the system are less considerable, because correlations between core identities are stable and strong as a rule. But if one of the short-term identities becomes salient, the imbalance within the system grows significantly; much time and restructuring effort are required to return it to a stable position. In many situations, a more numerous, authoritative, and powerful out-group will influence the development of a person's salient identity. But research shows that even the disproportion between groups can increase the salience of identity; for example, children who are in an ethnic minority in their classrooms have strong ethnic identity. Similarly, children who are raised in families in which there are more members of the opposite gender than of their own have stronger gender identity than do children raised in families in which most of the members are of the same gender (McGuire et al. 1978).

Identity and Conflict Readiness

Core identities are connected to stable attitudes and worldviews. Attitudes connected to short-term identities are less stable and tend to change very quickly. Research reveals that individuals who respond more rapidly to traits that are characteristic of both themselves and the in-group have stronger group identity

(Smith and Henry 1996). There is also an echo effect: the intention of a national minority to become autonomous or independent will provoke a nationalistic reaction among the indigenous majority (Hagendoorn et al. 2000).

Other results confirm the role of subjective group membership in shaping political attitudes and behavior (Conover 1988; Miller et al. 1981). Some researchers report a strong correlation between identification with an in-group and hostility toward an out-group (Branscombe and Wann 1994; Grant and Brown 1995). It has been shown that negative stereotypes can be reinforced, not only as a result of the attribution of antagonistic goals to out-groups, but also by the attribution of goals to the in-group when in-group members assume that out-groups will react in a hostile manner to these shared in-group goals (Hagendoorn et al. 1996). The longitudinal analyses of Duckitt and Mphuthing (1998) demonstrate that black Africans' in-group identification is impacted by their attitudes toward white Africans.

Thus, the salience of social identity affects attitudes: a more salient social identity strengthens attitudes and behavioral intentions to a greater extent than does a nonsalient identity. Moreover, salient identity is connected to the presence of more developed and numerous attitudes than is nonsalient social identity. People with salient national identity have a more developed system of negative attitudes toward and stereotypes about the residents of other countries than do people with a low level of national identity salience (Korostelina 2003a). A salient social identity can also moderate the impact of other social identities on attitudes by strengthening or weakening attitudes connected to it.

Minorities' attitudes toward other ethnic groups show the actual level of active prejudice in a society. Prejudice has been commonly defined as a negative attitude, "an antipathy based on faulty and inflexible generalization" that "may be felt or expressed" and "may be directed toward a group as a whole or toward an individual because he is a member of that group" (Allport 1954: 9). As an attitude, prejudice has three components: cognitive prejudice (thoughts and beliefs about other groups), affective prejudice (feelings and emotions about other groups), and conative prejudice (behavioral predispositions and intended actions) (Esses, Haddock, and Zanna 1993; Zanna and Rempel 1988). Some scholars note that attitudes do not necessarily have all three aspects and that they can be formed primarily or exclusively on the basis of only one component (Eagly and Chaiken 1993). Thus, each component can have a different level of development and a different role in defining the structure and nature of an individual's prejudice. Theories of stereotypes, prejudice, and discrimination posit a wide range of relations between and among the components of prejudice (Stephan and Stephan 2004).

Prejudice is typically measured using standardized scales that contain statements about the attributes of a group, the respondent's feelings about the group, and whether the respondent supports policies that affect the group (Dovidio et al. 1996). Other special methods measure single components of prejudice. Many scholars consider stereotypes to be cognitive components and measure them by asking respondents to provide descriptions of members of a group or by rating the extent to which specific traits are associated with the group. The affective component of prejudice contains different emotions, such as dislike, hate, discomfort, and anxiety, which interact with cognitive components and lead to negative intergroup perception (Hyers and Swim 1998). Emotions are measured by asking participants to indicate the level at which they experience each of a range of feelings.

Psychological research provides sufficient empirical information about stereotypes and emotions but sheds considerably less light on the conative component of prejudice. Although discrimination is described as a phenomenon separate from prejudice, the results of research on discrimination can in fact be used to understand the behavioral element of prejudice. Discrimination, for example, means denying equality of treatment (Allport 1954) or maintaining the favored position of one's own group at the expense of other groups (Jones 1972). Discrimination has been measured in terms of failure to help, self-disclosure, seating distances, and nonverbal behavior (Dovidio and Gaertner 1998). There is almost no research, however, on behavioral intentions related to the readiness for conflict with another group as a measure of the conative component of prejudice. The readiness for conflict aiming at the dominance of the in-group over out-groups or at defending the status and goals of the in-group is an extreme consequence of intergroup prejudice. It is important to extend research on prejudice to include the intention to fight with another group, since this intention reflects the conflict potential resulting from particular intergroup relations.

One's readiness for conflict with another group reflects one's willingness and eagerness to defend one's own group in situations of real or perceived threat from other groups, to control and prevent actions of the members of other groups that are potentially dangerous or unpleasant for one's own group (or that could increase the status of the other group), or to punish or take revenge against members of the other group. People with a high level of conflict readiness engage in harassment and fighting with members of other groups more often than they do with members of their own group.

Conflict readiness is interconnected with the cognitive and affective components of prejudice. Negative stereotypes, beliefs, feelings, and emotions reinforce it. Cognitive dissonance theory (Festinger 1957) leads us to expect, moreover, that conflict readiness will reshape negative stereotypes and feelings. It predicts that individuals will tend to seek consistency among their cognitions (i.e., their beliefs and opinions). When there is an inconsistency between behavioral intentions and stereotypes, something must change to eliminate the dissonance. In the case of such a discrepancy, it is most likely that stereotypes will be changed to accommodate behavior. Therefore, if people have a high level of conflict readiness, their stereotypes and attitudes will almost certainly become more negative and extreme to avoid dissonance.

When we approach social identity as a system, we can expect the salience of national identity to moderate the impact of ethnic identity on conflict readiness by strengthening or weakening individuals' readiness for conflict with the members of other ethnic groups. But the salience of identity itself cannot provide complete information about how attitudes and conflict readiness will be moderated. To understand the moderation effect of another identity (in this case, national identity), it is also important to analyze the meaning of this identity. Assessing the impact of concepts of national identity provides an opportunity to develop a deeper understanding of interrelations within the identity system and their effects on conflict intentions.

National and Ethnic Identities

Since a usual characteristic of nations is their residence in common territory, many people in newly nationalizing states become members of these states only because they reside within their borders. As Kelman (1997) pointed out, the establishment of new states creates incentives for the creation of ethnic homogeneity and thus systematic efforts to marginalize or destroy ethnic "others." Conflict can develop when the identity chosen by an individual is incompatible with the identity imposed by others or with the social context in which identity is constantly being re-created (Kelman 1982; Stein 1998; Stern 1995).

Yet national identity building may also create a tolerant new common identity and opportunities for the de-escalation of conflict. According to a common in-group identity model (Gaetner et al. 2000), possession of a new common identity changes people's conceptions of their membership—they shift from perceiving themselves as members of different groups to perceiving themselves as members of a single, more inclusive group—and it makes individuals' attitudes toward former out-group members more positive, even if the two groups have a long history of conflict. The new superordinate national identity provides a strong feeling of unity with other groups, self-esteem, confidence, and dignity, and it can reduce intergroup biases and conflict. For example, when American identity is the most important one for members of diverse ethnic and racial groups in the United States and they see themselves as members of their ethnic or racial groups only secondarily, they exhibit less conflict behavior (Citrin, Wong, and Duff 2000). Research on ethnic and racial identities in the United States and Israel also suggests that a sense of patriotism is connected to weak identity as a member of a subordinate group and to the possession of strong national identity (Sidanius et al. 1997). Thus, when an individual has salient national identity, national identity is important to that individual, who usually has strong feelings of belonging to the nation, shared positive attitudes toward the in-group, and shared negative attitudes toward the citizens of other countries. Salient national identity has a strong influence on behavior, and for some people national identity can become a central identity.

Concepts of National Identity

The meaning of a new national identity can have a significant impact on people's conflict readiness. Research stresses the importance of meaning in both shaping identities and determining whether behavior is conflict seeking or tolerant (Deaux 1993; Gurin, Hurtado, and Peng 1994; Huddy 2003; Simon and Hamilton 1994). Breakwell (2001) shows that the different meanings of identity in different European countries shape reactions to policies designed to create a European Union. The meaning of African-American identity influences African-Americans' readiness to support programs designed to improve the situations of other minority groups (Sellers et al. 1998). Research also shows that the meaning of national identity can influence attitudes toward other groups and toward those in other political situations. Thus, individuals with a nativist sense of American identity regard immigrants negatively and see the adoption of American customs as an obligation of immigrants (Citrin, Wong, and Duff 2000).

The central problem of national identity formation concerns the interrelations between the majority and the minority, between dominant and small minorities, and between natives and immigrants. The core question for the national identity concept is the position of ethnic minorities within the nation, that is, whether the minority will be oppressed by the majority or whether members of the minority will have opportunities to maintain their ethnic culture. The analysis of relations between ethnic groups shows that people can have three different concepts or ideas of national identity: an ethnic concept, a multicultural concept, and a civic concept. People with an ethnic concept of national identity perceive their nation as built around a core ethnic community into which ethnic minorities must assimilate. They see their nation as monoethnic and monolingual, and they believe that those who have inherited or assimilated the values and attributes of the ethnic core should have higher status within the nation. Those with a multicultural concept of national identity view their nations as offering equal rights—and even some elements of autonomy and self-governance—to all ethnic groups. They see their states as societies within which ethnic minorities should be guaranteed resources to maintain their ethnic cultures and communities. The different ethnic groups must have an opportunity to receive education in their native language, and their cultural heritage must be part of the country's heritage. Those with a civic concept, finally, perceive their citizenship as a contract between the people and the state that involves rights and obligations. They view the constitution, the rule of law, and civic responsibility as the main features of the nation, and they see ethnicity as insignificant. They perceive their nation as built on a distinctive nonethnic civic culture into which all citizens must integrate.

Citizens in countries such as France and Germany developed a common understanding of their nation and national identity over centuries.

But in newly developing nations, people often differ in their understanding of national identity, and this influences their estimations of their situation, their expectations, and their behavior (Korostelina 2003a). The meaning of national identity shapes people's attitudes and behavior toward different ethnic groups within their own nations as well as their approaches toward other nations. Research shows that concepts of the nation are associated with specific models of integrating immigrants into society; for example, they influence the process of integrating a nation into the broader European community (Münch 2001). Thus, an ethnic concept of national identity in Germany leads to the rejection of immigrants as members of the German nation and to the belief that they are granted too many rights. A multicultural concept of national identity in the United States produces the appreciation of different cultures and the acceptance of differences among citizens and other permanent and temporary residents. And a civic concept of national identity in Great Britain makes possible the integration of immigrants into society by providing them a place in the community of citizens. Because the meaning of national identity influences individuals' attitudes and behavior, the concept of national identity can influence the readiness of both majorities and minorities to fight with other groups and can increase or decrease the influence of other identities.

Ethnic Identity Salience

As Phinney (1991) shows, people with strong ethnic identity salience are more prejudiced and show greater readiness for conflict behavior toward other groups. Research demonstrates, for example, that South Africans' strong identification with their own racial and ethnic group influences their need for group solidarity and reinforces their antipathy toward out-groups and their feelings of threat and intolerance (Gibson and Gouwa 1998). Other results also suggest that salient group membership has a role in shaping political attitudes and behavior (Conover 1988; Miller et al. 1981) and find a correlation between salient group identification and hostility toward out-groups (Branscombe and Wann 1994; Grant and Brown 1995).

My previous research (Korostelina 2004) showed that salient ethnic identity itself—measured by responses to the statements "I am proud to be a member of my ethnic group" and "It is important for me to be a member of my ethnic group, and I share my values and ideas with other members of my ethnic group"—did not have a strong effect on conflict readiness. These statements measure internal sources of self-esteem (Korostelina 2003b) and identity salience. Individuals who agree with them have a strong sense of membership because they are proud of their own group; they do not have a need to compare their group to other groups or to view out-groups negatively. But combined with ethnocentrism—measured by responses to the statements "There are no people in the world better than those of my ethnic group" and "The more the culture of my ethnic group influences the culture of other nations, the better it is for these nations"—the salience of social identity *does* have a significant impact on conflict readiness. This second group of statements measures the degree to which the respondent has external sources of self-esteem and identity salience: the in-group itself does not provide a source of pride, and the individual instead tends to perceive out-groups negatively and to discriminate against them. Negative comparison provides a basis for strong identification with the in-group.

Ethnocentrism has the following characteristics: individual members give their primary loyalty to their own ethnic community; this loyalty supersedes their loyalty to other groups; and their ethnic community has a positive estimation of the in-group and negative attitudes toward out-groups. Ethnocentric individuals have a strong feeling of own-group centrality and superiority, and they attempt to maintain the security of their own-group stereotyping and their misplaced suspicion of others' intentions (Booth 1979). Most stereotypes are inaccurate and lead to all sorts of biases and prejudices (Allport 1954; Fiske and Taylor 1991). Ethnocentric attitudes cause people to understand events in ways that further strengthen their positive views of the in-group and their negative views of out-groups (Crocker and Luhtanen 1990). Pettigrew (1979) called such a predisposition the "fundamental attribution error": it involves a tendency to make internal attributions for in-group success and external ones for in-group failure and to make internal attributions for out-group failure and external ones for out-group success. Hewstone (1990) reviewed the many studies documenting this attribution error and found that it escalates conflict between groups. The greater the perceived differences in the typical characteristics of the in-group and out-groups, the greater the likelihood of hostility (Oakes 1987; Turner et al. 1994).

Intergroup dynamics and the need for positive identity both act to produce enemy images even in the absence of hostile intentions by the other party. They generate behavior that is hostile and confrontational, increasing the likelihood that the other party will respond with hostile action. Negative stereotypes can in fact be reinforced by the in-group's attribution of hostile goals to the out-group, and by the expectation that out-groups may react with hostility to the in-group's shared goals (Hagendoorn et al. 1996).

Research shows that in-group bias is stronger among minority groups than among majority groups (Brewer and Weber 1994; Ellemers, Kortekaas, and Ouwerkerk 1999; Simon and Hamilton 1994). In particular, members of lower-status minority groups show more discriminatory behavior (Espinoza and Garza 1985; Otten, Mummendey, and Blanz 1996). Minority group members experience a stronger collective self, have more elaborate positive and negative self-stereotypes, and process more group-level information than majority group members (Ellemers, Kortekaas, and Ouwerkerk 1999; Simon 1992; Simon and Hamilton 1994). They also perceive more in-group homogeneity and in-group similarity than do majority group members (Brewer and

Weber 1994). The stronger in-group bias of minority groups can be explained by minority group members' concerns about social identity (Gerard and Hoyt 1974; Mullen 1983) and their need to compensate for insecurity (Sachdev and Bourhis 1984). Minority groups are often low-status groups and therefore their members need more group support than do the members of majority groups. Their members are highly motivated to improve the fate of the in-group (Mummendey and Otten 1998) and identify more strongly with the in-group than do majority group members (Perreault and Bourhis 1999; Kinket and Verkuyten 1999; van Oudenhoven and Eisses 1998; Verkuyten and Masson 1995). The evidence on this matter is not conclusive, however. Mullen, Brown, and Smith (1992) found that in-group bias is weaker among low-status groups, and Ellemers et al. (1992) report a stronger sense of collective self among minority groups only when the status of the minority group is high. Nonetheless, if strong in-group identification contributes to in-group bias (Brewer 1996; Deaux 1996; Perreault and Bourhis 1998), then minority groups appear to be more prone to bias.

Some studies show that stronger in-group identification does not lead to more in-group bias in the same way for majority groups as it does for minority groups. The in-group identification of majority group members is provoked primarily by perceptions of intergroup conflict, while minority group members have high levels of in-group identification for a variety of reasons (Jackson 2002; Verkuyten and Masson 1995). Under conditions of perceived intergroup conflict or out-group threat, in-group bias may be stronger among majority group members than among minorities. This suggests that the relationship between identity and bias is contingent on the position of groups as majorities or minorities.

The Context of the Research

The research for this chapter took place in Crimea in Ukraine, where Russians and Crimean Tatars, both ethnic minority groups within Ukraine, are now in the process of adopting a new national identity. Crimea was a nominally independent khanate of the Ottoman Empire until 1783, when it was annexed by Russia. After the Russian Revolution, Crimea was independent from 1917 to 1918 and was then incorporated into the Soviet Union as an autonomous republic of the Russian Federation in 1921. Its autonomous status was abolished in 1944. In 1954, Crimea was transferred to the Ukrainian Soviet Socialist Republic, and its status as part of Ukraine continued when Ukraine became independent in 1991. The current population of Crimea is nearly 2.5 million. Ethnic Russians, though a minority in Ukraine, make up 64 percent of the Crimean population; of the remaining population, 23 percent are Ukrainians, 10 percent are Crimean Tatars, and 3 percent are Belorussians, Armenians, Greeks, Germans, Jews, and others.

The Crimea of the 1990s had substantial potential for ethnopolitical violence. Multiple "nested autonomies" conflicts arose due to the resettlement in Crimea of 250,000 Crimean Tatars who had been deported to Central Asia by Stalin in 1944. The resettlement changed the ethnic balance of the population by inserting an ethnically divergent group, and it resulted in land and property disputes as well as citizenship claims by the new arrivals. During the 1990s, approximately half of the remaining deported ethnic Tatars and their descendants returned to their "homeland," only to find that they were repeatedly denied citizenship rights and access to education, employment, and housing. In May 1999, 20,000 Crimean Tatars joined in protest against these discriminatory practices and in support of the idea of an autonomous Crimean Tatar republic, provoking a negative reaction from the ethnic Russian population. Russians fear that return migration and population growth will make the Tatars a numerical majority and that this will reinforce their claim for autonomy (Korostelina 2000; Sasse 2002; Shevel 2000). Russians also fear that Muslim fundamentalism will take root among Crimean Tatars (Helton 1996).

Crimean Tatars received state donations and funds for resettlement. This fact increased negative attitudes toward Crimeans among Russians, who had also experienced economic deprivation. Russians had better access to jobs and education than Crimean Tatars, but the collapse of the Soviet Union nonetheless engendered irredentist autonomy claims by the Russians as Crimea's majority ethnic group. The unraveling of the communist system of government posed challenges of new political institution building, social reorientation toward a market economy, and the definition of new concepts of post–Cold War national security for Ukraine as a newly independent state.

Russians and Crimean Tatars differ in their conceptions of the legitimacy of their positions in Ukraine (Korostelina 2000, 2003a). Crimean Tatars consider it legitimate to reclaim their possessions and re-establish national and territorial autonomy. Russians aspire to establish closer relations with Russia and perceive Crimean Tatar autonomy as a step toward Crimean incorporation into the Muslim world. Conversely, Crimean Tatars fear that local autonomy will never be granted if Crimea is part of Russia. Hence, the goals of Russians and Crimean Tatars are incompatible with the formation of a common national identity. The collective adoption of a Ukrainian national identity, however, could provide self-esteem and human dignity to these members of ethnic minorities, making them feel that they are equal citizens of an independent state. National shared identity may smooth away splits between the peoples of Ukraine and unite them in the development of a common state. The meaning of national identity is still in flux among politicians and peoples; thus, we expect that representatives of Russians and Crimean Tatars will have different concepts of national identity.

Empirical Study

Research Design

Schematically, the impact of the meaning of national identity building can be represented like this:

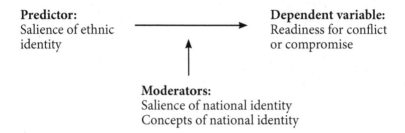

Predictor:
Salience of ethnic identity

Dependent variable:
Readiness for conflict or compromise

Moderators:
Salience of national identity
Concepts of national identity

Based on this scheme, I proposed some prospective interrelations between the independent and dependent variables and the moderator:

> *Proposition 1.* Possession of salient national identity will decrease readiness to fight with other groups and weaken the effect of ethnic identity salience on conflict readiness.
> *Proposition 2.* Possession of the ethnic concept of national identity will increase readiness to fight with other groups and strengthen the effect of ethnic identity salience on conflict readiness.
> *Proposition 3.* Possession of the multicultural concept of national identity will reduce readiness to fight with other groups and weaken the effect of ethnic identity salience on conflict readiness.
> *Proposition 4.* Possession of the civic concept of national identity will reduce readiness to fight with other groups and weaken the effect of ethnic identity salience on conflict readiness. This effect will be more significant than the effect of the multicultural concept.
> *Proposition 5.* The meaning of national identity will have a different effect on minority groups than on majority groups.

Method

Sampling. To test these propositions, I designed an opinion survey that was conducted between January and May 2003 in several towns and villages in Crimea. The sample was stratified by location, number of resettlements, and rural-urban status. The survey strata include the towns of Simferopol and Alushta and the counties of Bahchisarai (including the city of Bahchisarai), Krasnoperekopsk, and Sudak, with 997 respondents distributed across these locations in equal proportion.

Questionnaire Design. In addition to asking respondents to provide basic demographic and socioeconomic data about themselves (including estimated income level, occupation, age, level of education, gender, and indigenous language competence ranked in one of five categories from excellent to none), the questionnaire dealt with the following issues. First, it measured identity salience in two ways: (1) it measured the salience of ethnic identity with five statements such as "I am proud to be a representative of (ethnic group)" and "There are no people in the world better than those of my ethnic group"; (2) it measured salience of national identity with three questions such as "I am proud to be a citizen of Ukraine." Second, the survey measured the meaning of national identity in three ways: (1) it assessed the ethnic concept of national identity with three statements such as "The Ukrainian nation must be created on the basis of single Ukrainian culture" and "To be strong and independent, Ukraine should unite around the Ukrainian ethnonational idea"; (2) it assessed the multicultural concept of national identity with three statements such as "Ukraine has to provide an opportunity for each citizen to speak and study in every language" and "All ethnic groups in Ukraine must have the right to autonomy and self-governance"; (3) it assessed the civic concept of national identity with three statements such as "For citizens of Ukraine, ethnic identity should not play any role and cannot be used for political purposes" and "Citizenship of Ukraine is only a contract between citizens and the country about duties and rights." All statements were to be answered on a five-point scale from disagree to agree. Finally, the survey measured readiness for conflict with the questions "How will you behave to defend your ethnic group in a situation of out-group threat?" and "How will you behave to accomplish the aims of your ethnic group in Ukraine?" to be answered on a three-point scale (reject fighting, use legal methods of fighting, or use any methods of fighting). Five-point scales were recoded to four-point scales, excluding "No answer." All missing data and the "do not know" answers were deleted from the analysis.

Results

Crimean Tatars identify more strongly with the ethnic Tatar in-group (M=16.74 on a scale from 3 to 20) than Russians identify with the ethnic Russian in-group (M=12.46; $F(1,827)=50.52$; $p<.001$). Crimean Tatars also identify more strongly with the nation of Ukraine (M=7.29 on a scale from 3 to 12) than Russians do (M=6.64), but the difference is not significant ($F(1,828)=.50$; n.s.).

The multicultural concept of national identity is stronger among Crimean Tatars (M=9.29 on a scale from 3 to 12) than it is among Russians (M=8.81; $F(1,828)=8.74$; $p<.005$), while the civic concept of national identity is stronger among Russians (M=7.63 on a scale from 3 to 12) than it is among Crimean Tatars (M=7.51; $F(1,826)=5.35$; $p<.05$). The ethnic concept of national identity does not differ significantly between the groups ($F(1,827)=2.35$; n.s.). Crimean

Tatars and Russians have very similar levels of conflict readiness (M=4.52 and M=4.51; n.s. on a scale from 1 to 8).

A partially saturated general linear model was used to simultaneously test the effects of all the above-mentioned predictors on conflict readiness. For both ethnic groups, a salient ethnic identity strengthens conflict readiness, and a salient national identity reduces conflict readiness. The results also show that a salient ethnic concept of national identity among Russians contributes to conflict readiness, while among Crimean Tatars it substantially reduces conflict readiness (table 3.1).

TABLE 3.1 Significance and Effects of the Concepts of National Identity on Conflict Readiness

	Russians			Crimean Tatars		
		Mean readiness to fight score			Mean readiness to fight score	
	Beta	W/ concept	W/o concept	Beta	W/ concept	W/o concept
Ethnic concept	2.05*	4.67	4.14	3.44**	4.07	4.81
Multicultural concept	1.90*	4.33	4.51	3.92**	4.68	4.20
Civic concept	2.27**	4.28	4.56	3.04**	4.16	4.71

Notes: * = p<.05; ** = p<.01. Standardized Beta coefficients from a partially saturated general linear model of data from the 2003 Crimean survey. Scores on a scale of 1 to 8, where 8 is the highest readiness to fight. Model and data available from the author.

Among Russians, the multicultural concept of national identity reduces conflict readiness, while among Crimean Tatars, it makes a significant contribution to conflict readiness. The civic concept of national identity significantly reduces conflict readiness among both Russians and Crimean Tatars; this impact is more significant for Crimean Tatars.

The moderating roles of identity salience and of the different concepts of national identity were determined by comparing the direct effect of ethnic identity on conflict readiness relative to the model above, in which salience and each concept of national identity operated as a moderator. Identity salience and possession of the different concepts of national identity do have moderating effects on the impact of ethnic identity for Russians and Crimean Tatars (table 3.2).

Possession of a salient national identity and of the ethnic concept of national identity strengthens the influence of salient ethnic identity on conflict readiness among Russians and weakens it among Crimean Tatars. Possession of the multicultural concept weakens the influence of salient ethnic identity on conflict readiness among Russians and strengthens it among Crimean Tatars. Possession of the civic concept weakens the influence of salient ethnic identity on conflict readiness among representatives of both ethnic groups.

TABLE 3.2 The Moderating Effects of National Identity on Conflict Readiness among Russians and Crimean Tatars

Effects of Ethnic Identity	Russians	Crimean Tatars
Without salient national identity	2.56*	3.73**
With salient national identity	3.01**	2.20*
Without ethnic concept	1.95*	2.47*
With ethnic concept	2.54*	2.02*
Without multicultural concept	4.01**	2.23*
With multicultural concept	3.25**	3.03**
Without civic concept	4.02**	2.27*
With civic concept	3.12**	1.93*

Notes: * = $p<.05$; ** = $p<.01$. Standardized Beta coefficients from a partially saturated general linear model of data from the 2003 Crimean survey. Model and data available from the author.

Discussion

The results of my survey demonstrate that the possession of salient national identity increases the influence of ethnic identity on the personal and group conflict readiness of Russians. When Russians adopt a salient national identity and believe that they are the main and more powerful minority group in Ukraine, their readiness to fight with other ethnic minorities is strengthened. When Russians accept Ukrainian identity without adopting a salient ethnic identity and ethnocentric views, however, they perceive the Ukrainian identity as common to all ethnic groups in Ukraine. Conversely, ethnic identity among Crimean Tatars with low national identity salience leads to readiness to fight with other ethnic minorities who can compete with them, but if national identity is salient, it decreases the influence of ethnic identity on conflict readiness.

I expected to find that possession of the ethnic concept of national identity would increase conflict readiness and strengthen the negative impact of ethnic identity. This hypothesis was confirmed for Russians, but it failed for Crimean Tatars, for whom possession of the ethnic concept of national identity decreases conflict readiness and weakens the impact of ethnic identity. I also assumed that possession of the multicultural concept of national identity would reduce conflict readiness and weaken the impact of conflict indicators. This hypothesis, too, was confirmed for Russians but failed for Crimean Tatars, among whom the multicultural concept of national identity contributes to conflict readiness and strengthens the impact of ethnic identity. My hypothesis that possession of the civic concept of national identity would reduce the influence of conflict indicators was completely confirmed. Therefore, my research shows that different concepts of national identity *do* affect readiness for conflict with out-groups among ethnic minorities. They also moderate the impact of salient ethnic identity on conflict readiness.

These effects depend, however, on the position of an ethnic minority in Ukrainian society. Thus, Russians and Crimean Tatars have different ethnic conceptions of national identity: the Russians have a concept of Russian-Ukrainian national identity, while the Crimean Tatars have a concept of simple Ukrainian national identity. For Russians, a numerous and powerful minority particularly in Crimea, possession of an ethnic concept of national identity increases the impact of the salience of ethnic identity on the readiness to fight with other ethnic groups. When Russians have an ethnic concept of national identity, they perceive the nation as a single ethnic entity in which Ukrainian Russians must have the highest status among other groups (Korostelina 2003a). They think that national identity in Ukraine has to be built around the Russian community. Therefore, as the dominant minority (and even the absolute majority in Crimea), Russians are ready to fight other ethnic groups for their privileged position. When Crimean Tatars, a small minority in Ukraine, have an ethnic concept of national identity, on the other hand, they accept the leading role of the Ukrainian ethnic group in the nation. They feel themselves to be secure within the nation and are ready to accept Ukrainian culture and language if Ukraine will help the Crimean Tatars deter the pro-Russian movement in Crimea (ibid.). Thus, the possession of an ethnic concept of national identity weakens the impact of ethnic identity on the readiness of Crimean Tatars to fight with other groups.

Possession of a multicultural concept of national identity decreases the impact of ethnic identity on conflict readiness among Russians and increases its impact among Crimean Tatars. When Russians have a multicultural conception of national identity, they see Ukraine as a society within which ethnic minorities should be guaranteed resources to maintain their ethnic cultures and communities. As a numerous and powerful minority, Russians expect that they will receive major benefits from the state, and they want to preserve their position without having to struggle against other ethnic groups. Such beliefs reduce the influence of salient ethnic identity among Russians in Crimea. When Crimean Tatars, as a small minority, see the nation as multicultural one, however, they are more ready to fight against other ethnic groups for their rights and some privileges. They believe they can get more resources than other ethnic groups because of their history of deportation and their unique position as an endogenous people. In this case, the multicultural concept strengthens the impact of salient ethnic identity on readiness to fight for resources to maintain the ethnic culture and community of Crimean Tatars.

Possession of a civic concept of national identity reduces the impact of salient ethnic identity for both groups. When people perceive their nation as built on a distinctive nonethnic civic culture into which all citizens should integrate, their ethnic identity does not have an important influence on their conflict readiness. If representatives of both large and small minorities see civic responsibility as the main feature of the nation, their ethnicity is less significant. Thus, the civic concept of national identity mitigates readiness to fight among ethnic minorities and moderates the impact of ethnic identity. (This finding accords with David Brown's predictions in the first chapter of this volume.)

The hypotheses, which were derived from conventional theory, suggested that possession of the ethnic concept of national identity would increase readiness to fight with other groups and strengthen the effects of ethnic identity salience on conflict readiness. They also predicted that possession of the multicultural concept of national identity would reduce readiness to fight with other groups and weaken the effects of ethnic identity salience, ethnocentrism and economic deprivation on conflict readiness. My results show that such propositions are accurate for some groups and incorrect for others. The critical moderating variable, I would suggest, is the position of a minority within the state as a major or minor minority: For numerous and powerful minorities, possession of the ethnic concept of national identity strengthens their willingness to fight for the privileged position within the society; the multicultural concept, on the other hand, reduces their readiness to fight, because they expect to obtain the major benefits in a multicultural nation. For small minorities, possession of the ethnic concept encourages assimilation and reduces willingness to fight, while possession of the multicultural concept evokes competition with other ethnic groups for rights and social and economic position within the society. Generalizing from my findings, I would propose that the position of a minority within a nation regulates the impact of the ethnic and multicultural concepts of national identity on members of that minority's readiness to fight with members of other groups. The only proposition that appears to have been correct for both groups is my hypothesis about the moderation effect of the civic concept. My results show that possession of the civic concept of national identity significantly reduces conflict readiness among ethnic minorities.

Conclusion

The findings provide ample empirical support for my hypothesis that a salient social identity can influence the impact of other identities on conflict intentions. I have shown that possession of a salient national identity can mitigate the impact of ethnic identity on readiness for conflict with other ethnic groups. I have also demonstrated that the meaning of another social identity can be a powerful moderator of the influence of a particular identity on behavioral intention: the three different concepts of national identity, I argue, weaken or strengthen the impact of ethnic identity on the readiness for conflict among ethnic groups. Thus, my study confirms that analysis of the impact of social identity on attitudes or behavior requires assessment of the interconnections between different identities. To understand the effects of a single social identity, it is necessary to analyze the influence, salience, and meaning of other social identities.

References

Abrams, D. 1999. "Social Identity, Social Cognition, and the Self: The Flexibility and Stability of Self-Categorization." In *Social Identity and Social Cognition,* ed. D. Abrams and M. Hogg, 197–229. Oxford: Blackwell.

Adler, H. G. 1994. "A Mischling Attempts to Fight for His Rights." In *Displacements: Cultural Identities in Question,* ed. A. Bammer, 205–215. Bloomington: Indiana University Press.

Allen, V. L., and D. A. Wilder. 1975. "Categorization, Belief Similarity, and Group Discrimination." *Journal of Personality and Social Psychology* 32: 971–977.

Allport, G. W. 1954. *The Nature of Prejudice.* Reading, MA: Addison-Wesley.

Alwin, D. F., R. L. Cohen, and T. M. Newcomb. 1992. *Political Attitudes over the Life Span: The Bennington Women after Fifty Years.* Madison: University of Wisconsin Press.

Berry, J., U. Kim, S. Power, M. Young, and M. Bujaki. 1989. "Acculturation Attitudes in Plural Societies." *Applied Psychology* 38: 185–206.

Billig, M., and H. Tajfel. 1973. "Social Categorization and Similarity in Intergroup Behavior." *European Journal of Social Psychology* 3: 27–52.

Booth, K. 1979. *Strategy and Ethnocentrism,* New York: Holmes & Meier Publishers, Inc.

Branscombe, N., and D. Wann. 1994. "Collective Self-Esteem Consequences of Outgroup Derogation When a Valued Social Identity Is on Trial." *European Journal of Social Psychology* 24: 641–657.

Breakwell, G. M. 2001. "Social Representational Constraints upon Identity." In *Representations of the Social,* ed. K. Deaux and G. Philogene, 271–284. Malden, MA: Blackwell.

Brewer, M. B. 1991. "The Social Self: On Being the Same and Different at the Same Time." *Personality and Social Psychology Bulletin* 17: 475–482.

———. 1996. "When Contact Is Not Enough: Social Identity and Intergroup Cooperation." *International Journal of Intercultural Relations* 20: 291–303.

———. 2001. "The Many Faces of Social Identity: Implications for Political Psychology." *Political Psychology* 1: 115–126.

Brewer, M. B., and N. Miller. 1984. "Beyond the Contact hypothesis: Theoretical Perspectives on Desegregation." In *Groups in Contact: The Psychology of Desegregation,* ed. N. Miller and M. Brewer, 281–302. Orlando, FL: Academic Press.

Brewer, M. B., and M. Silver. 1978. "In-Group Bias as a Function of Task Characteristics." *European Journal of Social Psychology* 8: 393–400.

Brewer, M. B., and J. G. Weber. 1994. "Self-Evaluation Affects of Interpersonal versus Intergroup Social Comparison." *Journal of Personality and Social Psychology* 66: 268–275.

Brubaker, R. 1996. *Nationalism Reframed: Nationhood and the National Question in the New Europe.* Cambridge: Cambridge University Press.

Citrin, J., C. Wong, and B. Duff. 2000. "The Meaning of American Identity: Patterns of Ethnic Conflict and Consensus." In *Social Identity, Intergroup Conflict and Conflict Resolution,* ed. R. D. Ashmore, L. Jussim, and D. Wilder, 71–100. New York: Oxford University Press.

Conover, P. J. 1988. "The Role of Social Groups in Political Thinking." *British Journal of Political Science* 18: 51–76.

Crenshaw, K. 1998. "Demarginalizing the Intersection of Race and Sex: A Black Feminist Critique of Antidiscrimination Doctrine, Feminist Theory, and Antiracist Politics." In *Feminism and Politics,* ed. A. Phillips, 314–343. New York: Oxford University Press.

Crocker, J., and R. Luhtanen. 1990. "Collective Self-Esteem and Ingroup Bias." *Journal of Personality and Social Psychology* 58: 60–67.

Cross, W. E. 1991. *Shades of Black: Diversity in African-American Identity.* Philadelphia: Temple University Press.

Deaux, K. 1993. "Reconstructing Social Identity." *Personality and Social Psychology Bulletin* 19: 4–12.

———. 1996. "Social Identification." In *Social Psychology, Handbook of Basic Principles*, ed. E. Higgins and A. Kruglanski, 777–798. New York: Guilford.

Doise, W., and A. Sinclair. 1973. "The Categorization Process in Intergroup Relations." *European Journal of Social Psychology* 3: 145–157.

Dovidio, J. F., J. C. Brigham, B. T. Johnson, and S. L. Gaertner. 1996. "Stereotyping, Prejudice and Discrimination: Another Look." In *Stereotypes and Stereotyping*, ed. C. N. Macrae, C. Stangor, and M. Hewstone, 276–319. New York: Guilford.

Dovidio, J. F., and S. L. Gaertner. 1998. "On the Nature of Contemporary Prejudice: The Causes, Consequences, and Challenges of Aversive Racism." In *Confronting Racism: The Problem and Response*, ed. J. Eberhardt and S. T. Fiske, 3–32. Newbury Park, CA: Sage.

Duckitt, J., and T. Mphuthing. 1998. "Group Identification and Intergroup Attitudes: A Longitudinal Analysis in South Africa." *Journal of Personality and Social Psychology* 74: 80–85.

Eagly, A. H., and S. Chaiken. 1993. *The Psychology of Attitudes*. San Diego, CA: Harcourt Brace.

Ellemers, N., B. Doosje, A. Van Knippenberg, and H. Wilke. 1992. "Status Protection in High Status Minority Groups." *European Journal of Social Psychology* 22: 123–140.

Ellemers, N., P. Kortekaas, and J. W. Ouwerkerk. 1999. "Perceived Intragroup Variability as a Function of Group Status and Identification." *Journal of Experimental Social Psychology* 31: 410–436.

Espinoza, J. A., and R. T. Garza. 1985. "Social Group Salience and Interethnic Cooperation." *Journal of Experimental Social Psychology* 21: 380–392.

Esses, V. M., G. Haddock, and M. P. Zanna. 1993. "Values, Stereotypes, and Emotions as Determinants of Intergroup Attitudes." In *Affect, Cognition, and Stereotyping: Interactive Processes in Group Perception*, ed. D. M. Mackie and D. L. Hamilton, 137–166. New York: Academic Press.

Ethier, K. A., and K. Deaux. 1994. "Negotiating Social Identity When Contexts Change: Maintaining Identification and Responding to Threat." *Journal of Personality and Social Psychology* 67: 243–251.

Festinger, L. 1957. *A Theory of Cognitive Dissonance*. Stanford, CA: Stanford University Press.

Fiske, S. T., and S. E. Taylor. 1991. *Social Cognition*. 2nd ed. New York: McGraw Hill.

Gaertner, S. L., J. F. Dovidio, B. S. Banker, M. Houlette, K. M. Johnson, and E. A. McGlynn. 2000. "Reducing Intergroup Conflict: From Superordinate Goals to Decategorization, Recategorization, and Mutual Differentiation." *Group Dynamics: Theory, Research, and Practice* 4: 98–114.

Gellner, E. 1994. "Nationalism and Modernization." In *Nationalism*, ed. J. Hutchinson and A. Smith, 55–62. Oxford: Oxford University Press.

Gerard, H., and M. F. Hoyt. 1974. "Distinctiveness of Social Categorization and Attitude toward Ingroup Members." *Journal of Personality and Social Psychology* 29: 836–842.

Gerson J. M. 2001. "In Between States: National Identity Practices among German Jewish Immigrants." *Political Psychology* 22, no. 1: 179–198.

Gibson, J. L., and A. Gouwa. 1998. "Social Identity Theory and Political Intolerance in South Africa." Unpublished manuscript, University of Houston.

Grant, P., and P. Brown. 1995. "From Ethnocentrism to Collective Protest: Responses to Relative Deprivation and Threats to Social Identity." *Social Psychology Quarterly* 58: 195–211.

Gurin, P., A. Hurtado, and T. Peng. 1994. "Group Contacts and Ethnicity in the Social Identities of Mexicanos and Chicanos." *Personality and Social Psychology Bulletin* 20, no. 5: 521–532.

Hagendoorn, L., G. Csepeli, H. Dekker, and R. Farnen, eds. 2000. *European Nations and Nationalism: Theoretical and Historical Perspectives.* Aldershot, UK: Ashgate Publishers.

Hagendoorn, L., H. Linssen, D. Rotman, and S. Tumanov. 1996. "Russians as Minorities in Belarus, Ukraine, Moldova, Georgia and Kazakhstan." Paper presented to the International Political Science Association conference, Boone, NC.

Helton, A. 1996. *Crimean Tatars: Repatriation and Conflict Prevention.* New York: Open Society Institute.

Hewstone, M. 1990. "The Ultimate Attribution Error? A Review of the Literature on Intergroup Causal Attribution." *European Journal of Social Psychology* 20: 311–335.

Hirt, E. R., D. Zillmann, G. Erickson, and C. Kennedy. 1992. "Costs and Benefits of Allegiance: Changes in Fans' Self-Ascribed Competencies after Team Victory versus Defeat." *Journal of Personality and Social Psychology* 63: 724–738.

Huddy, L. 2001. "From Social to Political Identity: A Critical Examination of Social Identity Theory." *Political Psychology* 1: 127–156.

_____. 2003. "Group Identity and Political Cohesion." In *Oxford Handbook of Political Psychology,* ed. D. O. Sears, L. Huddy, and R. Jervis, 511–558. NY: Oxford University Press.

Huici, C., M. Ros, I. Cano, N. Hopkins, N. Emler, and M. Carmona. 1997. "Comparative Identity and Evaluation of Socio-Political Change: Perceptions of the European Community as a Function of the Salience of Regional Identities." *European Journal of Social Psychology* 27: 97–113.

Hyers, L. L., and J. K. Swim. 1998. "A Comparison of the Experiences of Dominant and Minority Group Members During an Intergroup Encounter." *Group Processes and Intergroup Relations* 1: 143–163.

Jackson, J. 2002. "The Relationship between Group Identity and Intergroup Prejudice Is Moderated by Socio-Structural Variation." *Journal of Applied Social Psychology* 32: 908–933.

Jones, J. M. 1972. *Prejudice and Racism.* Reading, MA: Addison-Wesley.

Kaiser, R. 1994. *The Geography of Nationalism in Russia and the USSR.* Princeton, NJ: Princeton University Press.

Kelman, H. C. 1982. "Creating the Conditions for Israeli–Palestinian Negotiations." *Journal of Conflict Resolution* 1: 39–76.

_____. 1997. "Nationalism, Patriotism, and National Identity: Social-Psychological Dimensions." In *Patriotism in the Lives of Individuals and Nations,* ed. D. Bar-Tal and E. Staub, 165–189. Chicago: Nelson-Hall.

King, D. 1988. "Multiple Jeopardy, Multiple Consciousness: The Context of Black Feminist Ideology." *Signs* 14: 42–72.

Kinket, B., and M. Verkuyten. 1999. "Levels of Ethnic Self-Identification and Social Context." *Social Psychology Quarterly* 60: 338–354.

Korostelina, K. 2000. "The Social-Psychological Roots of the Ethnic Problems in Crimea." *Democratizatsiya* 8: 219–231.

_____. 2003a. "The Multiethnic State-Building Dilemma: National and Ethnic Minorities' Identities in the Crimea." *National Identities* 5, no. 2: 141–159.

_____. 2003b. *Social'naya identichnost' i konflict* [Social Identity and Conflict]. Simferopol, Crimea: Dolya.

_____. 2004. "The Impact of National Identity on Conflict Behavior: Comparative Analysis of Two Ethnic Minorities in Crimea." *International Journal of Comparative Sociology* 45, no. 3–4: 213–230.

McGuire, W. J., C. V. McGuire, P. Child, and T. Fujioka. 1978. "Salience of Ethnicity in the Spontaneous Self-Concept as a Function of One's Ethnic Distinctiveness in the Social Environment." *Journal of Personality and Social Psychology* 36: 511–520.

Miller, A. H., P. Gurin, G. Gurin, and O. Malanchuk. 1981. "Group Consciousness and Political Participation." *American Journal of Political Science* 25: 495–511.

Mullen, B. 1983. "Egocentric Bias in Estimates of Consensus." *Journal of Social Psychology* 121: 31–38.

Mullen, B., R. Brown, and C. Smith. 1992. "Ingroup Bias as a Function of Salience, Relevance, and Status: An Integration." *European Journal of Social Psychology* 22: 103–122.

Mummendey, A., and S. Otten. 1998. "Positive-Negative Asymmetry in Social Discrimination." *European Review of Social Psychology* 9: 107–144.

Münch, R. 2001. *Nation and Citizenship in the Global Age: From National to Transnational Ties and Identities.* New York: Palgrave.

Oakes, P. 1987. "The Salience of Social Categories." In *Rediscovering the Social Group: A Self-Categorization Theory,* ed. J. C. Turner, M. A. Hogg, P. J. Oakes, S. D. Reicher, and M. S. Watherell, 117–141. Oxford: Blackwell.

Otten, S., A. Mummendey, and M. Blanz. 1996. "Intergroup Discrimination in Positive and Negative Outcome Allocations: Impact of Stimulus Valence, Relative Group Status, and Relative Group Size." *Personality and Social Psychology Bulletin* 22: 568–581.

Perreault, S., and R. Y. Bourhis. 1998. "Social Identification, Interdependence, and Discrimination." *Group Processes and Intergroup Relations* 1: 49–66.

_____. 1999. "Ethnocentrism, Social Identification, and Discrimination." *Personality and Social Psychology Bulletin* 25: 92–103.

Pettigrew, T. F. 1979. "The Ultimate Attribution Error: Extending Allport's Cognitive Analysis of Prejudice." *Personality and Social Psychology Bulletin* 5: 461–476.

Phinney, J. S. 1990. "Ethnic Identity in Adolescence and Adulthood: Review of Research." *Psychological Bulletin* 108: 499–514.

_____. 1991. "Ethnic Identity and Self-Esteem: A Review and Integration." *Hispanic Journal of Behavioral Science* 13: 193–208.

Rogers, C. R. 1961. *On Becoming a Person.* Boston: Houghton Mifflin.

Sachdev, I., and R. Y. Bourhis. 1984. "Minimal Majorities and Minorities." *European Journal of Social Psychology* 14: 35–52.

Sasse, G. 2002. "The 'New' Ukraine: A State of Regions." In *Ethnicity and Territory in the Former Soviet Union: Regions in Conflict,* ed. J. Hughes and G. Sasse, 69–100. London: Frank Cass.

Sears, D. O., and P. J. Henry. 1999. "Ethnic Identity and Group Threat in American Politics." *The Political Psychologist* 4, no. 2: 12–17.

Sellers, R. M., M. A. Smith, J. N. Shelton, S. A. J. Rowley, and T. M Chavous. 1998. "Multidimensional Model of Racial Identity: A Reconceptualization of African American Racial Identity." *Personality and Social Psychology Review* 2: 18–39.

Shevel, O. 2000. "Crimean Tatars in Ukraine: The Politics of Inclusion and Exclusion." *Analysis of Current Events* 12: 9–11.

Sidanius, J., S. Feshbach, S. Levin, and F. Pratto. 1997. "The Interface between Ethnic and National Attachment: Ethnic Pluralism or Ethnic Dominance?" *Public Opinion Quarterly* 61: 102–133.

Simon, B. 1992. "The Perception of Ingroup and Outgroup Homogeneity: Reintroducing the Intergroup Context." *European Review of Social Psychology* 3: 1–30.

Simon, B., and D. Hamilton. 1994. "Self-Stereotyping and Social Context: The Effects of Relative Ingroup Size and Ingroup Status." *Journal of Personality and Social Psychology* 66: 699–711.

Skevington, S., and D. Baker, eds. 1989. *The Social Identity of Women.* London: Sage.

Smith, E. R., and S. Henry. 1996. "An In-group Becomes Part of the Self: Response Time Evidence." *Personality and Social Psychology Bulletin* 22: 635–642.

Stein, J. G. 1998. "Image, Identity, and Conflict Resolution." In *Managing Global Chaos: Sources of and Responses to International Conflict*, ed. C. A. Crocker, F. O. Hampson, and P. Aall, 93–111. Washington, DC: United States Institute of Peace Press.

Stephan, W. G., and C. W. Stephan. 2004. "Intergroup Relations in Multicultural Education Programs." In *Handbook of Research on Multicultural Education*, 2nd ed., ed. J. A. Banks and C. A. M. Banks, 782–798. San Francisco, CA: Jossey-Bass.

Stern, P. 1995. "Why Do People Sacrifice for Their Nations?" *Political Psychology* 2: 217–235.

Stryker, S. 1969. "Identity Salience and Role Performance: The Relevance of Symbolic Interaction Theory for Family Research." *Journal of Marriage and the Family* 30: 558–564.

———. 2000. "Identity Competition: Key to Differential Social Movement Participation?" In *Self, Identity, and Social Movements*, ed. S. Stryker, T. Owens, and R. White, 21–40. Minneapolis: University of Minnesota Press.

Stryker, S., and R. T. Serpe. 1994. "Identity Salience and Psychological Centrality: Equivalent, Overlapping, or Complementary Concepts?" *Social Psychology Quarterly* 57: 16–35.

Swann, S., and R. S. Wyer. 1997. "Gender Stereotypes and Social Identity: How Being in the Minority Affects Judgments of Self and Other." *Personality and Social Psychology Bulletin* 23: 1265–1276.

Tajfel H. 1969. "Cognitive Aspects of Prejudice." *Journal of Social Issues* 25: 79–97.

Tajfel, H., and J. C. Turner. 1979. "An Integrative Theory of Intergroup Conflict." In *The Social Psychology of Intergroup Relations*, ed. W. G. Austin and S. Worchel, 33–48. Monterey, CA: Brooks/Cole.

———. 1986. "The Social Identity Theory of Intergroup Behavior." In *Psychology of Intergroup Relations*, ed. S. Worchel and W. G. Austin, 7–24. Chicago: Nelson-Hall.

Ting-Toomey, S., K. K. Yee-Jung, R. B. Shapiro, W. Garcia, T. J. Wright, and J. G. Oetzel. 2000. "Ethnic/Cultural Identity Salience and Conflict Styles in Four US Ethnic Groups." *International Journal of Intercultural Relations* 24: 47–81.

Turner, J. C., M. A. Hogg, P. J. Oakes, S. D. Reicher, and M. S. Watherell, eds. 1987. *Rediscovering the Social Group: A Self-Categorization Theory*. Oxford: Blackwell.

Turner, J. C., P. J. Oakes, S. A. Haslam, and C. McGarty. 1994. "Self and Collective: Cognition and Social Context." *Personality and Psychology Bulletin* 20: 454–463.

Van Oudenhoven, J. P., and A. Eisses. 1998. "Integration and Assimilation of Moroccan Immigrants in Israel and the Netherlands." *International Journal of Intercultural Relations* 22: 293–307.

Verkuyten, M., and K. Masson. 1995. "New Racism, Self-Esteem, and Ethnic Relations among Minority and Majority Youth in the Netherlands." *Social Behavior and Personality* 23: 137–154.

Zanna, M. P., and J. K. Rempel. 1988. "Attitudes: A New Look at an Old Concept." In *The Social Psychology of Knowledge*, ed. D. Bar-Tal and A. Kruglanski, 315–334. New York: Cambridge University Press.

4

Ethnic Identities of the Karen Peoples in Burma and Thailand

Kwanchewan Buadaeng

"Karen" is a generic term for speakers of Karenic languages and their descendants.[1] Members of this ethnic minority live mostly along the frontier between Burma and Thailand.[2] In Burmese statistics, the category "Karen" comprises many small groups. Since survey methods differ and, more importantly, different surveys include and exclude different subgroups, estimates of the Karen population in Burma vary widely. A 1911 survey counted 1.1 million Karen out of a total Burmese population of 8 million. The official census of 1931 found 1.4 million. The Karen National Union (KNU), a pan-Karen political organization, believes this to be an undercount, because the Burman officials who conducted the census counted Karen Buddhists as Burmans.[3] The KNU estimates that the current Karen population in Burma numbers between 8 and 10 million, with approximately 1 million in Karen State proper and the balance spread across the delta areas of southern Burma from Pegu to Rangoon to Mergui-Tavoy (Tharckabaw and Watson 2003; see also Enriquez 1933).

It is easier to count the number of Karens in Thailand, where their population is much smaller and comprises fewer subgroups. The 2002 Thai highland census found 438,131 Karens. They are the largest minority group in northern Thailand and make up 48 percent of the total highland ethnic population (Royal Thai Government 2002).

Differences in the historical processes of colonization and modernization in the two countries have caused Karen group identity to develop differently on

---

Notes for this chapter begin on page 92.

either side of the border. Karens in Burma developed a national consciousness, created national organizations, and sought to establish an autonomous Karen state. To that end, ever since Burma gained its independence in 1948, many of Burma's Karen have been at war with the country's government. Thai Karen, by contrast, attracted little notice from the outside world. In the 1970s, as armed fighting between the KNU and the Burmese government entered into its third decade, anthropologists who studied the Karen in Thailand still found it difficult to identify markers of their group identity. They debated questions such as: Who are the Karen? What are their identities? Do the Karen really exist? (Hinton 1983; Keyes 1979; Rajah 1986). Karens in Thailand did not begin to speak out until the 1980s, when they organized environmental movements, portraying themselves in the public media as nature conservationists in order to win forest land-use rights and gain equal status with the lowland Thai majority. Unlike Karens in Burma, they do not seek an autonomous state.

How did such distinct ethnic identities emerge among the Karen of Burma and Thailand? Ethnic identity can be defined as a constructed expression, communicated through textual descriptions, symbols, public displays, rituals, and other practices, which is intended to or acts to differentiate a group from other groups. An ethnic group's members usually share origins, history, cultural characteristics, or geographic territory. Ethnic identity is shaped from within the group by common experiences and heritage, and from without by the larger society's system of ethnic relations. Although that system, and the ethnic conflict that can arise within it, interacts with ethnic identity, and although political actors often manipulate ethnic identity to achieve their goals, ethnic identity does not by itself lead to intergroup violence. As can be seen in a comparison of the Karen of Burma and of Thailand, the roots of ethnic conflict, or its absence, can often be found in a society's recent history of ethnic relations.

The Construction of Karen Identity in Burma

Great Britain conquered southern and southwestern Burma in 1826, won control of the remaining southern lowlands in 1852, and finally conquered the northern half of the country in a two-week war in 1885, after which it exiled the former Burmese monarch. From 1886, the British ruled Burma as a province of India, although it took fifteen years to eliminate upland resistance. In 1937, in response to decades of agitation for self-rule, London granted the colony a separate constitution. Burmese rebels allied themselves first with the Japanese and later with the British during World War II and won independence for their country in the war's aftermath.

Colonization deeply changed power relations within Burma. First, imported religious beliefs and practices divided Burmese society. The British suppressed the monarchy, which had patronized Buddhism (and was itself legitimated by the Buddhist clergy). The British also supported Christian missionary projects just when the Buddhist establishment lost government support. These acts inspired Buddhist revolts throughout the colonial period. Second, the new rulers controlled their subjects and environs much more tightly than had the monarch. A centralized, bureaucratic, modern state enrolled members of the population in its schools, police, and military forces. The national borders were demarcated to better monitor both the national territory and its inhabitants. In 1868, after the representatives of the courts of Great Britain and Siam (today's Thailand) signed a convention designating the Moei River as the international boundary separating Siam and British territory, the first population census using ethnic classifications was conducted in southern Burma. Third, the British divided Burma into two parts: Burma proper, the lower part of the country, which was governed by Burmese under the control of the British government, and British Burma, the highland and frontier areas, where hundreds of diverse tribes lived, which the British governed directly. As a result, the frontier peoples, including the Karen, had British, not Burmese, rulers for more than a century. The Karen also received relatively privileged treatment from the British.

Ethnic groups emerged—that is to say, the formation of ethnic consciousness and identities began—only after ethnic classification by the British. Before colonization, the Karen as a group did not exist. Several of the small, scattered groups that would later come to compose the Karen had their own autonyms. The peoples who would come to be known as the Sgaw Karen and the Pwo Karen called themselves *pga gan yaw* and *phlong*, respectively. The speakers of Karenic languages did not have their own state. They lived mostly on the periphery of kingdoms ruled by other ethnic groups, the Burmese, the Mon, and the Shan, and were known to each by different names. The Burmese called them *kayin*. The Shan called them *yang*. The Mon referred to the group that would later become the Pwo Karen as *kariang* and to the group that would become the Sgaw Karen as *karang*.[4] These exonyms changed over time to delineate distinctions of dress, dialect, and places of settlement within the groups they described. For example, the Shan developed the terms *yang dam* (black Karen) and *yang khao* (white Karen) to distinguish two groups of Karen based on the color of their clothing.

Before the modern period, small tribes in Southeast Asia associated with one another for many reasons other than a common language or history; for example, economic exchange or settlement in the same watershed might bring about contact. They made no attempt to combine into larger ethnic groups, assign themselves names, or count their members. It was only after European conquest that the definition of ethnic groups living within a state's boundaries occurred. The colonizers, in a "comprehensive project of documentation and certification," studied diverse peoples and classified them into ethnic groups in order to fix their geographic territories, determine their relationships with other groups and with the state, and assign rights and duties to each group (Foster 1991: 245; cited in Keyes 1995).

Although the root of the English term "Karen" is the Burmese "Kayin," scientific criteria, not vernacular usage, is often used to justify the identification of some tribes but not others as Karen. One important criterion used to group the smaller groups together is language. A late-twentieth-century example is LeBar, Hickey, and Musgrave's (1964) *Ethnic Groups of Mainland Southeast Asia*. It defines four language groups: Sino-Tibetan, Austro-Asiatic, Tai-Kadai, and Malayo-Polynesian. The first group is divided into four categories: Sinitic, Tibeto-Burman, Karen, and Miao-Yao, which between them contain the 100–150 language groups found in Burma. Not all linguists assign Karen to the same category. In earlier works, Karen was classified under a Tai-Chinese grouping (Enriquez 1933: 76; Government of the Union of Burma 1949: 2).

Which small groups should be defined as Karen? Because of the political implications of the size of the Karen population and of the geographic regions occupied by the small groups, the answer to this question has always been disputed. Compare, for example, the claims of the KNU and the Burmese government. The KNU (1986) contends that the Karen include twelve subgroups—Sgaw, Pwo, Pa-Os, Paku, Maw Nay Pwa, Bwe, White Karens, Padaung (Kayan), Red Karens (Karenni), Keko/Keba, Black Karens, and Striped Karens—with a population of seven million in 1986. The Burmese government includes fewer groups in the Karen category—excluding, for example, the Pa-Os and the Padaung—and as a result, it estimates the Karen population to be much smaller.

Despite disagreements concerning membership, today the Karen are recognized as a single ethnic group. "It is clear," Jorgensen (1997: vi) explains, "that until the 19th century, the word 'Karen' was never used by the groups which constitute the category Karen today, until Christian missionaries and British colonial officers gave the term respectability. Since then it has gained itself a social reality as a term accepted by most educated Karens, Thai, and Burmese." As use of the term spread, ethnic consciousness and an ethnic identity developed in association with it. In less than one hundred years, the Karen became, according to the KNU (2000), "much more than a national minority. We are a nation ... [with] all the essential qualities of a nation. We have our own history, our own language, our own culture, our own land of settlement and our own economic system of life. By nature the Karens are simple, quiet, unassuming and peace loving people, who uphold the high moral qualities of honesty, purity, brotherly love, co-operative living and loyalty, and are devout in their religious beliefs."[5] Whenever Karen nationalist leaders explain Karen history and hopes for the future, they project a sense of high esteem, of pride in being a nation. This assertive ethnic identity evolved, in part, from the relatively privileged treatment that the Karen of Burma received from missionaries and the British government during the colonial period.

The first Christian missionary arrived in Burma from India in 1807. However, the first sizable outreach to the Karen began when the American Baptist mission started its work in 1826, the year in which Britain won the first Anglo-Burmese War and gained control of the Tenasserim (southwest) and Arakan (southern) coastal areas. Although evangelization of the Burmans had begun decades earlier, missionaries had been far less successful with them than with the Karen. By 1834, fewer than 125 Burmans had converted to Christianity, while between 500 and 600 Karen had done so (Trager 1966: 49). The Karen's higher conversion rate attracted the attention of missionaries. In subsequent years, more churches were established in Karen areas than elsewhere in Burma.

Along with the churches, the missionaries established schools. One evangelist wrote: "A great deal of the success and growth of the Karen work is due to their Christian schools. As soon as Karens became Christians they determined that their children should learn to read God's word for themselves, and were willing to give generously for the support of their schools. Every Karen field developed a system of Christian schools, usually primary school in the villages, and middle or high schools in the central town."[6] Tens of thousands of Karen moved from the mountains to urban areas to attend the higher-level schools. A Baptist college was established in Rangoon in 1875 and became the meeting place of many of the ethnic group's future leaders. There they discussed the history and hopes of their peoples, disseminated the ideas that became Karen nationalism, and, in 1881, founded the Karen National Association (KNA). The KNA trained Karen to be leaders, promoted education, and supported writers who speculated about the future of the Karen (Smith 1999: 44–45). In Karen, the organization was named *daw k'lu'*, which means "every group of people." This was the closest the language came to a word for "nation."

When the Karen defined themselves as a nation, they found it important to answer the key questions of any national history: Who are we? Where do we come from? Before any official histories had been written, the folklore and beliefs of some of the Karen provided explanations regarding their origin and present status. Missionaries were amazed to learn that the Karen called their God "Ywa," and that the stories of Ywa resembled the stories of the creation in the Bible. Karen myths even seemed to predict the coming of Europeans with holy scriptures. The story of the Golden Book (or the Book of Life) explains that the Karen (the eldest brother) were senior to the White Man (the youngest brother). However, the Karen were ignorant, and because they were, Ywa gave the Book to the White Man instead of to the Karen. The White Man went west and profited from the knowledge in the Book, becoming prosperous. The Karen remained poor but believed that some day the White Man would return and give them the Book. Christian missionaries credited this story for the Karen's relative eagerness to welcome missionaries and accept the Gospel. Genevieve Sowards (1951), in her article, "Folklore Aid to Missions," in a US national Baptist magazine, the *Watchman Examiner*, theorized that since the Karen story of the Book resembled the Old Testament, the Karen might have learned the story from one of the ten lost tribes of Israel. She supposed that one of the tribes wandered into China before the ancestors of the Karen migrated south. "Those who are inclined to this explanation," she wrote, "call attention to the Karen name for God, Ywa, which is strikingly like the old Hebrew name for God, Yahweh." Some missionaries even believed that the Karen were one of the ten lost tribes.

Modern histories of the origins of the Karen stem from another popular myth, "Thaw Me Pa," or the story of the wild boar's tusk father. In the tale, Thaw Me Pa, the eternal ancestor, led the people from an overpopulated country in the north to a new and better land in the south, beyond the "running sand river" (probably the Gobi Desert, which ancient Chinese texts refer to as the Sand River). Thaw Me Pa kept going, but the group stopped to cook shellfish. They were surprised when the green shells did not turn yellow after heating. "Why won't our food cook?" they wondered, and waited, hungry, until the Chinese came and taught them how to eat shellfish. Afterwards, they could never catch up with Thaw Me Pa (cf. Marshall [1922] 1997: 5).

This and other myths have been transformed, first by missionaries[7] and later by Karen intellectuals, into historical accounts with exact dates of migration and resettlement. They re-enter popular culture through accounts such as this one in a Karen newsletter published in Australia:

> The Karens migrated from Babylon in BC 2234 to go to the kingdom of Mongolia, arriving in BC 2197 ... then departed in BC 2017 for East Turkestan, arriving in BC 2013.... In BC 1866 ... they left to migrate to Tibet ... and reached Tibet in BC 1864. From Tibet in BC 1388 ... they left for the kingdom of Yunnan arriving there in BC 1385 ... in BC 1128 a first wave departed for Burma arriving there in BC 1125 ... a second wave departed Yunnan in BC 741 ... and arrived in Burma in BC 739.... This means that the total duration of Karen residence in Burma is in total 739 years plus 2000 years equals 2739. (Australia Karen Organization 2000: 2)

As a result, most Karen believe their ancestors came from southern China, although few are familiar with the exact dates when they are supposed to have moved from place to place. They also believe that history shows they settled in their present lands long ago.

In Burma, from 1937 forward, the British colonial government endorsed this history by declaring Karen New Year's Day a national holiday. In New Year's ceremonies organized in Karen communities across the country, the story of the migration was recounted, and their long centuries of residence in Burma were celebrated. The holiday confirmed that the Karen settlement in Burma predated the arrival of the Burmans. During the years when the KNU ruled a liberated area along the Thai-Burma border, New Year's celebrations in the region were grand and included army parades, salutations to and the raising of the Karen flag, dancing in national costumes, sports contests, and traditional rituals worshiping Phi Bue Yo, the rice goddess.[8] Even after the fall of their stronghold in the mid-1990s, the KNU continued to organize New Year's ceremonies, although on a much smaller scale. The Karen New Year remains an official holiday in Burma. In 2005, in Pa-an, the capital of Karen state, the biggest ceremony was held early in the morning at the Taungale monastery. It was followed by five days and nights of Karen cultural displays:

a Don dance contest, boxing, theatrical performances (*zat*), and music played on traditional instruments.

KNU accounts stress another fact that defines the Karen as a nation: they possess their own written language. Jonathan Wade (1781–1872), a missionary, invented written Karen in 1832 by adapting Burmese characters to the Sgaw Karen spoken language.[9] Wade finished his translation of the New Testament from English into Karen in 1843. Ten years later, another missionary, Francis Mason, completed a Karen translation of the Bible. In the intervening decade, the Karen Mission Press in Tavoy (Burma) published sixty-three books of Christian literature and distributed them to Karen Christians. These books, mostly printed in Karen, were produced in fairly large press runs totaling over ten million pages altogether. They included hymn books, scripture portions, books for pastors, books for teachers, school books, health lectures, and a four-volume Karen thesaurus.[10]

A monthly magazine printed in Sgaw Karen, the *Morning Star*, was first published by Dr. Mason in 1842.[11] The *Morning Star* played an important role by linking the Karen—especially the Christian Karen—together as members of the same imagined ethnic Karen community. When it was closed in 1962 by Ne Win's coup d'état, it was the oldest continuously published vernacular newspaper in the country (Smith 1999: 44).

The written Karen language was invented by missionaries to help spread Christian beliefs and practices. Its introduction brought about unintended changes in Karen society, for its use has helped to promote the reconstructed Karen history, traditions, and culture, and has provided a medium for communicating the ideas of Karen nationalists. The existence of these written characters makes the Karen proud of being a civilized nation and of possessing something other nations also have: their own written literature.

If missionaries in Burma found the Karen hospitable and eager to accept the Gospel, the colonial government came to consider them dependable allies. Karen served in the British Army in the first two Anglo-Burmese Wars in 1826 and 1852. Karen soldiers were employed to put down frequent revolts against the colonizers both before and long after the final war in 1885 completed Britain's conquest. Decades later, they helped to suppress the Saya San movement of 1930–1932. In World War II, Karen fought in cooperation with the British-organized underground movements against the Japanese and their sometime Burman allies. In 1942, after the British fled Burma and the colonial administrative structure collapsed, the Burma Independent Army—Burmans trained and armed by the Japanese, each side using the other to pursue its goal of defeating the British—reportedly killed numerous Karen in Papun, while local Burman leaders killed many Karens in Myaung-mya. Karen fighters also attacked and killed many Burmans until the Japanese military stepped in to stop the violence. These events and decades of Karen service in the British Army left a legacy of hatred, mistrust, and deep conflict between Burmans and Karens.

In his book, *The Loyal Karens of Burma*, D. M. Smeaton, a British government official who served in Burma from 1879 to 1884, praised the Karen for their bravery and for their sacrifice for "our government": "The Karen people are at heart loyal to us, and they have proved their loyalty by freely shedding their blood in defence of our rule and in the cause of order" (Smeaton 1887: 6). Smeaton recounted Karen history and culture in an attempt to educate British popular and official opinion. He urged his government to support the Karen both to reward their loyalty and to empower them so they could continue to serve as a counterbalance to the less tractable Burmans. He suggested employing more Karen officials, especially in Karen living areas. He recommended official sanction for three aspects of Karen culture: language, traditions, and organization. In each area, he proposed detailed alternative policies. For example, he thought the government should make Karen an official language, just like Burmese. Official texts should be produced in both Karen and Burmese; government representatives should communicate directly with Karen speakers in their own language; the Karen language should be taught in schools; and excellence in Karen should win students the same awards as those given for excellence in Burmese. "The Karens," his book concluded, "look on Christianity and education as inseparable factors in their civilization.... State encouragement to their schools should be accompanied by state aid to their churches and missions.... The government should endeavour by every possible means to draw the hill Karens down to the plains and settle them on good rice-growing lands" (ibid.: 235–236).

Smeaton's suggestions became official policy. During the colonial period, more Karens than Burmans held high-ranking positions in the Burmese government despite their smaller share of the population. In 1939, 1,448 Karens and only 472 Burmans served in the British Army (Smith 1999: 44). One of them, Smith Dun, began as an enlisted man, attended the India Military Academy, fought on the British side against the Japanese throughout World War II, and, when Burma was granted independence, was named commander-in-chief of the army and of the police forces. However, he was removed from his command when the Karen revolt began in 1949. Although he remained loyal to the national government, he also sympathized with the Karen rebels (Dun 1980).

Like military service, education was a path to advancement for Karens in Burma under British rule. In 1870, missionaries sent 14-year-old San C Po to study medicine in the United States. (Po took the surname of the female missionary who cared for him as a schoolchild, Crombie, as his middle name, later shortening it to the single letter C.) After returning to Burma twenty-four years later, Po worked as a medical doctor in the civil service for eight years. In 1915, he was the first Karen appointed to the Legislative Council, which advised the British government. In 1917, representing the Karen at a conference in India, he spoke against plans for a separate (Burman-governed) Burmese state and for continued rule by Britain. He helped recruit Karen soldiers to fight for the British Army in World War I, in honor of which he was named a Commander of the British Empire in 1924. The next year, while still serving on the Legislative Council, he was chosen KNA president. When Burma was granted its own constitution in 1937, he was elected to the Senate (Fink 2001; Po [1928] 2001). In the latter part of his life, Po argued energetically for the creation of a separate, self-governing Karen state and became "regarded as the 'Father' of the Karen nation" (Martin Smith, quoted in Fink 2001). Acknowledging the tutelage he and other Karen leaders received from foreigners, he wrote: "[T]he Karens are not ashamed or afraid to proclaim to the world publicly or in private that they owe what progress and advancement they have made, to the missionaries whom they affectionately call their 'Mother' under the protection of the British government whom they rightly call their 'Father'" (Po [1928] 2001: 58)..

After the Japanese were defeated in 1945, the quest for independence took center stage in Burma. Burmese nationalism was inseparable from Buddhism. Karen leaders, most of whom were Christian, worried that if the British left, the Karen would suffer. They sent a "goodwill mission" of four lawyers, all educated in Britain, to London to put the case for the Karens before the British government.[12] They proposed that after independence, Burma should be a federal state comprised of autonomous ethnic states, each of which would have its own parliament and army. Two options were envisioned for the Karen: an autonomous Karen state under British protection to include a seaport, or a Karen state in a federation of frontier area states within the British Commonwealth and separate from Burma. The answer was disheartening. The British government "would not and could not" support the mission's proposal (Dun 1980: 80; Smith 1999: 72–73, 469).

In February 1947, General Aung San convened the Panglong Conference. Representatives of several ethnic groups (the Shan, Kachin, and Chin) agreed to stay together as the Union of Burma for at least the first ten years after independence. After that, certain ethnic states could choose to secede. Karen representatives, attending the conference as observers, did not sign the agreement. The September 1947 constitution, by which the Panglong agreement became law, made some provisions for the Karens but did not grant them even a delayed right of secession.

Days before Panglong, representatives of the existing Karen organizations met to form the Karen National Union, which campaigned for a separate Karen state and called for a boycott of elections for the Constituent Assembly. Other Karen organizations disagreed, and their candidates represented the Karen in the assembly. As a result, Karen voter turnout was low, and no Karen nationalists were among the writers of the constitution.

The KNU continued to ask for self-determination after Britain granted Burma independence on 4 January 1948. The four slogans of the 11 February 1948 demonstrations, in which hundreds of thousands of Karen took part, were "Give the Karen State at once—Independence," "For the Burmese one *kyat* and the Karen one *kyat*—Equality," "We do not want communal strife—National Unity," and "We do not want civil war—Peace" (Smith 1999:

110). Despite this public stance and the loyalty of the Karen and other ethnic groups in the armed forces in the chaos of the summer of 1947 (when Aung San was assassinated) and 1948 (when the Communist Party of Burma [CPB] rebelled, joined by whole units of the army), armed conflict between the KNU's Karen National Defence Organization (KNDO) and the Burmese government became unavoidable once Karen civilians were killed and leaders were arrested at the end of 1948.[13] Since that time, fighting between the KNU and the Burmese government has ebbed and flowed but never ceased entirely.

Although Burmese nationalism and Karen nationalism developed concurrently under British rule, the KNU believes that the differences in the national characteristics of the two nations are irreconcilable: "[I]t is extremely difficult for the Karens and the Burmans, two peoples with diametrically opposite views, outlooks, attitudes and mentalities, to yoke together.... Unless we control a state of our own, we will never experience a life of peace and decency, free from persecution and oppression" (KNU 2000). There are numerous political, quasi-political, and political-religious Karen organizations, and many may not agree with the political aims and direction of the KNA or the KNU. But all of these organizations assert a Karen national identity, with a common history of origin, written languages, and selected cultural features as its foundation. Karen national consciousness and identity evolved during a century of relative privilege under British colonial rule and has continued to develop despite political arrangements in independent Burma (now Myanmar) that work against Karen national integration.

Themes repeat themselves in the writings of missionaries and in the KNU's history of the Karen. As these sources tell it, the Karens in Burma were severely oppressed and exploited by Burman feudal lords. Under colonial rule, their status improved dramatically, but after independence, they suffered once again at the hands of a Burman regime. Their only option was to fight to gain their own state. Similar stories are not told by Karen organizations in Thailand because the political and social context in which Karen identity has been constructed there is very different.

The Construction of Karen Identity in Thailand

Although at the end of the nineteenth century Thailand (Siam until 1939) had lost some western and southern territory to Britain and some eastern land to France, it remained independent. Aware of the threat of colonization, the kings of Thailand carried out administrative reforms that centralized the government and unified the country. Unlike the changes Britain imposed on Burma, no ethnic classification process was employed, nor was there an intensive effort to educate the Karen. A few missionaries, both foreign and Karen, came across the border from Burma to evangelize the Karens of Thailand. Their work was intermittent until it was curtailed by World War II.

Unlike Karen speakers in Burma, Thai Karen have not constructed a single history of their origins. All of the Karen in Thailand share a relatively positive view of their people's premodern treatment by the kings, but different tales of the historical past are told by Karens in the west and in the north. Communities in the north remember that their ancestors came from west of the Salawin River, in what is today Burma.[14] Some believe that their villages have moved from place to place within the region for many generations and do not know where they came from before that. Others remember that their ancestors were captured in a war toward the end of the eighteenth century and resettled in the present area. As subjects of the northern royalty, they sent tribute either directly to the northern lords or via the Lua people, who inhabited the land before them. Karen in western Thailand recall that their ancestors came from Tavoy, in present-day Burma, fleeing Burmese pursuit together with the Mon after the Burmese king conquered the Mon kingdom in the mid-eighteenth century, and settled in the lands of the Siamese king, in or around present-day Uthaithanee, Suphanburi, and Kanchanaburi Provinces. The king appointed a Karen leader to the position of Phra Sri Suwan Khiri (chief) to oversee the frontier area populated by the Karen. Prior to the late-nineteenth-century reforms, five Karen chiefs held the post in succession (Renard 1980). The last one became the first district officer of Sangkhlaburi District, Kanchanaburi Province in the new, centralized administrative structure, when Thai territorial space was organized into villages, districts, and provinces.

As late as the 1950s, when Karen nationalism had emerged in Burma and Burma's Karen were fighting for an autonomous state, Karens in Thailand in general continued their way of life with little interference from the Thai state. Living mostly undisturbed in still-verdant forests, they governed themselves at the village level. Some Karens in the west adopted Buddhism from the Buddhist Mon with whom they had emigrated from Burma. Karens in the north largely maintained their ancestor cults.[15]

The 1950s began a period of modernization driven by socioeconomic and political change in Thailand. The first Thai national economic development plan in 1961–1966 built infrastructure that improved transportation, telecommunications, and power generation and delivery in various parts of the country to promote privately financed resource extraction and import-substitution industries. A key factor was the construction of dams, which supported cash-crop expansion and produced electricity for industry and the service sector.

During the same period, state agencies extended their administrative control and their welfare and development efforts into remote mountainous areas. The Cold War had come to Southeast Asia, and the Thai government, fearing that the Communist Party of Thailand (CPT), backed by communist parties of neighboring countries, might seek converts among the upland peoples of the north, began to pay attention. "Hill tribe" emerged as an official category for nine northern ethnic groups—the Karen, Lisu, Lahu, Akha, Lua, Khamu, Thin, Hmong, and Mien. The Hill Tribe Welfare Committee was set up in 1955, and in 1961, the Provincial Hill Tribe Development and Welfare Center was established to coordinate research activities and carry out development projects in hill tribe villages. In 1965, the Ministry of the Interior, with the support of UNESCO and SEATO, began the Tribal Research Center to study each of the nine hill tribes.[16]

Also in 1965, the Dhammacharik Buddhist missionary program began working with the hill tribes. Its main goals were to convert to Buddhism hill people who still largely practiced their traditional religions, to induce a sense of being Thai among them, and thereby to secure their loyalty to the Thai nation. Its biggest achievement, however, has been in schooling. The Dhammacharik program sponsors hill tribe boys to be ordained as novice monks and provides them with a monastic education. Many go on to higher education, and some earn college degrees (see Hayami 1999).

Christian missionary work among the Karen in Thailand began seriously only in the 1950s, unlike missionary efforts in Burma, which reached the Karen as early as 1826 and continued for more than a century during the colonial period. Missionaries came to Thailand from China after being expelled by the Chinese government in the aftermath of the 1949 revolution. They also migrated from Burma during the chaos following that country's independence. As they had in Burma, Christian missionaries helped Karen children receive higher education by providing scholarships and accommodation in villages or in cities. However, they established far fewer separate Christian schools than in Burma because there was not the same need. In Thailand, primary education became mandatory in 1921, and since that time, the Thai had established many primary schools in rural areas.[17] Christian missionaries supported education among the Karen by constructing dormitories near government schools, in order to give Christian Karen children from remote villages a place to live while studying. They provided food and other necessities and taught the schoolchildren the Gospel and Christian practices.

Christian missionary influence among the Karen in Thailand is narrower than in Burma. The Bible is the same one published in Burma, with Karen written characters. But the use of the written languages *li wa* (based on Burmese script) and *li ro me* (based on Roman script) is limited mainly to religious activities. These languages are not widely used in daily communication. Because the Thai government school system teaches only one written language, Thai, Karen youth in general cannot read Karen characters. Poor rural Karen children in Thailand need not depend on Christian missionaries to support their schooling—the boys, at least, can receive support from the Dhammacharik Buddhist missionary project. In Thailand, unlike in Burma, missionaries have always been regulated at the national level; their organizations must register with, and are overseen by, public authorities. In Burma, Christian missionaries helped create a separate Karen consciousness (allied, it is true, with British colonial rule for many decades). In Thailand, by contrast, Christian missionaries have aided the Karen to better integrate into Thai society.

Prejudice against the hill tribes permeates Thai society. Decades of school texts, mass media reports, and public documents describe hill tribespeople as a problem for Thai society. Some did join the CPT Army, threatening Thai national security. Many others supported the Thai Army, but this is rarely mentioned in official documents (Prasit Leepreecha 2003). Once the CPT collapsed in the early 1980s, the problems of narcotics production and consumption were blamed on the hill tribes. Moreover, they have been held solely responsible for forest destruction in Thailand. This mainstream "hill tribe" discourse has convinced many people—including many of the hill peoples themselves—that this minority's ignorance and backward agricultural practices cause drug abuse and deforestation. Their non-Thai background is linked with disloyalty to Thai society and an inclination to do things that may be harmful to the nation.[18]

The national integration policy, which promoted schooling, research and development, and the Dhammacharik Buddhist missionary projects, also aimed to suppress the old attachments, beliefs, and practices of the hill tribes and to instill a sense of Thai national identity, so that the hill tribes, including the Karen, would become Thai and exhibit loyalty to the Thai nation. However, after four decades of national integration, the Karen in Thailand have not "become Thai." Instead, they have developed plural identities, thinking of themselves, for example, as a Thai citizen with Karen background and Christian or Buddhist beliefs. They identify themselves as Christian Thai Karen or Buddhist Thai Karen rather than as purely Karen or purely Thai.

Official discrimination has hindered integration. In perhaps the worst instance, the so-called Thai hill tribes are subjected to forced relocation. They lived for generations in forest areas in the north and the west of Thailand, making their living by cultivating upland fields and collecting forest products. Elsewhere in the country, forests have largely disappeared, destroyed by encroachment from residential, resort, and government agency office development, displaced by the expansion of cash-cropping, or clear-cut by logging concessions, a practice which was officially banned in 1989. In compensation, the government demarcated the northern and western forests, proclaiming them to be protected areas—national parks, wildlife sanctuaries, and class 1 watersheds—and in this way transformed the resident hill tribe farmers of these highlands into illegal inhabitants, threatened with removal to degraded forests. Swidden farming and cutting trees to build houses are now grounds for arrest.

Since the 1980s, more and more of the Karen have received higher education, and over time they began to participate in all sectors of Thai society. As they became less isolated, they learned that lowland Thais looked down on them and discriminated against them in many ways. Moved by this growing awareness of unequal treatment, and helped by domestic and international development organizations, the Karen and other hill tribes established associations to represent their interests, to preserve their cultures, and to sponsor development projects with the goal of ensuring their economic survival. Karen leaders, aided by allies in academia and the media, countered the official hill tribe discourse. They argued that the Karen are not recent migrants, that they settled in Thai territory many centuries ago. They demonstrated "local wisdom" in natural resource management by explaining how they classified forest areas and cared for forests, citing year-round ceremonies as further evidence of a life in harmony with nature. They rejected the term "shifting cultivation" and argued that what they actually practice is "rotational cultivation," a swidden cultivation system that allows soil fertility to regenerate on its own, making the farming of upland fields sustainable.[19] In addition, the Karen have promoted the conservation of their way of life as an instance of the international effort to preserve indigenous cultures. Many recent books by Karen authors explain the group's cultural practices and beliefs.

Distinct from Karens in Burma, the Karens of Thailand have not developed a national consciousness: they have not constructed a unitary national history, attempted to specify their original territory, or developed or adopted a widely used written language as their own. There is no pan-Karen political movement maneuvering for its own state in Thailand. Instead, facing the challenge of prejudice and discrimination, Thai Karens have organized themselves to assert their identity as (mainly) forest conservationists to counter the official stereotype of hill tribespeople as forest destroyers. They assert their place as citizens of Thailand who deserve to be treated no differently than the Thai majority. They seek recognition from, and equal respect alongside, lowland Thais, not separation from Thai society.

Ethnic Identity, Ethnic Conflict, and Resolution

Thus far, we have seen how Karen identity developed differently within different systems of ethnic relations in Burma and in Thailand. Ethnic relations, ethnic identity, and ethnic conflict influence and shape each other. Ethnic conflict, as I define it, is based on ethnic claims but always integrates itself into larger economic and political agendas. It takes place between two or more ethnic groups, or, as in the two cases studied here, it may pit an ethnic group against a modern nation-state. When it does, as Appadurai (2000: 162) explains, "nationalism and ethnicity thus feed each other, as nationalists construct ethnic categories that in turn drive others to construct counterethnicities, and then in times of political crisis these others demand counterstates based on newfound counternationalisms."

The evolution of nationalist aspirations among the Karen in Burma has been even more complicated than Appadurai suggests. Burmese nationalism and Karen nationalism each emerged during the colonial period. For decades, they confronted each other politically, attempting to enlist as allies powerful agents such as the colonial government, missionaries, the Japanese occupation government during World War II, and the leaders and organizations of other ethnicities and political ideologies.

In the aftermath of independence, many of Burma's ethnic groups gave birth to secessionist movements. The Karen movement, one of the strongest, has endured ever since. Karen ethnic identity, an important factor in its survival, has become a focal point for boosting the morale of the movement's members. Embedded in the rationale for continuing the armed struggle, it is implicit in the "four principles of the Karen revolution" announced by KNU leader Saw Ba U Gyi in 1950 at the first all-KNU Congress to meet after the war broke out, only days before he died in battle, ambushed by the *tatmadaw* (Burmese Army): "There shall be no surrender. The recognition of the Karen state must be completed. We shall retain our own arms. We shall decide our own political destiny" (Smith 1999: 143–144).

In this context, power relations, constructed Karen identity, and collective violence are interdependent: a change or manipulation affecting one may have an impact on the others. In the decades since the war for secession began, three actors have exerted the most influence over both Karen identity and the course of the conflict. The first is Burma's government. After a brief period of parliamentary rule, plagued by the difficulties of factionalism and of fighting multiple insurgencies, since the early 1960s the country has been governed— and terrorized—by military autocrats. Participation in public affairs is risky and difficult even for Burmans. Ever-present fear and oppression have forestalled reconciliation. Development toward a genuine federal union, in which all ethnic groups would share power fairly (as some on all sides hoped at the time of independence from Britain), has not occurred. The second important set of actors is comprised of Karen nationalist leaders, who have adjusted their vision, strategies, and projected identities in response to changing political conditions. The third key actor is the international community, which plays a role in sustaining, preventing, and terminating armed struggle.

When Karen nationalists finally rebelled in early 1949, a large segment of Burma's armed forces were under their control. They quickly took control of several large towns and came close to taking the capital, Rangoon. In June, the KNU established its short-lived provisional *kaw thoo lei*[20] government, naming Saw Ba U Gyi prime minister. The next year, as the KNU gradually lost its strongholds to the Burmese government due to poor coordination among its forces, the *kaw thoo lei* government had to be dissolved. Saw Ba U Gyi's death that summer left a vacuum in KNU leadership. When new leaders emerged in 1953 and established the Karen National United Party (KNUP), they adopted Maoist ideology and strategy. Although this permitted limited cooperation with the CPB, inspired the suppression of banditry (which won the KNUP support from Burman as well as Karen villagers), and led to important improvements in military organization and discipline, as the decade progressed, Marxist hostility to religion offended many Christian and Buddhist Karens.

While the insurrections regained strength, divisions in the Burmese government were settled by Ne Win's caretaker military rule in 1958–1960. Alarmed by the restored civilian government's moves toward federalism, Ne Win and the *tatmadaw* staged a coup in 1962. In the name of Burmese socialism and the defeat of the communist and ethnic armies, the new regime suppressed student associations, political parties, the press, religious organizations, and dissent in general. It expelled foreigners (including missionaries), provoked an exodus of ethnic Indians and Chinese, restricted travel into and out of the country, and nationalized much of the economy. The tensions within the Karen nationalist movement, which had begun over KNUP ideology, continued, leading some militants to retire from the rebellion and others to surrender, and causing geographic and organizational divisions among the majority of soldiers who kept up the fight.

The secessionist movement led by the KNU regained its power only in the late 1960s, under new leadership and with substantial support from international agents, amid fierce wars between communist forces and the rulers of Burma and its neighbors. In 1966, Bo Mya, the leader of the KNU's eastern units, had broken with the organization in disagreement over its relationship with the CPB. He founded a new organization, the Karen National United Front, in 1968, became a vice-chairman of the reunited KNU in 1975, and served as its chairman from 1976 to 2004. Bo Mya's reputation as a staunch anticommunist earned the KNU significant support from the Thai government, which in the late 1960s and 1970s was fighting the Communist Party of Thailand. The Thai government also intended to use the KNU's bases as a buffer zone to prevent the Burmese, a historical enemy of the Thai state, from threatening the border. Talks between Karen and Mon rebels and the Thai military authorities in Bangkok, and agreements permitting the former to set up camps along the 500-mile Thai border and buy supplies from Thailand, date back to 1954 (Lintner 1999: 441).

The revival of the KNU from the late 1960s to the early 1980s was not only due to international support. The Karen also took economic advantage of their geographic position.[21] When Ne Win closed the borders to lead Burma to "socialism" in 1962, shortages of consumer goods resulted, with many items being smuggled in. It is estimated that for a time, 80 percent of Burma's consumer goods passed through Karen-controlled areas on their way from Thailand, and the KNU levied a 5 percent tax on the traffic. The KNU also granted logging concessions to Thai, Singaporean, and Malaysian businesses. In 1984, there were 65 saw mills along the border. In 1989–1993, around 18,800 square kilometers of forest were logged under agreements with the KNU (see Boucaud and Boucaud 1992; Bryant 1996; Falla 1991; Lintner 1999; Rajah 1990; Renard 1990). As KNU income rose, so did its ability to buy weapons and expand the army. Thai brokers supplied weapons from Laos and Cambodia. Singaporean brokers smuggled arms from Belgium and Israel. At its greatest strength, the Karen National Liberation Army (KNLA) may have had 90,000–100,000 soldiers (Somchoke Sawasdiruk 1997: 28; Thammarat Thongrueng 2000: 31, 63, 77).[22]

As the Cold War ended, the situation in the region changed. The communists were no longer a threat. In Thailand, the economy boomed, and the government launched efforts to convert war zones into trading zones to further economic growth. Following the unrest of 1988, Burma's rulers began to open the country to market forces. In 1997, the Association of Southeast Asian Nations admitted Burma as a member, making it possible for the Thai and Burmese governments to cooperate in economic development. When logging in the south of Thailand was halted following flash flooding in 1989, a high-ranking member of the Thai government visited Burma and obtained an agreement to let Thai businesses log along the border. The KNU, which lost significant income as a result, faced a dilemma: opening more forest areas under Karen control for logging risked the forests' destruction and thus the loss of their refuges. Commerce began to flow in by sea from Singapore and by road from China, decreasing the demand for smuggled goods from Thailand. The Thai government ceased its support for the KNU in order to maintain good relations with Burma (cf. Corson-Knowles 2003; Gravers 1999: 63–64; Maclean, Myo, and Maung 2003; Smith 1999: 408–409).

Religious tensions among the Karen made conditions worse. The frontline Karen soldiers were mostly Buddhists or traditionalists, while almost all of their leaders were Christian—predominantly Baptist or, like Bo Mya, Seventh-day Adventist. Soldiers in the Pa-an region related that their local Christian Karen officers mistreated them, discriminated against them, and enlisted child soldiers. Similar stories were reported in other areas, as were tales of forced recruitment and of corruption and criminal actions on the part of KNLA officers. These conditions, the frustration of fighting a stalemated war, and Burmese government appeals led hundreds of KNLA fighters to join the Democratic Karen Buddhist Army (DKBA) in late 1994. Armed and supplied by the government, the DKBA fought against the KNLA. Attrition and DKBA intelligence helped the *tatmadaw* finally conquer the KNU stronghold of Manerplaw, the "land of victory," in 1995. Since then, the KNU has been forced to retreat to new, smaller camps established in forest areas near the border. Villages in the former KNU area fell under the control of Burmese forces and the DKBA. Caught in the crossfire, Karen noncombatants fled across the border. Today more than 100,000 displaced Karen live in Thailand, residing in refugee camps and villages on the border or working illegally in the interior (Corson-Knowles 2003: 17–18; Gravers 1999: 87–94; KHRG 1995, 1996; Smith 1999: 393–394, 445–447; Somchoke Sawasdiruk 1997: 182–183; Women's League of Burma 2005).

The camps survive with material support from several international organizations, which also facilitate the provision of education, health care, and development aid. As Sang Kook's (2001) research in the largest Karen refugee camp on the Thailand-Burma border shows, the nationalist cause is promoted in these camps in the education system, in ceremonies, and in everyday activities. The international organizations that support education projects at the high-school level have tried to reduce the nationalist content of the curriculum. For example, they have asked that Christianity not be taught in the schools and that any Karen history suggesting antagonistic relations with the Burmans be glossed over. The curriculum, according to these donors, should stress peace and coexistence with other groups.

In 1993, after the failure of an early *tatmadaw* attempt to take Manerplaw, Bo Mya, the chairman of the KNU, sent an open letter to the Burmese government demanding a countrywide ceasefire. The first meeting between KNU representatives and the Burmese government representatives was not held until 1995, when the Burmese again had the upper hand. There has been no concrete result from those meetings. In 1997, a few groups of KNU soldiers made their own ceasefire agreements with the Burmese government. The next year, Phado Aung San, a member of the KNU Central Committee, surrendered together with about seventy soldiers and their families. Despite these defections, the KNU did not disappear (*Irrawaddy* 2004b; Smith 1999: 445–450).

In January 2004, Bo Mya sent a delegation to Rangoon and obtained a verbal ceasefire agreement. The pact was mediated by the Thai government, which had backed the KNU for many years. In 2003, a ceasefire committee of senior Thai army officials had been formed with the purpose of ensuring that "Thai territory would not be used by armed groups to attack neighbors." The intent is to convert battlefields into areas open to trade and industry. An east-west development corridor, which will link Thailand with Burma, Vietnam, and Laos, is under discussion. Included in this plan is the development of an economic zone covering the area of Mae Sot and nearby Myawaddy Township in Burma (*Irrawaddy* 2004a: 11).

The KNU, and the Karen secessionist movement it leads, is at an important turning point. Its future direction is of major concern to everyone who is affected in one way or another by the movement. What kind of nationalism should the Karen have? One Karen refugee writes: "In general, nationalism combined with vision can produce prosperity and promote peace. While a broad-minded nationalism can preserve diversity and encourage creative ideas, a narrow-minded one maintains a 'we-are-better' attitude, is very trivial in essence and utterly divisive in nature. Hence, we shall embrace the former and reject the latter" (Saw Kapi 2005).

Ceasefire negotiations are an opportunity for the KNU leaders to alter the movement's strategy, although not without disagreement. "War is no good. It is meaningless for whoever dies—Burmese or Karen," Bo Mya said when he announced the January 2004 ceasefire, But, he added, the KNU was not ready to trust the government's honesty, and was prepared to resume fighting if promises were broken (Kyaw Zwa Moe 2003). When the Burmese prime minister who negotiated the ceasefires with the KNU and other organizations was arrested in October 2004 after a coup d'état, doubts increased. Bo Mya retired later that year. As of this writing, his successors continue to negotiate, and continue to refuse to surrender their weapons.

Conclusion

Power relations and the systems of ethnic relations in Burma and in Thailand differ greatly, and have shaped different Karen identities. In Burma, the Karen developed national consciousness and a national identity in the late nineteenth century, establishing the Karen National Association (KNA), writing their own history, and asserting their political rights as a group. Proud that they possessed all the characteristics of a nation, and emboldened by experience as soldiers and officers, many Karen leaders were reluctant to submit to the rule of the Burmans, their long-term rivals. When mutual distrust became open fighting in 1949, Karen nationalists, led by the KNA's successor, the Karen National Union (KNU), began an armed struggle for independence that still continues. They have endured and sometimes prospered despite changes in leadership, ideological disagreements, religious differences, the fluctuating strength of their opponents (the *tatmadaw* and its allies), changing economic and political conditions, and the fortunes of war. Their movement's successes and failures have affected the lives of millions, especially the residents of the frontier area once ruled by the *kaw thoo lei* government.

For over five decades, a peaceful life has been out of reach for soldiers, their families, and anyone who lives in areas affected by the fighting or by recruitment into the service of the opposing armies. When the government has on occasion talked peace, its conditions have been unacceptable, its promises have seemed untrustworthy, and its draconian control of the rest of Burma has warned the KNU and other rebels not to give up arms. In the last two decades, as the broader political context in Burma, Thailand, and the region has changed, the movement has faltered. It began losing major camps in 1984. Eleven years later, its Manerplaw headquarters fell, and in a short time it was driven out of its former refuges, and more than 100,000 Karen refugees were forced to flee across the border to Thailand. The KNU still leads one of Burma's largest rebel groups and still embodies a nationalist dream, but the path ahead is unclear.

By contrast, the Karen in Thailand have attracted the attention of the Thai public with a clear definition of "Karenness" only in the last two decades. Unlike in Burma, history and written language have played a small role in the creation of Karen identity in Thailand. The Thai Karen have recently defined themselves as people who live simple, self-sufficient lives in harmony with the forest. Discourses on Karen nature conservation practices and on their idyllic lifestyle, produced and disseminated by academics and non-governmental developmental organizations, continue to gain currency. The word *pga gan yaw* is increasingly used instead of *kariang* as it becomes more widely known that the Karen prefer the former term. Thai Karen identity has clearly been constructed from selected practices that counteract the state's labeling of hill tribes as forest destroyers and that justify granting the Karen equal rights with other lowland Thais. Though the intention makes sense, in practice the assertion of this identity has had little impact, I believe, on the important Thai government policies that control the granting of forest land-use rights to highland communities.

As I have shown, ethnic identities are defined in processes of negotiation, cooperation, and resistance involving both those who claim an identity and those who reject it. The Karen ethnic identity as projected and confirmed by the KNU of Burma is the result of a long interplay of powerful forces during the colonial period up to, and after, independence. The very different Karen identity kept in public view by the Karen of Thailand is of recent origin, an effort by a people only recently subjected to the power of the state to redefine their relationship to it. In each case, ethnic relations, ethnic identity, and ethnic conflict, whether violent or not, have influenced and shaped each other. These examples suggest that whether collective violence is prompted or hindered by a change in a system of ethnic relations or by changes in an identity itself depends largely on the actions of the national government, the ethnic organizations' leaders, and international communities.

Many solutions have been proposed by many actors and agents—locally, regionally, and internationally—to address ethnic conflict and violence in Burma and Thailand. The proposals sometimes contradict each other. The question that remains unanswered is, how can ethnic and national identities interact in a way that draws on the potentialities of each group, avoids violent conflict, and leads to human well-being and happiness in a just, peaceful, and prosperous society?

Notes

The author is a researcher at the Social Research Institute, Chiang Mai University, Chiang Mai 50200, Thailand. Research for this chapter was conducted under the auspices of Fulbright's 2003 New Century Scholars Program, "Addressing Sectarian, Ethnic and Cultural Conflict within and across National Borders," and as a Fall 2003 Visiting Fellow in Yale University's Program in Agrarian Studies.

1. While, as will be explained, a common written language played an important role in the development of Karen identity in Burma, today, after more than four decades of autocratic government in that country, many Karens there no longer speak, much less read and write, the languages of their grandparents (cf. Smith 1999: 35). As Cheesman (2002: 200) points out, the decline of Karenic languages does not necessarily mean the disappearance of the Karen ethnic group. Max Weber (1978: 364) defined ethnic groups as "human groups (other than kinship groups) which cherish a belief in their common origins of such a kind that it provides a basis for the creation of a community. This belief may be based on similarities of external custom or practice or both, or on memories of colonisation or migration. The question of whether they are to be

called an 'ethnic' group is independent of the question whether they are objectively of common stock. The 'ethnic' group differs from the 'kinship' group in that it is constituted simply by the belief in a common identity, whereas a kinship group is a genuine 'community', characterised by genuinely communal activity. By contrast, the sense of a common ethnic identity (as that expression is being used here) is not itself a community, but only something which makes it easier to form one." The Karen in Burma and in Thailand each developed distinct "common" identities.

2. In 1989, the official English name of the country, once called the Union of Burma, became the Union of Myanmar. At the same time, many cities and towns were renamed: Rangoon, Tavoy, and Pegu became Yangon, Dawei, and Bago. Since most of the events discussed in this chapter took place during the period of British rule (1885–1948) or after independence but before 1989, colonial place names are used throughout for the sake of consistency.

3. The term "Burmese" refers to the people of Burma in general. The term "Burman" refers to the country's majority ethnic group.

4. Suriya Rattanakul (1986) reasons that all of these exonyms may derive from a single ancient Burmese exonym, *karyan,* which itself may have derived from an even older autonym, *ke yaw* or *ke ya.* See also Lehman (1979) on the ethnolinguistic and historical evidence of Karen origins.

5. Saw Po Chit, one of the Karen delegates to London in 1946, made the same argument in similar terms a few years before Britain granted Burma independence: "It is a dream that Karen and Burman can ever evolve a common nationality, and this misconception of one homogeneous Burmese nation … will lead Burma to destruction. Karens are a nation according to any definition. We are a nation with our own distinctive culture and civilisation, language, literature, names, nomenclature, sense of value and proportion, customary laws and moral codes, aptitudes and ambitions; in short we have our own distinctive outlook on life. By all canons of international law we are a nation" (cited in Gravers 1999: 45).

6. Taken from "Our Baptist Heritage. Study Material for 1963, Section C; the Karen Work" (no date). From the archives of the American Baptist-Samuel Colgate Historical Library, Rochester, NY, catalog item #RG1160: Erville and Genevieve Sowards (Box 4).

7. Saw Aung Hla, a missionary-educated inspector of schools for the colonial state, first reconstructed the story of the Karen migration from "Karen, Burmese, and English texts, and Karen epic poems and oral histories" in his *Karen History*, published in Sgaw Karen around 1932 (Cheesman 2002: 205).

8. According to a Karen legend, a Karen orphan was kind to Phi Bue Yo. She rewarded him with a good rice harvest and promised to do so again every year if he invoked her in ritual.

9. It is possible that some groups of the Karen developed their own written characters prior to the early nineteenth century, but those characters were never widely used. At that time, the Karen had little need to communicate by written language and no mechanism to reinforce its use.

10. "Our Baptist Heritage."

11. The *Morning Star*, a Rangoon monthly, was published from 1842 to 1962. Contents principally include news and stories of Karen Christian communities. A more or less complete set is on file at the American Baptist-Samuel Colgate Historical Library, Rochester, NY.

12. The mission was led by the 64-year-old Saw Sydney Loo-nee, a member of Burma's House of Representatives (MP) since 1937 and its speaker for a brief period before the Japanese invasion. The other team members were Saw Po Chit, also an MP and minister of education in 1939; Saw Thra Din, the 51-year-old president of the Karen National

Association; and Saw Ba U Gyi, a 42-year-old barrister who had worked to bring about reconciliation with Aung San and the Burmese during the Japanese occupation.

13. Burmese police forces killed around eighty Karen who were celebrating Christmas in a village near Palaw in the Tavoy district of lower Burma. Christian Karens in other villages in Rangoon were killed or imprisoned by neighboring Burmese.

14. The Karens from Burma whom I interviewed in 2004 in a refugee camp believe that the Karen in Burma originally came from what is now Thailand. They refer to the myth that Chiang Mai was originally the center of the Karen kingdom.

15. Karens in Burma call the Karens of Thailand, who have a smaller population and live mostly in mountainous areas, *pga gan yaw ka jer* (hill Karens). They consider them less "civilized" because of their lower levels of formal education and lack of belief in a world religion.

16. In the beginning, foreign scholars served as the advisers of the Tribal Research Center (TRC). Eric Wolf and Joseph Jorgenson (1970) criticized anthropologists who worked in Thailand, especially those who studied hill tribes, as being implicated in intelligence work for the US. Hinton (2002), a one-time adviser to the TRC, reviewed the situation and denied that there was any involvement in intelligence work, as no data were considered secret. The TRC, which later became the Tribal Research Institute, was closed down in 2002 following the latest restructuring of the Thai bureaucratic system.

17. The Compulsory Primary Education Act of 1921 required that all Thai children attend school in the formal education system. Since 1960, six years of primary education have been compulsory.

18. Pinkaew Laungaramsri (1998, 2003) discusses the construction of the official discourse on hill tribes. The attribution of drug abuse problems to the Hmong is discussed in detail in Prasit Leepreecha (1998) and Aranya Siriphon (2003).

19. The Karen leader Joni Odechao, elected as one of the ninety-nine members of the first National Economic and Social Advisory Council (2001–2004), is the best-known national proponent of the ecological wisdom of Karen hill farming and forest management. Walker (2001) argues that the rotational cultivation Karen advocates describe is idealized and that the actual agricultural practices of the Karen are neither as environmentally sound nor as economically viable as advertised, although the story of Karen conservationism has succeeded as a strategy to protect the Karen's land-use rights. However, by constructing a counterdiscourse, one with the power to unite them "as 'children of the forest,' in their own eyes and in those of others," the Karen of Thailand have opened a symbolic space wherein they can maneuver for their rights (Yos Santasombat 2004: 119–120).

20. According to Tharckabaw and Watson (2003), *kaw thoo lei* translates as "the land of light" or, literally, "the country without evil." Smith (1999: 141) writes that "[t]he term first surfaced after the war and is a word play with several possible meanings. Veteran nationalists usually explain it as 'the country burnt black,' i.e., the country which 'must be fought for' (Kaw = country, Thoo = black, lei = bare), but it is also often described as 'flowery' or 'green' land. The 'thoolei' is a green, orchid-like plant common in the eastern hills."

21. Smith (1999: 391) describes the liberated zone in the early 1990s: "From the Mawdaung Pass to the Toungoo hills, an impressive network was established of KNU government departments, hospitals and clinics and hundreds of village schools, serving the seven main KNU administrative districts.... [M]ost of the teachers were university graduates."

22. Estimates of KNU troop strength vary widely. The 90,000–100,000 figure is from an interview that Thai Group Captain (and Royal Thai Air Force School Assistant Professor)

Somchoke Sawasdiruk (1997: 28) conducted with Bo Mya at the KNU's Manerplaw headquarters on 13 August 1994. Smith (1999: 394) believes that the combined enlistment of the groups' two fighting forces, the KNLA (regular soldiers) and the KNDO (village militia), peaked in the early 1980s and never exceeded 10,000.

References

Appadurai, Arjun. 2000. *Modernity at Large*. Minneapolis: University of Minnesota Press.

Aranya Siriphon. 2003. "Fin kap khon mong: Pholwat khwamlaklai lae khwam subson haeng atluk khong khon chai khob" [Opium and the Hmong People: Dynamics, Diversity, and the Complexity of Marginal People's Identities]. In *Atlak chatphan lae khwam pen khon chai khob*, a book of collected papers presented in 2002 at the First Annual Anthropology Meeting at the Princess Maha Sirindhorn Anthropology Centre in Bangkok, ed. Pinkaew Luangaramsri, 27–80.

Australia Karen Organization. 2000. *News* 3 (January): 1–8.

Boucaud, Andre, and Louis Boucaud. 1992. *Burma's Golden Triangle: On the Trail of the Opium Warlords*. Bangkok: Asia Books.

Bryant, Raymond. 1996. "Asserting Sovereignty through Natural Resource Use: Karen Forest Management on the Thai-Burmese Border." In *Resource, Nations and Indigenous Peoples*, ed. Richard Howitt, John Connell, and Philip Hirsch, 32–41. Oxford: Oxford University Press.

Cheesman, Nick. 2002. "Seeing 'Karen' in the Union of Myanmar." *Asian Ethnicity* 3, no. 2: 199–220.

Corson-Knowles, David. 2003. "Highway Robbery: How Road Construction Expanded the Burmese Military's Resource Access." *Journal of Politics and Society* 14: 10–34. http://www.columbia.edu/cu/helvidius/journal2003.html (accessed October 2005).

Dun, Smith. 1980. *Memoirs of the Four-Foot Colonel*. Ithaca: Cornell University Press.

Enriquez, C. M. 1933. *Races of Burma*. 2nd ed. Delhi: Manager of Publications.

Falla, Jonathan. 1991. *True Love and Bartholomew: Rebels on the Burmese Border*. Cambridge: Cambridge University Press.

Fink, Christine. 2001. "Introduction." In San C. Po, *Burma and the Karens,* ix–xliii. Bangkok: White Lotus.

Foster, Robert J. 1991. "Making National Cultures in the Global Ecumene." *Annual Review of Anthropology* 20: 235–260.

Government of the Union of Burma. 1949. *KNDO Insurrection*. 2nd ed. N.p.: Government of the Union of Burma Publications.

Gravers, Mikael. 1999. *Nationalism as Political Paranoia in Burma: An Essay on the Historical Practice of Power*. 2nd ed. Surrey, UK: Curzon Press.

Hayami, Yoko. 1999. "Buddhist Missionary Project in the Hills of Northern Thailand: A Case Study from a Cluster of Karen Villages." *Tai Culture* 4, no. 1: 53–76.

Hinton, Peter. 1983. "Do the Karen Really Exist?" In *Highlanders of Thailand*, ed. John McKinnon and Wanat Bhruksasri, 155–168. Kuala Lumpur: Oxford University Press.

_____. 2002. "The 'Thailand Controversy' Revisited." *The Australian Journal of Anthropology* 13, no. 2: 155–177.

Irrawaddy. 2004a. 12, no. 2 (February). http://www.irrawaddy.org/issuecontent.asp?v=3724&s=0 (accessed October 2005).

_____. 2004b. "Chronology of Meetings between the Karen National Union and Burma's Military Government." Updated March 2004. http://www.irrawaddy.org/aviewer.asp?a =445 (accessed November 2005).

Jorgensen, Anders Baltzer. 1997. "Foreword." In Harry Ignatius Marshall, *The Karen People of Burma: A Study in Anthropology and Ethnology,* v–xii. Bangkok: White Lotus Press.

Keyes, Charles F. 1979. "Introduction." In *Ethnic Adaptation and Identity: The Karen on the Thai Frontier with Burma,* ed. Charles F. Keyes, 1–23. Philadelphia: Institute for the Study of Human Issues.

_____. 1995. "Who Are the Tai? Reflections on the Invention of Identities." In *Ethnic Identity: Creation, Conflict, and Accommodation,* 3rd ed., ed. L. Romanucci-Ross, G. A. De Vos, 138. Walnut Creek, CA: AltaMira Press.

KHRG (Karen Human Rights Group). 1995. "SLORC's Northern Karen Offensive: An Independent Report by the Karen Human Rights Group." KHRG #95–10. 29 March. http://www.ibiblio.org/freeburma/humanrights/khrg/archive/khrg95/khrg9510.html (accessed October 2005).

_____. 1996. "Inside the DKBA: An Independent Report by the Karen Human Rights Group." KHRG #96-14. 31 March. http://www.ibiblio.org/freeburma/humanrights/khrg/archive/khrg96/khrg9614.html (accessed October 2005).

KNU (Karen National Union). 1986. *KNU Bulletin,* no. 7 (November).

_____. 2000. "Karen History in the Karen National Union (KNU) Narrative." http://www.Karen.org/history/knunarr.htm (accessed February 2000).

Kyaw Zwa Moe. 2003. "KNU Still Talking with Government." *Irrawaddy* online news alert, 17 December. http://www.irrawaddy.org/aviewer.asp?a=591 (accessed October 2005).

LeBar, F. M., G. H. Hickey, and J. K. Musgrave, eds. 1964. *Ethnic Groups of Mainland Southeast Asia.* New Haven, CT: Human Relations Area Files Press.

Lehman, F. K. 1979. "Who Are the Karen, and If So, Why? Karen Ethnohistory and a Formal Theory of Ethnicity." In *Ethnic Adaptation and Identity: The Karen on the Thai Frontier with Burma,* ed. Charles F. Keyes, 215–253. Philadelphia: Institute for the Study of Human Issues.

Lintner, Bertil. 1999. *Burma in Revolt: Opium and Insurgency Since 1948.* Boulder, CO: Westview Press.

MacLean, Ken, with Mahn Nay Myo and Shwe Maung. 2003. *Capitalizing on Conflict: How Logging and Mining Contribute to Environmental Destruction in Burma.* Earth Rights International (ERI) and Karen Environmental and Social Action Network (KESAN). http://www.wrm.org.uy/countries/Burma.html (accessed October 2005).

Marshall, Harry I. [1922] 1997. *The Karen People of Burma: A Study in Anthropology and Ethnology.* Bangkok: White Lotus Press.

Pinkaew Laungaramsri. 1998. "Wathakam wa duey chao khao" [On the Discourse of Hill Tribes]. *Social Sciences Journal* 11, no. 1: 92–135.

_____. 2003. "Constructing Marginality: The 'Hill Tribe' Karen and Their Shifting Locations within Thai State and Public Perspectives." In *Living at the Edge of Thai Society: The Karen in the Highlands of Northern Thailand,* ed. Claudio O. Delang, 21–42. London and New York: RoutledgeCurzon.

Po, San C. [1928] 2001. *Burma and the Karens.* Bangkok: White Lotus.

Prasit Leepreecha. 1998. "Klum chatiphan hmong kap panha ya sep tid" [The Hmong Ethnic Group and the Problem of Narcotics]. *Social Science Journal* 11, no. 1: 136–165.

_____. 2003. "Kwan ru lae mayakhati gieu kap klum chatiphan hmong" [Knowledge and Myth on the Hmong Ethnic Group]. In *Chatiphan lae mayakhati* [Ethnicity and Myth], 23–55. Bangkok: The National Cultural Committee Office.

Rajah, Ananda. 1986. "Remaining Karen: A Study of Cultural Reproduction and the Maintenance of Identity." PhD diss., Australian National University.

_____. 1990. "Ethnicity, Nationalism, and the Nation-State: The Karen in Burma and Thailand." In *Ethnic Groups across National Boundaries in Mainland Southeast Asia*, ed. Gehan Wijeyewardene, 102–133. Singapore: Institute of Southeast Asian Studies.

Renard, Ronald D. 1980. "Kariang: History of Karen-Tai Relations from the Beginning to 1923." PhD diss., University of Hawaii.

_____. 1990. "The Karen Rebellion in Burma." In *Secessionist Movements in Comparative Perspective*, ed. Ralph R. Premdas, S. W. R. de A. Samarasinghe, and Alan B. Anderson, 93–110. London: Pinter Publishers.

Royal Thai Government. 2002. *Thamnieb chumchon bon phuenti sung yisib changwat nai prathetthai* [Directory of Highland Communities in 20 Provinces of Thailand]. Bangkok: Social Development and Welfare Department, Ministry of Social Development and Human Security.

Sang Kook, Lee. 2001. "The Adaptation and Identities of the Karen Refugees: A Case Study of Mae La Refugee Camp in Northern Thailand." MA thesis, Seoul National University.

Saw Kapi. 2005. "Commentary: On Karen Nationalism: Towards a True Meaning of Patriotism." http://www.karen.org/news2/messages/326.html (accessed October 2005).

Smeaton, Donald Mackenzie. 1887. *The Loyal Karens of Burma*. London: Kegan Paul, Trench and Co.

Smith, Martin. 1999. *Burma: Insurgency and the Politics of Ethnicity*. London: Zed Books.

Somchoke Sawasdiruk. 1997. *Kwam samphan rawang thai bamar kariang* [Thai-Burmese-Karen Relations]. A publication in the series "Thailand's Neighbors in Southeast Asia." Bangkok: The Thailand Research Fund and the Foundation for the Promotion of Social Sciences and Humanities Textbooks Project.

Sowards, Genevieve Sharp. 1951. "Folklore Aid to Missions." *Watchman-Examiner*, 4 January, 10–11.

Suriya Rattanakul. 1986. *Thai-Sgaw Karen Dictionary*. Research report of the Graduate School and the Language and Culture for Rural Development Research Institute, Mahidol University.

Thammarat Thongrueng. 2000. *Kariang: Chanuan rue chanuan songkram thai-phama yuk mai* [Karen: Buffer or Catalyzer of Thai-Burmese War in Present Days?] Nonthaburi: Than Bua Kaew.

Tharckabaw, David, and Roland Watson. 2003. "The Karen People of Burma and the Karen National Union." November. http://www.dictatorwatch.org/articles/karenintro.html (accessed June 2005).

Trager, Helen G. 1966. *Burma through Alien Eyes: Missionary Views of the Burmese in the Nineteenth Century*. Bombay: Asia Publishing House.

Walker, Andrew. 2001. "The 'Karen Consensus,' Ethnic Politics and Resource-Use Legitimacy in Northern Thailand." *Asian Ethnicity* 2, no. 2: 145–162.

Weber, Max. 1978. "Origins of the Belief in Common Ethnic Identity: Communities Based on Language and Cult." In *Max Weber: Selections in Translation*, ed. W. G. Runciman, trans. E. Matthews, 316–369. Cambridge: Cambridge University Press.

Wolf, Eric R., and Joseph G. Jorgenson. 1970. "Anthropology on the Warpath in Thailand." *New York Review of Books* 15, no. 9 (November): 26–35.

Women's League of Burma. 2005. "Members: Karen Women's Organization." http://www.womenofburma.org/kwo.htm (accessed November 2005).

Yos Santasombat. 2004. "Karen Cultural Capital and the Political Economy of Symbolic Power." *Asian Ethnicity* 5, no. 1: 105–120.

5

EUROPEAN ATTITUDES
TOWARD IMMIGRANTS

Thomas F. Pettigrew

A growing research literature in the social sciences focuses on prejudice and discrimination against Europe's millions of new immigrants (Pettigrew 1998b). Past results from this work can be divided into two distinct categories of research literature and disciplinary theories. Interestingly, the findings and conclusions from these two traditions often appear to be in conflict.

In the first category—individual and intergroup levels of analyses—social psychologists show that patterns of anti-immigrant prejudice and discrimination closely resemble the forms of prejudice and discrimination against nonimmigrant minorities described in the general literature (Jackson et al. 2001; Pettigrew et al. 1998). In basic outline, the anti-immigrant findings track most of the phenomena documented by Gordon Allport (1954) in his classic volume, *The Nature of Prejudice*.

At this level, then, anti-immigrant prejudice and discrimination share many features in common with out-group prejudice and discrimination in general. For example, prejudice against out-groups—immigrant or nonimmigrant—is characteristically correlated *positively* with authoritarianism, social dominance orientation, group relative deprivation, nationalism, political conservatism, and age. In addition, intergroup prejudice typically relates *negatively* with education, high income, political interest, and extensive contact with the out-group (Pettigrew 2000a).

In the second category—cultural and structural levels—however, anthropologists, political scientists, and sociologists demonstrate that resistance to

---

Notes for this chapter are located on page 117.

immigrants often reveals patterns that differ sharply from prejudice and discrimination against other out-groups. Consider six such cultural and structural examples.

1. *Prior national experience with immigration.* The New and Old Worlds have different experiences with immigration. For the New World, in-migration from throughout the world is a centuries-old phenomenon. To question the belongingness of another group can raise questions about one's own group. For instance, in the United States even the most intense racists, such as George Wallace, have never questioned the belongingness of African Americans. In Western Europe, by contrast, the belongingness of the new immigrant groups—from the Turks to the Vietnamese—is often the first barrier for them to overcome. Although there has been far more immigration into Western Europe in earlier eras than current popular thinking allows (Poles to Germany, Russians to France, etc.), there remains a vast difference between North America and Western Europe in prior experience with immigration.

2. *Structural and cultural differences among host countries.* Related to the belongingness issue are the contrasting ways ethnicity and citizenship are conceptualized in the countries receiving immigrants. In striking contrast to the New World, the Germans and British have an informal "blood" notion of their national identities. This conceptualization makes it difficult for immigrants to gain citizenship in Germany and for immigrants even with citizenship to gain full entry into the dominant group in Great Britain. It also means that ideologies of assimilation and segregation held by the host population closely relate to attitudes toward immigrants (Zick et al. 2001).

3. *Prior history of receiving population with out-group.* Earlier colonial history also shapes European responses to its new immigrants. For example, there is a sharp difference between French attitudes toward Vietnamese and Algerian immigrants. France lost colonial wars to both peoples, but the French harbor far greater prejudice against the Algerians (Pettigrew and Meertens 1995). One possible explanation is that the French had considered Algeria as a *département*—an integral part of France itself. They had not regarded Indochina in this manner. By violently breaking from France, Algerians became a special target of abuse for Jean-Marie Le Pen and his extreme right-wing Nationalist Front.

4. *Multiple distinguishing characteristics.* Native European minorities, such as the Basques, Scots, or Frisians, typically share a language, religion, and physical appearance with their national majorities. But the new immigrants often differ markedly with regard to many of these traits. This difference with other out-groups makes the new immigrants appear conspicuous and far more numerous than they actually are.

5. *The speed of entry.* Perceived threats—to jobs, housing, education, welfare payments, and potential violence—underlie prejudice against many minorities (Stephan et al. 2002). An immigrant group arriving suddenly in the host country can increase such threats dramatically. Italy witnessed this phenomenon in the years between 1989 and 1992 (Pettigrew 1998b), during

which time immigration into Italy spiked, closely followed by a sudden rise in anti-immigrant attitudes.

6. *The size and concentration of the immigrant group.* In aggregate analyses, the size of the immigrant population is positively related to anti-immigrant attitudes, especially in poorer countries. Quillian (1995) found that the interaction of high non–European Union minority percentage and low gross national product accounts for 70 percent of the variance in anti-immigrant prejudice means across twelve European Union nations (see also Fuchs, Gerhards, and Roller 1993). The concentration of immigrants in particular urban areas—such as Frankfurt, Marseilles, and Rotterdam—enhances this effect. This result coincides with similar aggregate findings concerning anti-black prejudice and discrimination across counties in the southern United States (see, e.g., Pettigrew and Campbell 1960; Pettigrew and Cramer 1959).

There is a need, then, to bring these two sets of literatures and theories together. Each offers invaluable insights. Indeed, as one who has contributed to both research literatures, I believe each tradition supplies what the other lacks. In short, the two approaches are complementary rather than conflicting. Aggregate data on structural and cultural factors require links with intergroup and individual data to avoid the ecological fallacy—the erroneous assumption that aggregate phenomena will be directly reflected at the individual level of analysis. Similarly, individual and intergroup data require links with the broader aggregate data tapping cultural and structural contexts to avoid the compositional fallacy—the erroneous assumption that individual phenomena will be directly reflected at the societal and cultural levels of analysis.

Following this view, we will attempt to untangle one of the most important discrepancies between the two research traditions. Complex processes arise from the differential effects of the size of the minority population on majority prejudice. On the one hand, sociological theory and research has long held that the larger a minority's population ratio, the greater the threat to and prejudice of the majority (e.g., Fuchs, Gerhards, and Roller 1993; Pettigrew and Campbell 1960; Pettigrew and Cramer 1959; Quillian 1995). But greater numbers of immigrants also lead to greater contact between the host population and the new arrivals. Thus, this aggregate finding appears at variance with the research results at the individual level. It directly conflicts with the standard social psychological finding that more intergroup contact typically leads to reduced prejudice (Pettigrew and Tropp 2000, 2006).[1]

Research Methodology

We shall focus on Western Europe in general and Germany in particular for several reasons. First, the social science literature on intergroup relations is heavily weighted with American research on black-white relations. African Americans are a unique minority group. Unlike most immigrants, African

Americans endured two centuries of slavery and a century of legalized segregation, yet they now share a religion, language, and national culture with other Americans. These differences make it difficult to apply generalizations from research on African Americans to reactions toward immigrants in Europe. Social science needs more work on diverse intergroup relations around the globe.

Second, there is an abundance of survey data on the topic in Europe using the same questions across a range of different countries with contrasting immigrant populations and cultural and structural contexts. One of these studies is referenced in chapter 2: the Eurobarometer 30 survey, conducted by the European Union in 1988. We shall refer to this study as Euro88 (Reif and Melich 1991). Numerous other publications on the basic findings of Euro88 are now available (e.g., Meertens and Pettigrew 1997; Pettigrew 1997, 1998b, 2000a, 2000b, 2001a, 2001b; Pettigrew and Meertens 1995, 1996, 2001; Pettigrew et al. 1998). Since 1988, the Eurobarometer has been repeated each year, often using many of the same components.

In 2002, the European Social Survey provided fresh data on the subject from probability samples of nineteen European nations and of Israel (Jowell et al. 2003).[2] It, too, allows cross-national comparisons on a wide range of attitudes toward immigrants. We shall refer to this study as ESS02. It boasts 34,500 respondents who are citizens of the country in which they live and were born within its boundaries. (The total sample is 38,500 with about 10.5 percent immigrants and others born abroad.) Our analyses will be restricted to native-born citizens.

In addition, European countries have conducted numerous national surveys of the phenomenon. This is especially the case in Germany, where surveys have repeatedly uncovered sharp differences between residents of the former East and West Germanys (Wagner et al. 2003). Recently, the Volkswagen Foundation funded a massive ten-year investigation of German prejudice toward immigrants, headed by Professor Wilhelm Heitmeyer (2002, 2003) of the University of Bielefeld. Two studies have now been conducted as a result of this inquiry. As in chapter 2, data from the 2002 initial survey, which we will refer to as GMF02, will be employed.

Western European nations—and Germany in particular—also have excellent structural data available. These data allow us to combine levels of analysis and study the effects of structural and aggregate factors together with data from individual Europeans.

In addition to traditional, single-level analyses, we will apply mediational analyses. We will view the cultural and structural variables as distal predictors of anti-immigrant attitudes and behavior whose effects are mediated by individual and intergroup variables acting as proximal predictors. For example, the effect of education on reducing European prejudice toward immigrants can be shown to be partly mediated by the fact that educated respondents are younger, less authoritarian, and less politically conservative, and have more intergroup friends than the poorly educated (Pettigrew 2001a). In particular, we will investigate in detail the complex role of the immigrant percentage in an area—a structural variable—on prejudice against immigrants—an individual variable. These analyses will follow the work of Baron and Kenney (1986) and employ structural equation modeling using the EQS software (Bentler 1992).

Clarifying the Role of Intergroup Proportion

Contact and Prejudice on the Individual Level

Our first goal is to assess the prediction that intergroup contact reduces prejudice against immigrants throughout Europe. To start to untangle the apparent conflict between levels of analysis on the role of group proportions, we must first test to see if contact does indeed routinely diminish prejudice against the varied groups of immigrants in the many countries tested.

Table 5.1 provides an initial test using all three major surveys. The correlations show the links between having an immigrant friend and various measures of anti-immigrant prejudice. Chapter 2 introduced the two scales of prejudice—blatant and subtle—that we will use in these analyses. It also discussed the Euro88 survey in some detail and provided some commentary on the GMF02 survey that will not be repeated here.

The ESS02 utilizes an extensive 28-item anti-immigrant scale that consists of four subscales: a 4-item social distance subscale, a 9-item scale of beliefs about immigrants, an 8-item scale listing preferred qualifications for admitting immigrants, and a 7-item scale consisting of beliefs about refugees. While each of these subscales provides adequate reliabilities (alphas from .68 to .81), the total 28-item prejudice scale has a strong alpha of .89. Moreover, when the four subscales are factor analyzed, they produce a single factor.

Here are sample items of the extensive ESS02 measure of prejudice. The social distance items tapped how much the respondent "would mind having an immigrant boss" and "having an immigrant ... marrying" into the family. The immigrant-beliefs scale asked if the respondent believed "immigrants take jobs away" and "undermine cultural life." Positively worded items also are in the scale and reverse scored. Thus, respondents were asked if they thought that "immigrants should have the same rights as everyone" and that "richer countries are responsible for accepting persons from poorer countries." The qualifications questions sought to learn what conditions the respondent thought immigrants should meet in order to enter their country: should immigrants be Christian, white, rich, able to speak the nation's language, have needed skills, be "committed to the country's way of life," have a good education, and have "close family" already living in the nation? Finally, the beliefs about refugees subscale asked the survey's respondents whether they thought that refugees really "don't fear persecution" as they claim and whether they should be kept

TABLE 5.1 Contact-Prejudice Correlations

	Blatant Prejudice	Subtle Prejudice	Anti-foreigner	Anti-immigrant
Euro88—Total	-.357 (-.267)	-.333 (-.262)		
British on Asians	-.279 (-.205)	-.305 (-.231)		
British on blacks	-.344 (-.271)	-.330 (-.264)		
Dutch on Surinamers	-.272 (-.189)	-.248 (-.180)		
Dutch on Turks	-.247 (-.143)	-.293 (-.243)		
French on Asians	-.453 (-.349)	-.413 (-.304)		
French on North Africans	-.403 (-.290)	-.386 (-.272)		
Germans on Turks	-.348 (-.261)	-.276 (-.218)		
GMF02—Total			-.371 (-.341)	
ESS02—Total				-.318 (-.254)
Belgium				-.301 (-.227)
Czech Republic				-.267 (-.216)
Denmark				-.287 (-.191)
Finland				-.294 (-.217)
Germany				-.346 (-.283)
Greece				-.280 (-.218)
Hungary				-.215 (-.142)
Ireland				-.280 (-.212)
Israel				-.277 (-.235)
Italy				-.248 (-.210)
Luxembourg				-.271 (-.201)
Netherlands				-.251 (-.180)
Norway				-.275 (-.183)
Poland				-.236 (-.158)
Portugal				-.215 (-.165)
Slovenia				-.277 (-.203)
Spain				-.312 (-.212)
Sweden				-.336 (-.239)
Switzerland				-.322 (-.249)
United Kingdom				-.292 (-.195)

Notes: The measure of contact in all samples is whether the respondent reports having immigrant or minority-group friends. The data in parentheses provide the partial correlations between having an immigrant friend and exhibiting prejudice, with education, age, and political conservatism controlled.

Sources: Euro88 data from Eurobarometer 30 (Reif and Melich 1991). GMF02 data from GFE Survey (Heitmeyer 2002). ESS02 data from European Social Survey 2002 (Jowell et al. 2003).

in "detention centers." And, more positively, this subscale asked if "the government should be generous in judging applications."

Table 5.1 provides the correlations between having an immigrant or ethnic friend and exhibiting prejudice across all three surveys. These results provide definitive evidence that having out-group friends relates consistently with exhibiting less prejudice. In every instance, the correlation is statistically significant at better than the .001 level of confidence. Few basic findings in social science so consistently and repeatedly replicate—in this case, across twenty-one nations, a time period of fourteen years, twenty-eight independent samples, more than a dozen different target groups, and four different measures of prejudice. Indeed, even the range of the mean correlations for the three studies is quite narrow—varying from −.32 to −.37.

But two alternative explanations for this replicated finding are possible. First, the association may reflect only that the two variables—out-group friends and prejudice against the out-group—relate the same way to numerous social variables. In fact, both having an immigrant friend and being relatively tolerant of immigrants do relate similarly to education, age, and political conservatism. That is, the less educated, older, and more conservative members of the native population are less likely to have an immigrant friend and more likely to be relatively prejudiced against immigrants. Table 5.1 tests for this possibility by providing in parentheses the partial correlations between the two variables with education, age, and political conservatism controlled. As expected, the correlations are lowered in each case, but all of the partial correlations remain statistically significant at better than the .005 level of significance.

The second alternative possibility concerns the causal direction between the two variables. Contact theory posits that having the immigrant friend reduces prejudice against the friend's group (Allport 1954; Pettigrew 1998a; Williams 1947). But perhaps more tolerant people seek out-group friendships, and more bigoted people shun such friendships. Indeed, research reveals that bigots do avoid intergroup contact (see, e.g., Herek and Capitanio 1996).

Three principal methods are available to untangle the meaning of the contact-prejudice correlation. Longitudinal designs offer the best approach, yet such designs are rare in intergroup research—with Sherif's (1966) Robbers' Cave study a striking exception. This famous study revealed optimal contact as the cause of reduced prejudice while eliminating the possibility of a participant selection bias.

Statistical methods borrowed from econometrics allow researchers to compare roughly the reciprocal paths (contact lowers prejudice versus prejudice decreases contact) with cross-sectional data. They demonstrate that the path from contact to reduced prejudice is much stronger (Pettigrew 1997; Powers and Ellison 1995). Thus, these methods suggest that while both causal sequences operate, the significantly more important effect is intergroup contact reducing prejudice.

A final method consists of finding intergroup situations that severely limit choice (e.g., Link and Cullen 1986). By eliminating the possibility of initial attitudes leading to differential contact, such research provides a clearer indication of how intergroup contact alters prejudice. In their meta-analysis of 515 intergroup contact studies, Pettigrew and Tropp (2006) found that research that did not allow the participants any choice in whether to engage in intergroup contact yielded slightly larger results than studies that did allow the selection bias. In other words, the studies that allowed the participant selection bias to operate did not typically yield larger effect sizes. Thus, each of the three methods suggests the same conclusion: contact in itself leads to greater tolerance of immigrants.

From these considerations, we conclude that the social psychological contention is correct: intergroup contact—especially when it leads to cross-group friendships—reduces prejudice. But to translate this striking microphenomenon into a societal-level finding with policy relevance, we must employ three steps to connect it to the larger social context. The social psychological side of the puzzle contends that (1) a larger proportion of immigrants will lead to greater contact, (2) which in turn is a prerequisite for more cross-group friendships, and (3) that these friendships will then lead to less prejudice directed against immigrants.

Now we turn to the other part of the puzzle. Note that placing the social psychological contentions concerning intergroup contact in social context makes its prediction conditional on the links between these steps. That is, we must now also ask whether an increase in the percentage of immigrants actually leads to more contact and whether this contact is of a nature that is likely to result in cross-group friendships.

Contact and Prejudice on the Societal Level

We must now assess the prediction that larger proportions of immigrants lead to a greater sense of threat in the receiving population that in turn causes greater prejudice toward immigrants. Note that this societal-level prediction also involves a three-step argument: (1) the larger the immigrant proportion, the greater the perceived immigrant proportion and (2) the greater the perceived threat, which leads in turn to (3) greater prejudice against immigrants. Note also that just as the individual-level prediction requires a social context, this societal-level prediction requires an individual context. After all, perceiving the immigrant population proportion and sensing a threat from immigrants are psychological phenomena. Even when we speak of collective threat (Pettigrew 2003), we are referring to a mass phenomenon involving threatened individuals.

The social science literature that tests this prediction typically suffers from a failure to test directly, at the individual level, for perceptions of minority proportions and perceptions of threat. As in the study by Quillian (1995) described earlier, much of this research infers such perceptions as intervening variables but does not directly test them.

Moreover, areas with large proportions of the target minority often do not reveal greater prejudice among their inhabitants than do other areas. Much of the original research that established this prediction was done on anti-black prejudice in the southern United States (e.g., Pettigrew and Campbell 1960; Pettigrew and Cramer 1959). Later research confirming these early findings has also been typically conducted on anti-black attitudes in the American South (e.g., Taylor 1998). But increasingly, new studies done elsewhere and on other minority targets question the universality of the prediction that larger minority percentages correlate positively with prejudice (e.g., Foreman 2004; Hood and Morris 1997; Taylor 1998).

Similarly, in the German sample under study here (GMF02), the anti-immigrant prejudice scale correlates negatively (-.27, p<.000) with the proportion of immigrants across the more than four hundred German districts. A large part of this effect is due to the striking differences between eastern and western Germany. Although it has far fewer immigrants, the east is nonetheless significantly more anti-immigrant than the west (for an explanation of much of this prejudice differential in terms of intergroup contact, see Wagner et al. 2003). Yet the negative relationship between immigrant proportion and anti-immigrant attitudes remains statistically significant within each region—a correlation of −.10 in the east and −.15 in the west. Hence, there is *less* prejudice against immigrants in each of these areas where the proportion of immigrants in the local population is relatively large.

Why this reversal of the standard structural prediction? Two measures that show Germany to be strikingly different from the American South suggest initial answers: out-group population ratios and economic prosperity. First, the percentage of immigrants in Germany—about 8 percent—is considerably smaller than the proportion of African Americans in the South, which is 20 percent and higher in the states of the Deep South (US Census Bureau 2000). Second, in the United States, high percentages of black Southerners are often found in the poorest parts of the region—the old plantation areas of the Deep South known as "the Black Belt." By contrast, German immigrants are typically found in the nation's most prosperous areas—West German cities and industrial belts, where their labor as "guest workers" has been most needed. In the GMF02 data, taxes (+.87) and wages (+.85) are highly and positively correlated with immigrant percentages across German districts. Indeed, when these two indicators of economic prosperity are controlled, the negative nationwide correlation between the anti-immigrant prejudice scale and immigrant percentage falls sharply from −.27 to −.04. Similarly, controlling for these two economic indicators deflates this correlation for the east (to −.01) and the west (to −.04). A comparable pattern emerges for responses throughout Germany to scales tapping anti-Semitism and racism. These measures also correlate negatively with immigrant percentages across districts by −.07 and −.16, respectively; the correlations decline to −.01 and −.02 once district taxes and wages are controlled.

In addition, German respondents who live in districts with fewer immigrants are *more* likely to agree that there are "too many foreigners in Germany" (−.20, p<.000). This finding suggests that it is the subjective perception of immigrant presence rather than the reality of immigrant proportions that shapes threat and prejudice.

A recent study with yet another German probability survey (the German General Social Survey of 1996) tested these issues directly. This study (Semyonov et al. 2004) measured the actual immigrant proportion in a district, the perceived immigrant proportion, the perceived threat from immigrants, and exclusionary attitudes toward immigrants. Again, as in the GMF02 results, an expected positive correlation is absent: no relationship was uncovered between the actual immigrant proportion and either perceived threat or anti-immigrant attitudes. But *perceived* immigrant proportion did correlate with both perceived threat and exclusionary attitudes. Surprisingly, the actual immigrant percentage in the area and the perceived percentage were essentially unrelated. Note that threat, as sociological theory asserts, mediates the effect between the perceived proportion and prejudice. But it is the perceived—and not the actual—proportion of immigrants that is the critical predictor of anti-immigrant opinions.

Thus, the predicted effect of out-group percentage on prejudice is also a conditional hypothesis. It assumes that people accurately perceive the actual out-group proportion. Moreover, in Germany, the prediction does not hold in large part because the immigrant population is centered in the more urban, prosperous, and tolerant areas of the country. Though their regions actually have fewer immigrants, residents of intolerant and less prosperous districts exaggerate the immigrant percentage in their midst, perceive greater threat, and express greater prejudice against immigrants.

There is, however, one striking exception to this trend. Perhaps as a result of the September 11 terrorist attacks in New York City and Washington, DC, minority percentages across Germany's districts correlate positively with prejudice against Muslims (+.07 with taxes and wages controlled). In general, it appears that prosperous urban areas in modern Germany have developed norms of tolerance concerning minorities. But a particular targeted threat can still arise, as in the case of attitudes against Muslims.

Toward a Solution of the Out-Group Proportion Puzzle

Our analysis provides a tentative explanation for the apparently conflicting predictions concerning the effects on prejudice of the population proportion of a minority group. We can advance our approach with a set of interlocking claims.

1. *Minority population proportion has dual effects.* The proportion and size of a minority group can lead to either a decrease or an increase in prejudice against the minority. Increased contact can diminish prejudice, while increased perceived threat can trigger greater prejudice. Both processes operate, but each is dependent on a set of optimal conditions. Conditions for the two processes tend to be reciprocal.

2. *The intergroup contact prediction is conditional.* The intergroup contact prediction has three interconnecting contentions: (1) larger proportions of immigrants lead to greater contact, (2) which in turn is a prerequisite for more cross-group friendships, (3) which then leads to less prejudice directed against immigrants. For the prediction to be validated, each of these contentions must hold. As we reviewed in table 5.1, only the third contention—namely, that cross-group

friendship with immigrants substantially reduces anti-immigrant prejudice throughout Western Europe—is solidly supported by extensive research.

But any factor that lessens the probability of the first two contentions will obstruct the prediction. Consider two such impediments—intergroup segregation and threat. If a district has both a high percentage of immigrants and intensive segregation between natives and immigrants in housing, education, and work, little contact will result—violating the first contention. If what contact there is occurs under threatening conditions, it is unlikely that many cross-group friendships will form—violating the second contention.

3. *The threat prediction also is conditional.* Similarly, the threat prediction of greater prejudice with larger out-group proportions has three basic contentions: (1) the larger the immigrant proportion, the greater the perceived immigrant proportion and (2) the greater the perceived threat, which in turn causes (3) greater prejudice against immigrants. The third of these contentions is well grounded in experimental research—threat has been shown to elevate prejudice (Stephan et al. 2002). But the first two links in the chain are less certain. We saw in the German case that the perception of the size of the immigrant population and the perceived threat are not related to the actual proportion of immigrants in the district's population. This remarkable reversal of "conventional wisdom" appears to be related to the fact that in Germany immigrants are concentrated in relatively prosperous areas—which introduces other factors that may be involved in the complex relationship between immigrant population percentages and anti-immigrant prejudice.

4. *An area's prosperity is critically involved.* Using broad national data from the EU's members, Quillian (1995) noted that immigrant population percentages interacted with a country's gross national product. Thus, relatively high immigrant proportions correlated positively with anti-immigrant attitudes most strongly in relatively poor EU nations. We noted earlier a similar phenomenon in Germany. It was respondents in the poorest German districts who harbored the strongest anti-immigrant opinions, even though they had fewer immigrants in their midst. Prosperity dampens threat, makes intergroup contact and friendship more likely, and reduces prejudice.

5. *An area's norms of tolerance advance intergroup contact and friendship while diminishing threat. By contrast, norms of intolerance restrict intergroup contact and friendship while accentuating threat.* The GMF02 survey estimated the norm guiding opinions about immigrants by asking the respondents if their friends had made anti-immigrant remarks. This one item proved to be highly predictive of the respondent's own views of immigrants—the correlation with the seven-item anti-immigrant scale was +.46. It remains +.38 even after the education, age, and political conservatism of the respondent and taxes and wages in the area are all controlled.

Utilizing these contentions, figure 5.1 provides a structural equation model of anti-immigrant prejudice in Germany. The model indicates a moderately good fit with the results from the GMF02 survey.

FIGURE 5.1 Model of German Prejudice against Immigrants

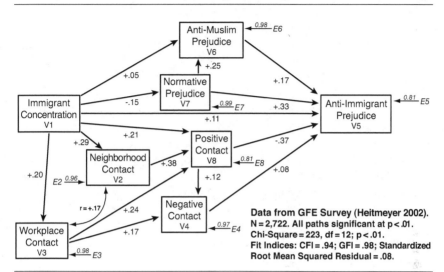

Data from GFE Survey (Heitmeyer 2002).
N = 2,722. All paths significant at p < .01.
Chi-Square = 223, df = 12; p < .01.
Fit Indices: CFI = .94; GFI = .98; Standardized
Root Mean Squared Residual = .08.

Note first that both positive and negative effects of the immigrant population proportion emerge. Two positive effects lowering anti-immigrant prejudice are present. First, more immigrants in an area leads to more intergroup contact, both on the job (standardized coefficient = +.20) and in neighborhoods (standardized coefficient = +.29). In turn, neighborhood contact appears especially beneficial, with only its effects on positive contact attaining significance (standardized coefficient = +.38). This positive contact is measured in the GMF02 survey by three items—having immigrant friends, receiving help from immigrants, and engaging in interesting conversations with immigrants. Contact at work has dual effects with respondents reporting both positive (standardized coefficient = +.24) and negative (standardized coefficient = +.17) encounters with immigrants. Finally, positive contact has a large, negative effect on anti-immigrant prejudice (standardized coefficient = −.37), while negative contact has only a small, positive effect (standardized coefficient = +.08). Witness, too, that a greater percentage of immigrants also relates to positive contact apart from work and neighborhood situations (standardized coefficient = +.21).

Separate from the intergroup contact process, an area's intergroup norms also play an important role. In these 2002 German data, respondents living in areas of high concentrations of immigrants report friends making anti-immigrant remarks less often than other respondents (standardized coefficient = −.15). This normative process reduces anti-immigrant prejudice at a level approaching that of positive contact (standardized coefficient = +.33). It is here that these German results probably differ most sharply from those of the often-studied American South, where the normative effects—especially in the rural

Deep South with its high black population ratios—are likely to be anti-black and produce greater levels of prejudice (Pettigrew 1958, 1959).

In addition to negative contact leading to greater prejudice in figure 5.1, note also two other processes associated with higher scores on the anti-immigrant prejudice scale. The exceptional case involving enhanced anti-Muslim feelings in areas of high immigrant concentration (standardized coefficient = +.05), not surprisingly, is related to greater anti-immigrant prejudice in general (standardized coefficient = +.17). Finally, after these mediating effects are entered into the model, there remains a positive, direct path between an area's immigrant percentage and anti-immigrant prejudice (standardized coefficient = +.11). This means that there are additional processes operating not captured by this model that associate higher immigrant population ratios with heightened anti-immigrant prejudice. The size of this residual effect, however, is small in comparison with that of positive contact (standardized coefficient = −.37) and of prejudice norms (standardized coefficient = +.33).

In summary, this model supports our contentions concerning the dual effects of immigration population percentages on prejudice. Social psychologists are correct that intergroup contact, made more possible by an enlarged minority population ratio, tends to diminish anti-immigrant prejudice. But structuralists are also correct when they maintain that a rising immigrant presence can trigger threat and intensify anti-immigrant feelings. Both processes are present, and they can operate simultaneously.

Two additional points must be added. The threat posed by immigrants is perceived by individuals but is not necessarily reflected in reality. Hence, we have seen that in Germany the perceived threat is not even related to the actual immigrant population ratios in an area. Finally, the role of intergroup norms is important and can easily tip the balance between the contact and threat processes. Germany's immigrants are concentrated in prosperous, urban areas with relatively tolerant intergroup norms. Immigrants and other minorities in other regions where this is not the case are likely to witness a negative process of hostile norms that amplify anti-minority prejudice, intensify threat, and curtail positive contact.

Policy Implications

The policy implications of these European findings are straightforward, even if their implementation is difficult. The delicate balance between the two entwined processes—threat and contact—can be approached by the same social policies. Creating optimal intergroup contact situations in a society requires many of the same remedies needed to deter intergroup threat, discrimination, and conflict. This is hardly surprising for we are dealing with a tightly interwoven system of intergroup relations that involves prejudice, discrimination, and conflict.

Four Critical Societal Indices

Policymakers must keep a close eye on four important intergroup indices: measures of (1) intergroup segregation in the labor force, (2) intergroup residential segregation, (3) intergroup educational segregation, and (4) intergroup marriage. Increasing intergroup separation on two or more of these indices may well signal future intergroup conflict. Such trends also indicate increasing group discrimination and a dangerous decline in optimal intergroup contact situations. When groups live largely segregated existences residentially, educationally, and in the work force, optimal contact is severely restricted. Intergroup friendships are limited, and intergroup marriages remain rare and stigmatized.

Apartheid in South Africa and racial segregation in the Southern United States highlight this process. By making equal status contact between races and intermarriage illegal, these regions guaranteed massive discrimination and conflict. Although these systems of separation have formally ended, their negative legacies distort current interracial relations. Hence, African Americans are far more residentially segregated from European Americans than any other minorities in modern urban America. And intermarriage between blacks and whites remains rare in a nation that otherwise witnesses rapidly increasing intermarriage rates for other ethnic and racial groups.

Group differences other than race also can lead to sharp separation and act to impede optimal contact. In Latin America, social class is highly correlated with color and forms the key differentiating variable. In Western Europe, culture and citizenship become focal lines of division. A continent more accustomed to out- than in-migration has found it difficult to embrace new cultures in its midst. Prejudice, discrimination, anti-immigrant political parties, and violence have erupted throughout Western Europe (Pettigrew 1998b).

In addition to thwarting beneficial intergroup contact, intergroup separation triggers a series of interlocking processes that make group conflict more likely. Negative stereotypes not only persist but are magnified. Distrust cumulates, and misperceptions and awkwardness typify the limited intergroup interaction that does take place. The powerful majority comes in time to believe that segregated housing, low-skilled jobs, and constrained educational opportunities are justified, even "appropriate," for the minority.

Consider Western Europe's misnamed "guest worker" system in this light. Foreign workers were officially invited to supply a vitally needed cheap labor force when declining natural population growth could not sustain a rapidly expanding economic base. Yet the newcomers were cast as problematic and stigmatized out-groups, suitable for low-status jobs but often not for citizenship. The very name—"guest worker"—implied this problematic status. From the start, such a system established segregated minorities, restricted intergroup contact, and led inevitably to conflict.

Current remediation efforts are made difficult by the system's negative effects, now deeply entrenched after two generations. But recent steps are encouraging: anti-discrimination legislation in the United Kingdom, the Netherlands, and Sweden; affirmative action policies, such as the Netherlands' concerted attempts to hire minority police; and Germany's efforts to make citizenship easier (Appelt and Jarosch 2000). While insufficient alone, these measures will not only reduce intergroup conflict but will also enhance opportunities for optimal intergroup contact.

Three Objections to This Policy Analysis

Critics of this approach raise three objections. First, they ask, "What about Bosnia? Is it not a disconfirming case for this analysis?" Second, some stout proponents of multicultural policies wonder if this view is actually a subtle argument for assimilation. Does this policy recommendation not ignore cultural differences? Does it not ask minorities to surrender their distinctiveness in the name of intergroup harmony? Finally, critics in political science, such as McGarry and O'Leary (1995), claim that intergroup contact is more likely to result in conflict than in reduced prejudice. Besides, they argue, reducing prejudice does not reduce intergroup conflict and other needed structural-level changes. We must address each of these objections in turn.

At first glance, Bosnia appears to raise problems for the intergroup contact perspective advanced here. Whatever else may be said about him, the late Marshall Tito followed an intergroup policy in the former Yugoslavia that resembled the policies outlined in this chapter. Of mixed Slovenian and Croatian heritage himself, Tito attempted to increase optimal intergroup contact in housing, jobs, education, sports, and other areas. Indeed, at least in Bosnia's major cities, these policies succeeded in making intergroup housing, education, and even intermarriage more commonplace. Yet, as we know, armed intervention in Bosnia quickly toppled these integrated structures, set the major ethnic groups against each other, and resulted in horrendous carnage.

Why? Was it inevitable, as some claim, given the tortured history of the Balkans? Did the conflict expose the failure of Tito's integration policies? I believe the answer to both questions is no. There are reasons to believe that Bosnians, had they been left alone, would not have begun intergroup warfare. Prior to military incursions, a massive demonstration occurred in Sarajevo involving the three major ethnicities. The demonstrators made it clear that they strongly identified with a superordinate group; they identified first as Bosnians who intended to live in peace. A national survey conducted just before violence erupted supports the generality of this view. Of the eight republics of the former Yugoslavia, Bosnia was both the most ethnically diverse and the most tolerant (Hodson, Dusko, and Massey 1994: table 1). From these and additional data, specialists believe that had a referendum been held at that point, Bosnians of all stripes would have voted for an independent and ethnically integrated state. But they were never allowed such a vote. Tito's policies had succeeded within their scope, but these new intergroup ties could not withstand the armed intervention and "ethnic cleansing" initiated by Bosnia's neighbors.

Turning to the second criticism, are the policy implications of contact theory simply a modern disguise for insistence on minority assimilation? Some advocates of multiculturalism in North America think so and come perilously close to advocating intergroup separation as a means of maintaining cultural purity. Reactionary politicians in Europe have seized on this argument to resist intergroup schools.

But other multiculturalists understand that their goals and the objective of providing greater societal access to minorities need not conflict. Indeed, integration and multiculturalism combined are stronger than either policy alone (Pettigrew 2004). Some degree of assimilation is, of course, necessary for new groups to thrive. But this process is more complex than critics concede. Assimilation, after all, is a two-way street; majority cultures also change from intergroup contact. Witness shifts in European eating habits and the arts, which reveal the direct influence of the new immigrants over the past two generations. And the process of expanding integrated opportunities for minorities must entail structural changes in the broadened institutions themselves—schools and the workplace—that reflect their culturally diverse participants.

The third criticism, raised by political scientists including McGarry and O'Leary, questions the effectiveness of intergroup contact. These critics appear to ignore the actual contentions of the theory and the massive research literature that supports it (as seen in table 5.1). "Sometimes," write McGarry and O'Leary (1995: 210), "good fences make good neighbors." At first blush, one might not regard such a claim seriously. Consider the repeated failures of "fences" from the Great Wall of China and Hadrian's Wall on Scotland's border to the modern examples of the Warsaw ghetto wall, the Berlin Wall, the Green Line of Cyprus, and Israel's new West Bank Wall. "Good neighbors" hardly resulted from any of these prominent experiments with "good fences." But we must dig deeper to understand the skepticism of these two political scientists.

McGarry and O'Leary focus on the tragic "troubles" between Roman Catholics and Protestants in Northern Ireland. They emphasize that contact can, under the hostile normative conditions that have long characterized Ulster, actually confirm and enhance rather than allay prejudice. Of course, contact theory amply allows for this, and we have noted it in figure 5.1's model from negative encounters generated from work contact with immigrants. But the two critics seem unaware of the actual theory and its supportive research. Instead, they stress how those Northern Irish who lived in neighborhoods predominantly occupied by members of the other religion were among the most seriously victimized—often forced to move out under threats of violence. But this process was not largely a process of neighbors evicting their neighbors. Extremist and violent groups of both religious communities orchestrated most of the removal (Darby 1986). One suspects that these efforts were motivated both by a desire to form tight, segregated communities under the groups' control and by the realization that neighborhood contact had the potential to undermine the intense prejudices on which the movements depended. In any event, these hostile activities of extremist organizations hardly constitute a refutation of contact theory.

More fundamentally, McGarry and O'Leary advance two major criticisms: (1) intergroup contact does not typically reduce prejudice—at least not in Northern Ireland; and (2) even if it did, the reduction of prejudice is irrelevant to larger structural policy and to the reduction in violence and conflict. The first claim is easily refuted. Just as we saw in table 5.1 for Western Europe, a recent meta-analysis found that 94 percent of over 500 studies from all over the world show that contact diminishes prejudice with an average r of −.21 (Pettigrew and Tropp 2006). To be sure, under especially harsh conditions, intergroup contact can increase prejudice—just as contact theory predicts. But these instances are far less common than those involving positive intergroup contact and friendship. Moreover, studies by social psychologists in Northern Ireland itself repeatedly find that Catholic-Protestant contact typically lessens prejudice at much the same level as intergroup contact in other parts of the globe (see, e.g., Hewstone et al. 2005, 2006; McClenahan et al. 1996; Niens, Cairns, and Hewstone 2003; Paolini et al. 2004). Indeed, this work has even demonstrated the beneficial effect of *indirect* contact (Wright et al. 1997). Thus, even those Northern Irish respondents who had a co-religion friend who had a friend of the other religion revealed less religious bigotry (Paolini et al. 2004).

More important is the second claim of McGarry and O'Leary—that intergroup contact is irrelevant to policy. Note that this claim is an assertion that microphenomena (i.e., intergroup prejudice) have little to do with macrophenomena (i.e., intergroup conflict and violence). This is a recurrent debate between largely micro- and mesolevel disciplines such as social psychology and largely macrolevel disciplines such as political science. This chapter maintains that such claims are dubious on their face; the various levels of analysis are in concert, not conflict. It is the task of social science to put the levels together in broader and more useful multilevel models.

No social psychologist has ever claimed that intergroup contact and a reduction in intergroup prejudice constitute a panacea for macrolevel conflict (see, e.g., Hewstone 2003). But positive intergroup contact can be part of the solution; in fact, it most likely is a *necessary* part of the solution. To argue that prejudice has little or nothing to do with intergroup conflict is an extreme position, to say the least.

Table 5.2 addresses this issue with data from the GMF02 survey. It tests three contrasting though interrelated individual-level theories about intergroup violence with two three-item scales measuring the acceptance of violence (alpha = .74; sample item: "Violence can be morally justified when political goals need to be attained") and personal readiness for violence (alpha = .72; sample item: "To enforce my claims, I have to use violence sometimes"). One explanation is basically psychiatric; violent individuals are thought to be more socially

TABLE 5.2 Predictors of Acceptance and Readiness for Intergroup Violence

	Acceptance of Intergroup Violence	Readiness for Intergroup Violence
Psychiatric scale	+.23 (+.22)	+.21 (+.20)
Social dominance orientation scale	+.34 (+.31)	+.16 (+.16)
Generalized prejudice scale	+.39 (+.36)	+.25 (+.26)
Anti-homeless scale	+.20 (+.18)	+.12 (+.11)
Anti-immigrant scale	+.34 (+.31)	+.24 (+.24)
Anti-Muslim scale	+.17 (+.15)	+.10 (+.11)
Anti-Semitism scale	+.30 (+.28)	+.23 (+.24)
Racism scale	+.29 (+.26)	+.17 (+.18)

Note: The data in parentheses provide the partial correlations, with education, age, and political conservatism controlled.

Source: Data from GFE Survey (Heitmeyer 2002).

isolated, more anomic and unhappy. This explanation is tested by use of an eighteen-item scale labeled "Psychiatric." It has an alpha of .77 and contains items such as "Nobody helps me with my real problems"; "I often feel lonely, afraid, and helpless"; and "I often feel like an outsider."

A second explanation for intergroup violence posits social dominance as the key cause. It holds that intergroup violence erupts when a threatened group attempts to maintain its superior status. The German survey measures this at the individual level with a three-item scale boasting a reliability alpha of +.60. Labeled SDO (for "social dominance orientation"; see Sidanius and Pratto 1999), this scale has items such as "Groups at the bottom of society should stay there."

A third explanation involves a generalized propensity for prejudice against a variety of targets. Labeled "General Prejudice," this concept is formed by combining five different prejudice measures: (1) the scales for anti-immigrant attitudes used earlier, (2) anti-Semitism (two items, $r = .53$; sample item: "Jews in Germany have too much influence"), (3) anti-homeless beliefs (two items, $r = 46$; sample item: "Homeless people in the cities are unpleasant"), (4) anti-Muslim bias (two items, $r = .28$; sample item: "With their many mosques in Germany, the Muslims want to demonstrate their power"), and (5) racism (two items, $r = .36$; sample item: "White people are rightfully leading the world"). Together this combined scale uses fifteen items and obtains an alpha of .84—demonstrating how these diverse measures of prejudice are routinely intercorrelated (median correlation = +.26). For example, our basic scale tapping anti-immigrant prejudice correlates strongly with the anti-Semitic (+.46), anti-Muslim (+.40), and racism (+.55) measures. This strong consistency of prejudice across sharply different types of target out-groups is one of the principal findings of social psychologists in this area (Allport 1954). It forms the basis of studying prejudice at the individual level of analysis.

Table 5.2 reveals that all three theories have merit. But note that the generalized prejudice measure correlates significantly higher with both the acceptance of and readiness for intergroup violence than either the social dominance or the psychiatric measures. And this consistent difference remains after age, education, and political conservatism are controlled. Moreover, in analyses not shown in table 5.2, the general prejudice indicator remains a significant correlate of both violence scales even after the psychiatric and social dominance scales are controlled (+.24 for the acceptance of violence scale and +.16 for the readiness for violence scale).

To be sure, table 5.2 reports an individual-level result. Yet it is difficult to imagine that neither acceptance of nor readiness for intergroup violence among individuals is an important ingredient in actual collective violence. A new study using German survey data collected in 2003 underlines this point empirically (Wolf et al. 2003). In this study, the pro-violence norm for German districts is estimated by averaging the scores on the acceptance of intergroup violence scale of the respondents surveyed in each district. Employing a multilevel analysis, Wolf and her colleagues then demonstrate that in districts with a high acceptance of violence, the relationship between generalized prejudice and the readiness for intergroup violence is significantly higher among the violence-prone subgroup of young males than in other German districts. From these considerations, we conclude that none of these criticisms of intergroup contact theory detracts from the policy implications of our findings.

A Final Word

In sum, two broad policy generalizations emerge from this intergroup contact perspective. First, separation in housing, schools, and employment limits intergroup contact and triggers a series of interlocking processes at both the psychological and social structural levels that enhance intergroup threat, prejudice, discrimination, and conflict. Second, social policies that increase minority access to wider societal opportunity automatically create more optimal situations for intergroup contact. Such efforts then trigger a benign cycle that leads to less intergroup threat, prejudice, discrimination, and conflict.

Notes

1. In chapter 2 we explored the role of group identity in the acceptance of immigrants in Western Europe. Social identity is widely regarded in social psychology as a critical variable in intergroup relations. But the structural tradition of prejudice theory and research tends to assume that virtually all members of both national majorities and the new minority groups are highly identified with their groups. Such an assumption is obviously too simple. The famous tension between first- and second-generation immigrants underscores the complexity of group identity.
2. Data from the 2002 European Social Survey (Round 1) are available online from the Norwegian Social Science Data Services (http://ess.nsd.uib.no/).

References

Allport, G. W. 1954. *The Nature of Prejudice*. Reading, MA: Addison-Wesley.

Appelt, E., and M. Jarosch, eds. 2000. *Combating Racial Discrimination: Affirmative Action as a Model for Europe*. New York: Berg.

Baron, R., and D. A. Kenney. 1986. "The Moderator-Mediator Variable Distinction in Social Psychological Research: Conceptual, Strategic, and Statistical Considerations." *Journal of Personality and Social Psychology* 51: 1173–1182.

Bentler, P. M. 1992. *EQS: Structural Equations Program Manual*. Los Angeles: BMDP Statistical Software.

Darby, J. P. 1986. *Intimidation and the Control of Conflict in Northern Ireland*. Dublin: Gill & Macmillan.

Foreman, T. 2004. "From Pet to Threat? Minority Concentration, School Racial Context and White Youths' Racist Attitudes." Unpublished paper, Dept. of Sociology, University of Illinois, Chicago.

Fuchs, D., J. Gerhards, and E. Roller. 1993. "Wir und die Anderen: Ethnozentrismus in den zwölf Ländern der europäischen Gemeinschaft" [Us and Them: Ethnocentrism in the Twelve Countries of the European Community]. *Kölner Zeitschrift für Soziologie und Sozialpsychologie* 45: 238–253.

Heitmeyer, W., ed. 2002. *Deutsche Zustände* [The German Situation]. Part 1. Frankfurt am Main: Suhrkamp Verlag.

———. 2003. *Deutsche Zustände* [The German Situation]. Part 2. Frankfurt am Main: Suhrkamp Verlag.

Herek, G. M., and J. P. Capitanio. 1996. "'Some of My Best Friends': Intergroup Contact, Concealable Stigma, and Heterosexuals' Attitudes Toward Gay Men and Lesbians." *Personality and Social Psychology Bulletin* 22: 412–424.

Hewstone, M. 2003. "Intergroup Contact: Panacea for Prejudice?" *Psychologist* 16: 352–355.

Hewstone, M., E. Cairns, A. Voci, J. Hamberger, and U. Niens. 2006. "Intergroup Contact, Forgiveness, and Experience of 'The Troubles' in Northern Ireland." *Journal of Social Issues* 62: 99–120.

Hewstone, M., E. Cairns, A. Voci, S. Paolini, F. McLernon, R. J. Crisp, and U. Niens. 2005. "Intergroup Contact in a Divided Society: Challenging Segregation in Northern Ireland." In *The Social Psychology of Inclusion and Exclusion*, ed. D. Abrams, J. M. Marques, and M. A. Hogg, 265–292. Philadelphia: Psychology Press.

Hodson, R., S. Dusko, and G. Massey. 1994. "National Tolerance in the Former Yugoslavia." *American Journal of Sociology* 99: 1534–1558.

Hood, M. V., III, and I. L. Morris. 1997. "¿Amigo o Enemigo? Context, Attitudes, and Anglo Public Opinion Toward Immigration." *Social Science Quarterly* 78: 309–323.

Jackson, J. S., K. T. Brown, T. N. Brown, and B. Marks. 2001. "Contemporary Immigration Policy Orientations among Dominant-Group Members in Western Europe." *Journal of Social Issues* 57: 431–456.

Jowell, R., and the Central Co-ordinating Team. 2003. *European Social Survey 2002/2003: Technical Report.* London: Centre for Comparative Social Surveys, City University.

Link, B. G., and F. T. Cullen. 1986. "Contact with the Mentally Ill and Perceptions of How Dangerous They Are." *Journal of Health and Social Behavior* 27: 289–303.

McClenahan, C., E. Cairns, S. Dunn, and V. Morgan. 1996. "Intergroup Friendships: Integrated and Desegregated Schools in Northern Ireland." *Journal of Social Psychology* 136: 549–558.

McGarry, J., and B. O'Leary. 1995. *Explaining Northern Ireland: Broken Images.* Oxford: Blackwell.

Meertens, R. W., and T. F. Pettigrew. 1997. "Is Subtle Prejudice Really Prejudice?" *Public Opinion Quarterly* 61: 54–71.

Niens, U., E. Cairns, and M. Hewstone. 2003. "Contact and Conflict in Ireland." In *Research the Troubles: Social Science Perspectives on the Northern Ireland Conflict,* ed. O. Hargie and D. Dickson, 123–140. Edinburgh: Mainstream Publishing.

Paolini, S., M. Hewstone, E, Cairns, and A. Voci. 2004. "Effects of Direct and Indirect Cross-Group Friendships on Judgments of Catholics and Protestants in Northern Ireland: The Mediating Role of an Anxiety-Reduction Mechanism." *Personality and Social Psychology Bulletin* 30: 770–786.

Pettigrew, T. F. 1958. "Personality and Socio-Cultural Factors in Intergroup Attitudes: a Cross-National Comparison." *Journal of Conflict Resolution* 2: 29–42.

_____. 1959. "Regional Differences in Anti-Negro Prejudice." *Journal of Abnormal and Social Psychology* 59: 28–36.

_____. 1997. "Generalized Intergroup Contact Effects on Prejudice." *Personality and Social Psychology Bulletin* 23: 173–185.

_____. 1998a. "Intergroup Contact Theory." *Annual Review of Psychology* 49: 65–85.

_____. 1998b. "Responses to the New Minorities of Western Europe." *Annual Review of Sociology* 24: 77–103.

_____. 2000a. "Systematizing the Predictors of Prejudice." In *Racialized Politics: The Debate about Racism in America,* ed. D. O. Sears, J. Sidanius, and L. Bobo, 280–301. Chicago: University of Chicago Press.

_____. 2000b. "Placing Authoritarianism in Social Context." *Politics, Groups and the Individual* 8: 5–20.

_____. 2001a. "Intergroup Relations and National and International Relations." In *Blackwell Handbook of Social Psychology: Intergroup Processes,* ed. R. Brown and S. Gaertner, 514–532. Oxford: Blackwell.

_____. 2001b. "Summing Up: Relative Deprivation as a Key Social Psychological Concept." In *Relative Deprivation: Specification, Development and Integration,* ed. I. Walker and H. Smith, 351–373. New York: Cambridge University Press.

_____. 2003. "Peoples under Threat: Americans, Arabs, and Israelis." *Peace and Conflict* 9, no. 1: 69–90.

_____. 2004. "Intergroup Contact: Theory, Research, and New Perspectives." In *Handbook of Research on Multicultural Education,* 2nd ed., ed. J. A. Banks and C. A. M. Banks, 770–781. San Francisco: Jossey-Bass.

Pettigrew, T. F., and E. Q. Campbell. 1960. "Faubus and Segregation: An Analysis of Arkansas Voting." *Public Opinion Quarterly* 24: 436–447.

Pettigrew, T. F., and M. R. Cramer. 1959. "The Demography of Desegregation." *Journal of Social Issues* 15: 61–71.

Pettigrew, T. F., J. Jackson, J. Ben Brika, G. Lemain, R. W. Meertens, U. Wagner, and A. Zick. 1998. "Outgroup Prejudice in Western Europe." *European Review of Social Psychology* 8: 241–273.

Pettigrew, T. F., and R. W. Meertens. 1995. "Subtle and Blatant Prejudice in Western Europe." *European Journal of Social Psychology* 57: 57–75.

———. 1996. "The Verzuiling Puzzle: Understanding Dutch Intergroup Relations." *Current Psychology* 15: 3–13.

———. 2001. "In Defense of the Subtle Prejudice Concept: A Retort." *European Journal of Social Psychology* 31: 299–309.

Pettigrew, T. F., and L. Tropp. 2000. "Does Intergroup Contact Reduce Prejudice? Recent Meta-Analytic Findings." In *Reducing Prejudice and Discrimination: Social Psychological Perspectives,* ed. S. Oskamp, 93–114. Mahwah, NJ: Erlbaum.

———. 2006. "A Meta-Analytic Test of Intergroup Contact Theory." *Journal of Personality and Social Psychology* 90, no. 5: 751–783..

Powers, D. A., and C. G. Ellison. 1995. "Interracial Contact and Black Racial Attitudes: The Contact Hypothesis and Selectivity Bias." *Social Forces* 74: 205–226.

Quillian, L. 1995. "Prejudice as a Response to Perceived Group Threat." *American Sociological Review* 60: 586–611.

Semyonov, M., R. Raijman, A. Y. Tov, and P. Schmidt. 2004. "Population Size, Perceived Threat and Exclusion: A Multiple-Indicators Analysis of Attitudes toward Foreigners in Germany." *Social Science Research* 33, no. 4: 681–701.

Sherif, M. 1966. *In Common Predicament.* Boston: Houghton Mifflin.

Sidanius, J., and F. Pratto. 1999. *Social Dominance: An Intergroup Theory of Social Hierarchy and Oppression.* New York: Cambridge University Press.

Stephan, W. G., K. A. Boniecki, O. Ybarra, A. Bettencourt, K. S. Ervin, L. A. Jackson, P. S. McNatt, and C. L. Renfro. 2002. "The Role of Threats in the Racial Attitudes of Blacks and Whites." *Personality and Social Psychology Bulletin* 28: 1242–1254.

Taylor, M. C. 1998. "How White Attitudes Vary with the Racial Composition of Local Populations: Numbers Count." *American Sociological Review* 63: 512–535.

US Census Bureau. 2000. *Current Population Survey, March 2000.* Washington, DC: US Government Printing Office.

Wagner, U., R. van Dick, T. F. Pettigrew, and O. Christ. 2003. "Ethnic Prejudice in East and West Germany: The Explanatory Power of Intergroup Contact." *Group Processes and Intergroup Relations* 6: 22–36.

Williams, R. 1947. *The Reduction of Intergroup Tensions.* New York: Social Science Research Council.

Wolf, C., J. Stellmacher, U. Wagner, and O. Christ. 2003. "Druckvolle Ermunterungen: Das Meinungsklima fordert menschenfeindliche Gewalt-bereitschaft" [Powerful Encouragement: The Climate of Public Opinion Promotes Readiness for Group-Focused Violence]. In *Deutsche Zustände* [The German Situation], part 2, ed. W. Heitmeyer, 142–157. Frankfurt am Main: Suhrkamp Verlag.

Wright, S. C., A. Aron, T. McLaughlin-Volpe, and S. A. Ropp. 1997. "The Extended Contact Effect: Knowledge of Cross-Group Friendships and Prejudice." *Journal of Personality and Social Psychology* 73: 73–90.

Zick, A., U. Wagner, R. van Dick, and T. Petzel. 2001. "Acculturation and Prejudice in Germany: Majority and Minority Perspectives." *Journal of Social Issues* 57: 541–557.

6

Tibetan Identity in Today's China

Badeng Nima

In this chapter, I examine the problem of social identity that faces Tibetans in the People's Republic of China. Drawing on personal interviews conducted in western China, I highlight Tibetans' major concerns about their traditional beliefs, economic circumstances, religion, and education. Ultimately, my goal is to consider how Tibetans can achieve a meaningful identity that draws upon their past traditions while still prospering in the modern world. Only by doing so can they achieve a peaceful resolution to their turbulent status as an ethnic minority in contemporary China.

The Tibetan situation can be productively situated within the context of a conceptual model developed by Stevan Harrell (1995) in *Cultural Encounters on China's Ethnic Frontiers*, a study of ethnic minorities in China. Harrell describes Chinese efforts to develop Tibet and acculturate its people as a typical "civilizing project." He defines a "civilizing project" as "a kind of interaction between peoples, in which one group, the civilizing center, interacts with other groups (peripheral peoples) in terms of a particular kind of inequality." He continues: "In this interaction, the inequality between the civilizing center and the peripheral peoples has its ideological basis in the center's claim to a superior degree of civilization, along with a commitment to raise the peripheral people's civilization to the level of the center, or at least closer to that level." While Harrell is particularly interested in China, he emphasizes that civilizing projects are to be found in many places where there is a dominant civilization and distinct minority communities at its periphery.

References for this chapter are located on page 129.

According to Harrell, civilizing projects seek to rid the minority society of what the majority community considers its inferior cultural features. In response, minorities "develop an ideology of ethnicity, or ethnic consciousness," which has two features: "First, [the minority group] sees itself as a solidarity, by virtue of sharing at least common descent and some kind of common custom or habit that can serve as an ethnic marker.... Second, an ethnic group sees itself in opposition to other such groups, groups whose ancestors were different and whose customs and habits are foreign, strange, sometimes even noxious to the members of the subject group" (Harrell 1995: 27). Members of the persecuted minorities respond with active resistance to the civilizing projects that the majority community seeks to implement.

Herein lies the nature of the conflict between the dominant Han Chinese and the minority Tibetans. Since the People's Republic of China annexed Tibet in 1959, the Chinese government has attempted to "civilize" Tibetans by eroding the institutions of their traditional culture and supplanting them with "modern" substitutes. In conducting interviews between March and July 2003, I probed the effects of this Chinese civilizing project on Tibetans and sought an answer to the question of whether, through the development of mutual understanding between the two communities, Tibetan ethnic resistance might take shape as a peaceful, educated response rather than a destructive force.

I visited many areas in Ulzhang, Amdo, and Kham, the three regions of the former nation of Tibet. In the Ulzhang region, I toured Lhasa and Dam-gzhung (Dangxiong). In the Amdo region, I traveled through Khri-kha County (Guide Xian), Chap-cha County (Gonghe Xian), and Re-skong County (Tongren Xian) in Qinghai Province; Bsang-chu County (Xiahe Xian), Rma-chu County (Maqu Xian), and Brug-chu County (Zhouqu Xian) in Gannan Tibetan Prefecture in Gansu Province; and Bar-khams County (Maerkang Xian), Rnga-ba County (Aba Xian), Mdzod-dge County (Ruoergai Xian), Btsan-lha County (Xiaojin Xian), Cha-chen County (Jinchuan Xian), and Khyung-mchu County (Hongyuan Xian) in Ngawa Tibetan and Qiang People's Prefecture in Sichuan Province. In the Kham region, I journeyed into Dar-mdo County (Kangding Xian), Rtau County (Daofu Xian), Drag-go County (Luhuo Xian), Dkar-mdzes County (Ganzi Xian), Nyag-rong County (Xinlong Xian), Le-thang County (Litang Xian), Nyag-chu County (Yajiang Xian), and Rong-brag County (Danba Xian) in Ganzi Tibetan Prefecture in Sichuan Province.

The people I interviewed were all ethnic Tibetans, though they varied widely in age, educational background, and occupation. They can be grouped into the following categories:

1. *Young, educated Tibetans.* These individuals, all of whom had graduated from high school in the last few years, were among the most vocal of those I spoke to, and I found them to be generally frustrated and angry. I interviewed more than thirty young people.

2. *Exceptionally well-educated Tibetans.* This group consists largely of graduates of programs in Tibetan literature and philosophy. These individuals speak Chinese well and have an excellent understanding of Chinese attitudes toward Tibetans, but because they do not speak English or other languages as well, it is difficult for them to explain their views to a sympathetic international audience.

3. *Tibetans in reasonably good positions in government administration.* These individuals work for the Chinese Communist Party (CCP), the Religion Department, the Police Department, and in hospitals in Mdzod-dge County, Sichuan, Co-ne County and Hezuo City, Gansu, and Dar-lag County, Qinghai. It must be noted that none of the individuals I spoke to in this group occupies a position of power.

4. *Other educated Tibetans.* This category includes seven people from Amdo in Sichuan and Gansu, ranging in age from 20 to 35, who travel abroad. It also includes twenty-four graduates of monastic educational institutions between the ages of 25 and 35 and thirty graduates of a Tibetan Department at a minority college. Most of the latter are 25 to 30 years old and are chronically unemployed. Indeed, in 2002 they organized a demonstration protesting their situation and demanding equal employment opportunities in Khyung-mchu County, Amdo.

5. *Uneducated and less educated Tibetans.* The members of this group did not reach middle school, though some have low-grade primary school educations.

6. *Religious persons.* Finally, I interviewed fifty people, including monastic leaders, acolytes, and common people, with particular attention to their attitudes toward religion.

I asked the Tibetans whom I interviewed about their attitudes toward their current social, economic, and political situations, with special attention focused on problems within the education system for ethnic Tibetans, a topical issue of central importance. In the sections that follow, I consider the results of the interviews with regard to the informants' perceptions of the Chinese civilizing project, economic inequality, and the state of religion and education. After summarizing my respondents' ideas about what the future will bring, I end by proposing one possible avenue toward a peaceful, prosperous, and fulfilling future for the Tibetan people.

Perceptions of the Chinese

In the responses of those I interviewed, it was easy to detect anger toward and disgust with the Chinese, as well as an ethnic consciousness of Tibetan heritage and the need to protect it—both typical responses to a civilizing project, according to Harrell. Consider, for example, the views of the group of young, high-school educated Tibetans whom I interviewed. They are convinced that the Chinese authorities have failed in every way to promote the equality of ethnic Tibetans and to safeguard their human rights in the communities in which they live. The problem, they believe, is that the Chinese authorities do not accept Tibetan culture nor do they consider it to be a valid alternative to Chinese culture. Because of this cultural prejudice, young Tibetans maintain, the Chinese authorities have created a situation in which ethnic Tibetans do not have the same rights and privileges enjoyed by ethnic Han Chinese.

Young Tibetans feel that the Tibetan way of life is one among many valid options in the modern world, and thus they see no need to discard it and "become Chinese." They would prefer for Tibetans to live according to the cultural principles of their heritage while also adopting some aspects of a modern lifestyle. Defying Chinese prejudice and asserting their own ethnic consciousness, they insist that traditional Tibetan philosophy and thought—the storehouse of the Tibetan cultural heritage—must be preserved among the Tibetan people. It is therefore imperative that all Tibetan scholars safeguard this teaching and pass it on to the next generation.

Highly educated Tibetans, too, see the conflict between Chinese and Tibetans as rooted in Chinese cultural attitudes, but they also blame the corrupt nature of Communist politics. They are angry about what they perceive as gross political inequalities between ethnic Tibetans and Han Chinese and the obvious Chinese attempts to simply dispose of Tibetan culture by preventing the Tibetan cultural heritage from being passed on to the next generation.

Tibetans who work for the government told me that they have tried to use their positions to stress the need for programs to improve educational opportunities for ethnic Tibetans and to encourage financial support for the preservation of the Tibetan cultural heritage, but they feel that all their efforts in this direction are rendered futile by the corrupt nature of their employers. Though they seldom used the term "human rights" in speaking to me, they certainly perceive their own rights to have been infringed upon, and they strongly support the advancement of equality and economic opportunity for all ethnic Tibetans. The diverse group of "other educated Tibetans" with whom I spoke are similarly disgusted by what they see as a corrupt and prejudiced system.

Uneducated Tibetans were perhaps less likely to discuss systemic problems and more likely to express their total contempt for the current government and its policies, specifically singling out corrupt and arrogant government officials and the seemingly ubiquitous cadres of the CCP. These Tibetans dismiss government pronouncements, pointing out that they have attended many meetings with government officials yet nothing that was promised ever happened.

One issue that many of those I interviewed mentioned as symptomatic of the Chinese disregard for Tibetan culture—and as urgently requiring redress—was the treatment of the physical environment in Tibetan regions. The Tibetans I interviewed feel that the environment must be protected in order to preserve the unique natural habitat of the Tibetan plateau, the landscape within which Tibetan culture emerged and upon which it depends. Tibetan views of the environment have much in common with those of North American Indians: they believe that a partnership exists between human beings and the natural environment in which they live. But despite Tibetans' frequent calls for changes in Chinese environmental policy, environmental degradation is horrendous in the Tibetan regions. Chinese companies are reportedly allowed to cut forests with abandon and to implement mining projects with total disregard for environmental effects. That the government seemingly allows and even encourages such behavior is one of many reasons that Tibetans are both angry with the Chinese and determined to preserve their ethnic heritage.

Economic Inequality

Most of the Tibetans I spoke to maintained that the economic situation of the average ethnic Tibetan must be improved. They complained of both the near total lack of government support for economic development in those regions where ethnic Tibetans are in the majority and of an educational system in which Tibetans devote so much time and effort to mastering the tools they require to understand fully the Tibetan heritage that it hinders them from acquiring the skills necessary to obtain well-paying jobs in a Chinese-dominated employment market. An in-depth knowledge of Tibetan language and culture is not, unfortunately, viewed as an asset by Chinese employers. I will return to this matter below in the section on education.

A wide spectrum of Chinese goods floods Tibetan markets. From buildings and clothing to trucks and bicycles and food and sewing thread, Chinese products are dominant, and their availability encourages many Tibetans to adopt a more Chinese lifestyle. Many of the uneducated Tibetans I interviewed genuinely hate the Chinese who come to trade or do other forms of business within the Tibetan region. Such traders are now everywhere in Tibet, taking advantage of support from the Chinese government that encourages Chinese entrepreneurs to travel to Tibet. Such inducements are not available to Tibetan entrepreneurs; consequently, the Tibetans feel that Chinese businesspeople have simply been given a license to steal. Moreover, the flow of cheap goods hinders the development of Tibetan industry, forcing local Tibetan enterprises to struggle for small rewards. The Chinese argue that these problems are the result not of unfair economic policies but rather of the backward and uncivilized nature of Tibetans.

The Chinese approach to economic development in Tibet seems to be working. Tibetans frequently express the feeling that their inability to compete economically is partly their own fault, and this conviction is producing an inferiority complex. Tibetans are troubled most by their limited incomes and high expenses. They believe that traditional products and the time-honored means of producing them are uncompetitive when compared to cheap Chinese industrial imports.

Religion

For thousands of years, the aim of Tibetan education in monasteries has been to teach monks and scholars age-old spiritual beliefs as well as medicine, philosophy, astrology, architecture, the arts, and so forth. The Tibetan people venerated the religious leaders and scholars trained in the monasteries. But since the Chinese annexed Tibet, Tibetan religious beliefs have sometimes sat uneasily with politics. When I interviewed Tibetan religious figures, I learned that while belief in the Buddha is unquestioned among the monks, there are some significant differences between the views of the current monastic leaders and those of previous generations with regard to the traditional Buddhist worldview.

The monastic leaders, who include the so-called living Buddhas and senior monastery managers (*kanbus*), possess truly religious views of life. They believe in Buddhism and its practices in the same way as did previous generations of Tibetan religious figures. Even so, there are differences: There is a manifest feeling among many that the living Buddha system lacks transparency and is rife with political manipulation. And unlike their predecessors, many monks do not view monastic life as the single road to success; some have accepted government positions. Nonetheless, those with whom I spoke cherish their Buddhist beliefs, and neither monks nor nuns really obey government administrators, although they put on a show of subservience. The government is known to deal with different monasteries in different ways. Many monks said they had little doubt that some monks are government spies and that some living Buddhas advocate government policies.

Younger monks live in tension. On the one hand, they are genuinely committed and work hard at their studies. On the other hand, most are skeptical of the living Buddha system due to how it is politically manipulated, and many are critical of the customary management structure of monasteries and the system of ranking monks. Though they would never dare to question them aloud, they do not believe in the "low-living Buddha," because too many low-living Buddhas work for the government. Such Buddhas are often of no help to the Tibetan people and have little understanding of Buddhism; they are viewed as living profligately at the expense of the common people.

Some former monks to whom I spoke also feel strongly that the government-chosen living Buddhas do not properly represent the religion. Despite their disillusionment, they tend to abide by traditional Buddhist ways more strictly than do other people.

Finally, the common people of Tibet whom I interviewed about their religion live far away from modern society in a milieu of bygone concerns and practices. Their belief in Buddhism has remained largely unchanged from that of their forefathers. They respect monks and nuns, venerate the Dalai Lhama, and send their children to monastery schools—even though education in such schools may be detrimental to their children's futures.

Education

Educational strategy is perhaps the single most important issue for the Tibetans whom I interviewed. Currently, the Chinese government in Beijing imposes the Law on Nine-Year Compulsory Education on the whole country. This means that every family must send their children to a government school or pay a fine of Rmb 1000 (approximately US$125). The national public school curriculum is developed to further both socialist values and Chinese culture. The vast majority of interviewees consider this system to be inherently unfair to Tibetan students and believe that it amounts to a systematic attempt to wipe out Tibetan culture. One role of education is to reinforce and promote a people's cultural identity, even to attempt to improve that culture. But the Chinese education system that exists in Tibet today, many feel, is not suitable for the development of Tibetan society.

Since 1959, modern schools have been established by the Chinese authorities in Tibetan areas. During the early years of Chinese schooling, the Tibetan language was included in the curriculum; in some schools, it was used alongside Chinese. But the Cultural Revolution of the late 1960s and 1970s changed the course of education in Tibet. The Tibetan language came to be associated with religious superstition (*zongjiao mixin*), and it was removed from the Tibetan public school curriculum for a decade. Many schools were closed, and people who were caught reading or writing in Tibetan were punished.

In the past twenty-five years, however, public schools have reopened in Tibet, and bilingual education has been reintroduced in most schools. Tibetan children are educated by the Chinese in schools of three types.

In areas where most students are Chinese and in cities that have been included in Tibetan regions by allocation, classes are conducted in Chinese, and the Tibetan language is not used or taught as a subject. The educational standard at such schools is lower than that of regular Chinese schools, but the students are prepared to attend minority nationality colleges. Increasingly, such schools are being replaced by schools of the second type, as described below.

In areas where Tibetan children speak Chinese and their own local dialect but not standard Tibetan, Tibetan courses have been established in the schools, but all other courses are conducted in Chinese. Children graduate from such schools with some knowledge of standard Tibetan, but because they take on the burden of coursework in Tibetan in addition to their standard coursework, they often do not score as well on examinations as their Chinese peers. Nonetheless, schools of this type are increasingly coming to predominate in Tibetan public education.

In the third type of school, all courses are conducted in Tibetan, and Chinese is taught as a separate course. For many years, such schools have served ethnic Tibetan students who come from families of nomadic herders or who live in distant farming villages. The schools provide boarding facilities for students, as they cannot return home on a daily basis. Though classes are conducted in Tibetan, the students are removed from their home environment and kept in what amounts to a totally Chinese environment. Their textbooks are direct translations of Chinese textbooks, and the aim and content of the classes is the same as it is in Chinese schools. The students at such schools acquire a thorough knowledge of standard Tibetan, but their Chinese language skills remain relatively undeveloped, and the educational standards of the schools of this type are lower than the government requires for entry into the minority nationality colleges. This type of school is also being replaced by schools of the second type.

Each of the three existing types of schools has advantages and disadvantages for Tibetan children. Being educated solely in Chinese is the only form of education that provides a means to a satisfactory livelihood, yet being forced to use Chinese in school improves Tibetans' Chinese to the detriment of their native Tibetan language. It is difficult for Tibetans to live among Chinese people without extensive knowledge of Chinese, because Chinese is used almost exclusively in the administration of Chinese government in Tibetan areas. In every department of the government, most documents, informal letters, notes, certificates, and so on are in Chinese. The post office requires letters to be addressed in Chinese, long-distance telephone calls made via the switchboard operator have to be placed in Chinese, and all telegrams must be sent in Chinese. The instructions for electrical appliances are in Chinese.

The Tibetan language, moreover, is not always an adequate substitute for Chinese even among those who know it, because it does not have words for many modern concepts and lacks a modern technical vocabulary. Students who study in Tibetan find it difficult to get good jobs after they graduate. Studying Tibetan in addition to the other required subjects imposes a great burden, and Tibetan students who do so usually have poor grades, making them even less economically competitive. Such students do not wish to return to the farming or nomadic life from which they came, however, so they are stranded between the lives of their parents and those of modern Chinese. The current education system forces Tibetan children and their parents to choose between their cultural heritage and a viable economic future, and as the Tibetan language loses its value in daily life, the proportion of children who attend schools conducted in Chinese increases.

It is the function of education to transmit the culture of a society to its young people. The ethnic Tibetans in China to whom I spoke agree that Tibetan cultural heritage must be preserved, and they maintain that the education of Tibetan children requires improvement. The present system of education, which promotes the Chinese government's socialist agenda, does not do an adequate job either of transmitting Tibetan cultural heritage or of preparing Tibetan children to be competitive in the modern economy. Schools that educate Tibetan children in their own language prepare them poorly for the job market; schools that educate them in Chinese fail to teach them what it means to be Tibetan. Thus, it seems that education is central to the problem of Tibetan ethnic identity in present-day China.

What the Future Holds

Young Tibetans feel very pessimistic about the future of Tibetan culture and see no signs that the economic, educational, or linguistic situation of ethnic Tibetans who are unwilling to abandon their cultural heritage will soon improve. They believe that the only long-term solution to their problems is an autonomous government of their own. While they hope for a peaceful future, they are willing to consider the use of violent means to preserve their heritage. Many of the other Tibetans I interviewed see the future in similar terms. Highly educated Tibetans believe that peaceful negotiation with the Chinese to improve the Tibetans' situation is absolutely useless. They see violent confrontation between ethnic Tibetans and the Chinese as unavoidable. Many Tibetans are convinced that should the Chinese security apparatus loosen its grip, violence will surely erupt. All of the ethnic Tibetans I interviewed are confident that the future will bring a harmonious, genuinely autonomous Tibetan society, but they feel equally strongly that a peaceful change in the current political situation is very unlikely. As one interviewee said, "A stone cannot be a pillow; the Chinese cannot be friends." Thus, as another person put it, "the people must react with violence to show that we are still here."

This chapter commenced with the question of how the Tibetan people may retain a meaningful social identity in the face of the Chinese civilizing project. The growing anger among most of the people I interviewed is a very worrying development. However, there remains a strong security presence in the region, there is little external support for forceful opposition, and the Tibetans are by nature a peaceful people. It is therefore unlikely that direct opposition from the Tibetan community will emerge in the near future. It seems more likely that the Chinese civilizing project will succeed: Tibetan culture will gradually be lost and the Tibetan people absorbed into the wider Han society.

But perhaps both the disappearance of Tibetan culture and violent conflict can be avoided through reform of the education system. If education is central to the problem of Tibetan identity, perhaps it could also be central to the solution: a new type of school might be developed that draws directly upon Tibetan skills and philosophy such that it becomes an integral part of the life of the people. Traditional techniques and practices need to be recorded and young people encouraged to learn them from the older artisans before they are lost. Young people, likewise, need to regain a pride in their ancestral culture while seeking creative ways to put its strengths to use in the modern world. Tourism, for example, could both provide economic benefit and assist Tibetans in preserving their heritage. In addition, the young must develop business sense if they are to seize the opportunities that exist in western China. Tibetans must also find ways of raising the issue of ecological damage at local, national, and international levels. To this end, it would be preferable if Tibetan children learned English directly rather than as a third language taught to them in Chinese. This would enable them to access the resources of the English-speaking world and express their views in an international forum, and it would also revitalize the value of the Tibetan language and culture.

Dominant communities have overwhelmed many small-scale societies, and their cultures and languages have been relegated to anthropological texts. More robust societies on the periphery continue to resist civilizing projects. Old traditions re-emerge as the world changes and the strength of the dominant community ebbs and flows. The Tibetan situation looks bleak, but the Tibetan people have a long history, a great literary heritage, and a persistent common identity. The hope for a society, polity, and viable economy centered around their language and respect for their cultural and religious inheritance may yet be fulfilled.

References

Harrell, Stevan, ed. 1995. *Cultural Encounters on China's Ethnic Frontiers.* Seattle: University of Washington Press.

7

CROSS-CUTTING IDENTITIES
IN SINGAPORE
Crabgrass on the Padang

James L. Peacock and Wee Teng Soh

Picture a smooth, green lawn on the grounds of the Singapore Cricket Club, founded in 1852. In 1963, Singapore celebrated its new nationhood on this site. The lawn is called "the Padang," a precolonial Malay name, and it remains a ceremonial center of the postcolonial national government. The last thing you would expect to find here is crabgrass, a hardy weed that crops up in lawns, growing in tufts and swirls.[1]

Singapore's official policies and institutions articulate a well-managed society with an intentionally global, multicultural identity. Within this society, less controlled yet vital and hardy identities crop up here and there as seemingly unplanned growths, nurtured, it appears, by organic energies that surge beneath placid surfaces. Our focus is on these identities. What are they? Who are the individuals who express them? How do they do so? How do these varied and singular identities connect to the larger identities shaped and defined by the structures of Singapore's government and society?

Such questions address themselves to the informal, slightly unruly and uncontrolled aspects of an otherwise formal and well-controlled society—to crabgrass growing on the Padang. The character of this essay also resembles crabgrass: images, observations, and comments gleaned from brief fieldwork in July and August 2003 are presented with enough context and analysis to be suggestive. What follows is not a full ethnographic or sociological analysis but a series of snapshots. The persons and situations discussed are involved

---

primarily in two spheres, the religious and the artistic, and represent major ethnic, religious, and cultural streams. But the essay also presents evidence derived from Peacock's interviews with psychologists and his explorations of some civic spaces common to Singaporeans, regardless of their particularized identities, including marketplaces, public parks, and national attractions. This analysis is also informed by wider contexts and backgrounds: Peacock did fieldwork in Singapore in 1969 and in Indonesia before and after that. In this study, he is aided by Soh, a native Singaporean.

Context: Singapore

Singapore is a small island surrounded by larger nations. To the south is Indonesia, approaching 200 million persons spread over a string of islands nearly 3,000 miles long. To the north are Malaysia (just across the narrow Johore Strait) and Thailand. Each dwarfs Singapore's population of some 4 million yet struggles to equal its achievements in economic development and political stability. Each has natural resources that Singapore lacks, most notably land and water. Roughly half of the city-state's water is imported from Malaysia (Mauzy and Milne 2002).

Entering Singapore through its airport, one is struck by its well-organized cleanliness (and perhaps also by the entry card, which promises that those who bring in drugs will be hanged). Driving into the central business district, one passes a bustling port and numerous banks and hotels, all framing a historic area that carefully preserves monuments to British colonialism as well as historically ethnic districts: Indian, Chinese, and Arab-Muslim. An excellent subway system leads out past the major shopping centers on Orchard Road to the botanical gardens, racetrack, and national universities. High-rise residential buildings, grouped into community estates, each with their own markets, community centers, shopping malls, and places of worship, are evident everywhere. Farther out is Changi Prison and the army camp. Off the main island are smaller islands, including one formerly called Belakang Mati (Behind Death) that is now Sentosa, a complex comprising amusements, hotels, historic exhibits, and an aquarium. Ships and small boats head out to the China Sea, the Indian Ocean, the Pacific, and most immediately to Indonesia. Trains, trucks, and buses go across the causeway to Malaysia and overland to Thailand. Airlines connect Singapore to Hong Kong, Taiwan, China, India, Australia, Britain, the United States, and the rest of the world.

Overseeing this city-state is a parliamentary system headed by a prime minister. The People's Action Party (PAP) has ruled Singapore throughout its four decades as an independent nation. The PAP's vision combines a tightly controlled, stable, yet multicultural local society and global reach. The world market and international society are orienting points to which Singapore necessarily forges links in commerce, manufacturing, and tourism—and, as we shall see, in its inhabitants' prayers, artistic creations, and psyches.

In an authoritative characterization of the development and functioning of the city-state since it was established as an independent nation in 1965, following its initial nationhood associated with Malaysia in 1963, Chua and Kuo (1998: 39) focus on "Singaporean identity as a discursive object of very recent origin." They trace its development from a time of high unemployment and dubious economic prospects in 1959, when Singapore obtained from the British self-government in domestic affairs under the leadership of Lee Kuan Yew's PAP, to current economic achievements accompanied by strong values of "discipline at the work place and, by extension, generalized social discipline" and a "general orientation to constant upgrading of educational qualifications which embodies a deep sense of competition with others for relative advantages in consumption" (ibid.: 41). At the same time, the PAP has attempted to define and foster a "multiracialism"—a society for all "races," not just the Chinese majority, and a society whose policies are meant to be race-neutral (ibid.: 45).[2]

English became the dominant common and first language. The other official second, or mother tongue, languages are Malay, Mandarin, and Tamil, representing the three major ethnic groups—Malay, Chinese, and Indian—while flattening dialect and cultural diversities within them (Chua and Kuo 1998: 48; Pendley 1983; Purushotam 1998). Vernacular streams were accorded separate but ostensibly equal school systems in the 1960s; they are now unified into a "national stream." (In a parallel change, the residents of ethnically clustered semirural villages were resettled into ethnically mixed high-rise apartment buildings.) National rituals were introduced, including a pledge of allegiance, initially recited in four languages, now only in English. The national anthem is in Malay, which most non-Malay students no longer speak.

In its third decade of development, economically and culturally, write Chua and Kuo, Singapore's integration of a unified national identity that subordinated diverse ethnic or cultural identities took a new turn. Fears surfaced that ethnic cultures might be lost and that the "westernization" of the entire populace would bring moral decline. In response, in the late 1970s the government began to encourage the Singaporean Chinese to speak Mandarin as their second language. It also launched an experiment in fostering religion, promoting Confucianism among the Chinese and introducing religious studies as a formal examination subject at the secondary level. Although state support for Mandarin has continued, the teaching of religion soon vanished from the schools. In the 1990s, the government began to endorse mores ostensibly common to Chinese, Malays, and Indians under such labels as "Asian values," "shared values," and "Singapore's family values" (Chua and Kuo: 61–63; Hill and Kwen Fee 1995: 156–157).

To summarize, Chua and Kuo argue that Singaporean society encompasses diversity, which, however, it compresses and categorizes into an ordered system to facilitate governance and prosperity. Led by Prime Minister Lee Kuan Yew, who was born in Singapore of Chinese descent, educated at Cambridge, and inspired by the other new nations emerging after World War II, Singapore adopted the concept of *Bhinekka Tunggal Ika* ("Diversity leading to unity," a slogan it shares with Indonesia) to anchor its centralized, parliamentary system of government to an abiding model of multiculturalism. Although it has made gestures toward a pan-Asian identity, it primarily asserts its own distinctive national identity, uniting Malay, Chinese, and Indian ethnicities within a Chinese-dominated global city-state.

In 2000, Prime Minister Goh Chok Tong named the low birth rate and emigration as Singapore's "two major challenges." Women bear children late, if at all, because the "dominant social values emphasize work achievement and material success" and because, in every field except politics, opportunities for women are wide open. Well-educated Singaporeans, many of whom speak two international languages, English and Mandarin, leave, seeking lower costs of living, lower levels of competition and stress, a less "restrictive political atmosphere," and fewer "rules and regulations." For the most part, the government and the PAP accept emigration as an unavoidable aspect of globalization, although students who accept bonded government scholarships to study abroad and then fail to return to serve their bonds are condemned. In the 1980s, in response to these problems, immigration restrictions were eased selectively. Recruitment of "foreigners who [are] educated and skilled, and in a productive age group" has increased ever since. Goh explained in 1997 that "the inflow of foreign talent will expand at all levels, from CEOs and professionals to blue collar workers." More than one-fourth of Singaporean residents are now foreign born (Mauzy and Milne 2002: 187–192). A local social scientist told us that government policy appears to envision that as much as 25 percent of the population in the future will be experts imported for their special skills who will not become long-term residents.

This much of the story is well known. Many accounts are available of the city-state's intentional efforts to promote harmony and preserve an idealized set of ethnic and religious traditions, and, by so doing, to maintain independence from much larger neighbors and retain a precarious, rewarding position as a center of regional and international trade, banking, and industry.[3] Our question is, within the history and ideals of Singapore as a society—an economy, a polity, a nation—caught between two poles, the global and the local, and in the mix of nationalities, ethnicities, religions, and cultures that eddy around those poles, how do Singaporeans forge their individual identities? And what do differently situated persons tell us about how this society is knit together and about the cultural fault lines along which it might break apart?

Some Portraits

In order to explore these questions, we spoke with persons working in religion and the arts. We chose informants representing major streams within religion (Buddhism, Islam, Christianity, and Hinduism) and major ethnicities (Indian,

Chinese, and Malay), though their perspectives and experiences cut across and transcend orthodox religious and ethnic categories. While we organize the vignettes according to standard labels, within and across these categories, dynamic and complicating relations are apparent.

Usually, organizations were selected by first looking at Web sites and phone directories. Initial contact was made through e-mail or phone calls, and we made appointments with representatives who agreed to speak to us. We also drew on some of Soh's informal contacts in Singapore, with whom we visited a few organizations. Each formal interview was conducted on site—at the temple, mosque, church, office, school, organization headquarters, home, or coffee shop. To put informants at ease, notes were taken without the use of a tape recorder. Interviews were conducted primarily in English, although Soh occasionally employed Mandarin and Peacock, Malay. In this chapter, organization names, where given, are real, while pseudonyms are used for all individual interlocutors.

Religion

Three Buddhist Societies. Although Christianity has made strong inroads among the educated middle class, Buddhism in its various modes remains the religion with the largest number of practitioners in Singapore. Its adherents are mostly Chinese. The majority of Buddhist organizations in Singapore are of the Mahayana school, of which Tibetan Buddhism represents a branch, but not the most popular one.

Mrs. An, a middle-aged Chinese woman who heads a small, private Tibetan Buddhist temple, was the first person who expressed a willingness to talk with us. We found the temple in the guise of an unimposing bungalow located in a quiet suburban street in Geylang. Entering through a side door, we were welcomed by An, a somewhat shy and down-to-earth woman. She soon warmed up and began to tell us about her life and work within the Tibetan Buddhist movement. Her quest began when her husband, a jockey, suffered a crippling back injury. Acquaintances told her of a Tibetan lama (Buddhist monk) in India who was a powerful healer. With a group of fellow pilgrims, she traveled to India, bringing her spouse along to seek the lama's aid. The master treated her husband by blowing smoke on his back through a pipe made of PVC. Her husband, she said, was cured some "60 to 70 percent." After that, she became the lama's disciple and has since traveled many times to Bangalore in India to visit him.

She also told us how the lama had restored a mute boy's speech by cleansing from him a "formless being" of a "past life." "This Tibetan can look at you and tell who you are, read your mind," she claimed. Evaluating her own progress on the ladder of spiritual evolution, she said, "I do not have wisdom, so I make merit, then gradually gain wisdom." She expressed a clear belief in the existence of a supernatural realm beyond the physical: "I gain power from [supernatural] beings, not from psychic energy." It is this power, she said, that enables her to step out from the confines of her family home in order to gather the funds for, set up, and run this Buddhist center as a service to the community. She hopes that one day a Tibetan Buddhist *sangha* (religious community) can be created in Singapore.

An showed us the main temple, a room across from her office that features a shrine and functions as a meditation and prayer hall. In the main hallway by the entrance, we saw a notice board prominently exhibiting photographs of a large-scale religious ceremony, a traditional Tibetan Buddhist *puja* (offering) held at the center to help the country through the SARS epidemic that had Singapore in crisis just two months before. Mrs. Goh, the wife of the prime minister, presided over the function.

An's experiences suggest how the commitment to religious life can lead an individual to pursue activities that lift her outside the confines of the ethnic, national, and familial contexts she was born into, forging international connections that make her part of global networks. Religious life led An, who would otherwise have been, in her own words, a "Chinese housewife," to become a leader in a Buddhist movement with cultural ties to Tibet and geographic ties to India. Individuals and local organizations with transnational ties also actively participate in national life, bringing to bear upon it the cultural perspectives they tap into, as we see strikingly in the case of the SARS *puja*.

The second Tibetan Buddhist center in Singapore that we visited was different. This center, located downtown, has as its spiritual leader a Caucasian lama based in the United States. It offers a certified course in Tibetan Buddhism for interested lay people. In talking with its representatives and in looking through its publications, which are in English, we found that the organization emphasizes its Western associations. It reaches out to an English-educated middle class using Western symbols and secular modes of disseminating information that are meant to confer legitimacy upon a traditional non-Christian religion, offering a modern bridge to Eastern religious beliefs and practices as an alternative to Christianity.

The third Buddhist society we paid a visit to was the Metta Welfare Association, which is affiliated with two Chinese Mahayana temples in Singapore.[4] It has ten centers in Singapore and organizes a variety of social service activities. Its main center is housed in an old government school that Metta now operates as a school for the mentally disabled. At the center, we spoke to the young monk, Fa-Hsin, and to a representative, Mr. Chan, who worked within the administration. They informed us that the religious head of the organization is a Singaporean abbot who at the time was on a retreat, traveling to Thailand, Sri Lanka, Myanmar, and Nepal in succession for a "multiplier effect." Chan explained the association's mission: "We do outreach to Burma and elsewhere, helping to rebuild a temple in Burma, working with the locals. It feels good." We gathered that the master is a charismatic teacher and an innovative leader who is respected for, and inspires others by, his moral example. His is a powerful message that emphasizes social service as an essential component of spiritual practice.

The organization itself includes members from the lay community and from the *sangha* (as they refer to their monastic order), which provides spiritual leadership. The abbot himself initiates monks into the *sangha* in Singapore. The young monk we talked to was one such initiate. Like most Singaporeans of his generation, Fa-Hsin, now in his mid-thirties, went to an English medium school where he learned English as the first language and Mandarin as the second. When he was in school, his Mandarin teacher, who was a Buddhist, involved him in social work by asking him to help the school's psychiatrist. In that early encounter, Buddhism influenced his life not through religious instruction but through the moral practice of helping others. "There was no dharma talk," he explained, "only service." Fa-Hsin's words gave us an insight into how the emphasis on social service for many Buddhists becomes a powerful medium that cuts across not only ethnic and geographical lines but also religious ones, helping to bring out the message of universal spirituality that is in Buddhism. "Care is care, no matter what religion," Fa-Hsin declared.

Chan showed us around the center and its school for mentally handicapped children. The school takes in children regardless of ethnicity or religion. These children, who are not accommodated within the competitive mainstream educational system, are given an innovative education that includes music and art. We looked at a music room that includes an *angklung*, an Indonesian instrument from West Java, among other instruments. Chan told us of a Malay boy who cannot do multiplication yet "knows musical scores after one or two exposures and can play the most difficult musical instrument." Chan's words underlined the organization's philosophy, reflected in its take on education, which affirms the worth of each individual. At the same time, he called our attention to the Malay boy's ethnicity.

Metta illustrates more extensively the global, transcendent, and cross-cutting mode of Buddhism. Although the monk we met, the administrator, and apparently the master are all Chinese Singaporeans, their outreach extends to Burma and elsewhere, and to Singaporeans in need, crossing national and ethnic lines.

A Muslim Sect. Ahmadiya is a sect that regards itself as within Islam, even though many Muslims see it as heretical. It was founded in Pakistan (in Lahore and Kadiane) by Mirza Ahmad, who is considered by Ahmadiyans as a successor to Muhammad, and has branches throughout the world, including in Singapore. When we visited the local headquarters in Geylang, two men met us at the entrance—Syed, a thickset man in his forties, and Hamid, an earnest young man in his twenties. They brought us inside and introduced us to Raphael, who had just come from Indonesia.

Raphael was originally a Christian pastor from Bantam, West Java, who later converted to Islam. He told us: "I came to be a Muslim, then felt peace in my heart. Christians say you cannot hold a Bible and Koran in the same hand. But I did not hate Islam. I joined Ahmadiya, met a friend in Bantam who led me to it. I moved to Bogor. Mirza Ahmad faced temptation and persecution, but we always seek common ground. Wherever you go among Ahmadiyans, you feel like a brother. Muslims love the prophet Muhammad, so they hate Ahmad."

Syed and Hamid told us about the Ahmadiya chapter in Singapore: "We have 360 members. We believe our founder was a Messiah. We are persecuted by [some Muslims in] Singapore, even though [we are] recognized in a Christian nation, Great Britain." Syed and Hamid emphasized that Ahmadiya does not support or approve of terrorism. The call for noon prayer came, and as they left to go into their mosque, they handed us some literature explaining Ahmadiya's global vision of peace.

This contact was with the second major ethnic and religious group in Singapore: Malay and Muslim. Ahmadiya is a special case, however, another example of cross-cutting rather than an accepted orthodox category. In the Malaya-Singapore context, "Malay" is often equated with "Muslim" (*masuk melayu* means both to "become Malay" and to "become Muslim"). Ahmadiya is anomalous both because it is ambivalently Muslim and because it includes non-Malays. One of its leaders was a Chinese Muslim from the Uigur tribe in China. Peacock is acquainted with a Singapore Chinese, Tan (later Talib), who confounded his relatives by converting to Ahmadiya, and who went on to create a new multiethnic Indo-Muslim-Chinese family with thirteen children.

With representatives from London to Washington, from Yogyakarta to Research Triangle, North Carolina, Ahmadiya is a global organization. It seems especially open to converts from Christianity, such as Raphael. It abjures identity with hard-line Islamic terrorism. In short, within the Islamic category, Ahmadiya is liminal, a bridge to other identities.[5]

Four Christian Churches. Wesley Methodist Church, one of the oldest churches in Singapore, is perched at the side of the road that winds its way up Fort Canning Hill.[6] Jim and Florence Peacock attended a packed English-language service there one Sunday. The congregation seemed composed entirely of ethnic Chinese. We returned to the church on Monday, where we met with an administrator, Andrew, an energetic and articulate Chinese man in his late thirties or early forties. He told us that this Methodist Church is one of forty in Singapore, adding: "God bless, a vibrant, crowded church." Services are conducted in various languages, and the Methodists have both traditional and praise services, as do the Anglicans. During praise, young boys pray and speak in tongues. There are Methodist mission schools in Singapore wholly supported by the church that are, according to Andrew, among "the strongest schools in Singapore." He continued: "Mission students always do well. Mission schools provide a place where Christ can be preached openly. We plant seeds and sow, and the harvest comes when the youths grow up. They are confident, vocal, and loyal. They question authorities and have solidarity." He said that mission students "tend to go into the professions," in contrast to the boys and girls who attend the three elite schools named after Sir Thomas Stanford Raffles, the founder of Singapore, and are more inclined to "go into government."

We asked about ethnic diversity in the church. Andrew replied: "We have services in English, Tamil, Mandarin, and Hokkien [a South Chinese dialect]." What about Malay? "Malays who convert from Islam are ostracized; however, the church serves Malays socially. Many who utilize our social services are Malay." How do church members relate to a larger Singaporean identity? "They are not typical, mostly middle class and professional."

On the following Sunday, the Peacocks attended the service at Saint Andrews, an old, mainline Anglican Church that occupies a cathedral located in the downtown area. The service was in English, conducted according to liturgies with hymns and prayers not unlike those used in English or American Anglican or Episcopal services. A Rev. Nam delivered a sermon to the congregation, which is primarily Chinese. Jim left him a note, and he visited the Peacocks in their apartment, where he spoke about his background. Originally from Malaysia, Nam is a vicar of Chinese descent. He was educated as a Baptist, by, among others, a teacher from North Carolina. What struck Peacock most about Nam was one of the sermons he heard him preach. In it, Nam discussed the threat of Islam surrounding Singapore, homosexuality as an issue, and the civic nature of Singaporean society, expressed by allusion to another city-state, Smyrna.

> Smyrna was like Singapore, aspiring to be excellent. However, Christians in Smyrna feared the spirit of the age at work. Christians were persecuted in Smyrna just as today some Christians are persecuted in our neighboring countries. In Indonesia right now a Christian pastor is accused of illegal possession of arms. This is fraud. Arms were placed in his car. Now he is sentenced to death.
>
> In Smyrna, in AD 155, a bishop was martyred on a Saturday afternoon. Why? The bishop was the sacrificial lamb, the holy cow, the martyr. This bishop, Polycarp, was arrested. The captain of the guard instructed him: "Just say Caesar is Lord." He would not. Wood was gathered to burn him.
>
> The challenge for Smyrna is the same as for us today: to answer the call. Jesus kept the faith, faithful unto death. Jesus looks for all-weather friends. One evidence of love is loyalty, despite persecution and suffering. Yes, Christians should learn to succeed, but I say to you, they need also to learn how to die. That is discipleship.

The context for this sermon is the threat to Christians living in the countries neighboring Singapore—notably, the large, predominantly Muslim nations of Indonesia and Malaysia—and the threat to Singapore itself from these same nations and the larger Islamic world. Christians in these societies are predominantly ethnic Chinese and are thus akin, by familial as well as ethnic ties, to Singapore Chinese. Singapore itself stands as an oasis of Chinese ethnicity, Christianity, and prosperity in this large expanse of Malayo-Indonesian ethnicity, Islam, and poverty. At the time this sermon was preached, not only had the incident with the pastor in Indonesia occurred, but some Singaporean Chinese had just been killed in a bombing by Indonesian Islamic terrorists in the Marriott Hotel in Jakarta, and the threat of Islamic terrorism loomed in the region generally. Thus, Smyrna and the early Christians symbolize both an encircled city-state and a threatened minority religious group. Both are called to keep the faith, if necessary by martyrdom. The sermon, then, expresses a certain "siege mentality" that echoes official statements and implicitly and understandably frames Singaporean identity.

A Presbyterian and a Pentecostal church rounded out the spectrum of Christian churches we visited. The Presbyterian Church holds services in various languages, including Indonesian and German. Its Australian minister compared the vitality of churches in Singapore favorably to those in Australia. On another Sunday, we visited the Pentecostal Church with Sita, an Indian girl. The church is a large one housed in a modern building located in a residential neighborhood. The service resembled more closely many Peacock has seen in the United States than those in England. The congregation is Chinese, as is the minister. The most striking experience at the Pentecostal Church, however, was hearing Sita's own testimony. An Indian citizen and a Brahmin, she is currently working in Singapore. One day, she had a dream: Christ entered the room. She felt ashamed because as a Brahmin, she put herself above everyone, whereas Christ was crucified for everyone. The dream led to her conversion to Christianity. Today, she attends this Pentecostal Church in Singapore dominated by Chinese. Her conversion, therefore, entailed both a shift of religion and a bridge to the Chinese ethnicity.

Hindu Temples and a Neo-Hindu Organization. Hindu temples, associated with Singapore's diasporic Indian community, are found all over Singapore. But when we visited one of the oldest of these temples in the middle of Serangoon Road, the heart of the historic district popularly known as "Little India," it was with Lily, a Chinese girl. We attended a *bhajan* (devotional singing session) organized by the Sathya Sai Organization, which has regularly rented space at the temple for this purpose since the 1960s. Its spiritual leader is a guru in India, Sai Baba, whom devotees consider an avatar (divine incarnation) and whose message emphasizes the unity of all religions and service to humankind. The organization has its headquarters in India but is global in its reach. In Singapore alone, it has over thirty registered centers and many more unregistered ones. Its members include people from all ethnicities and religions.

The session began with the communal chanting of Om, after which the *bhajan*s began. It ended with a "universal prayer" in which the names of God from all major religions were invoked, the offering of *aarthi* (waving of camphor flame) was made, and two traditional Sanskrit *sloka*s (short prayers) were chanted, first in Sanskrit, then in English. The first *sloka* prayed for personal enlightenment, the second for world peace.

The *bhajan*s transform the ultimate Hindu place, the temple precincts, into a space of multicultural friendliness and religious inclusivity. Many boundaries—caste, ethnicity and race, culture, geography, language, and religion—are broken down, and bridges are made between different faiths, emphasizing the unity of all faiths and the oneness of all religions through a synergetic combination of song, prayer, and ritual. The most pervasive influence within the religious service we witnessed appeared to be Hindu, but a Hinduism divested of caste and sect and expanded to encompass other religious influences and cultures—truly a neo-Hinduism, although its affirmation of the similarity, equality, and unity of all religions makes the very category "Hindu" in "neo-Hindu" problematic.

Such mixing of different religious practices is visible elsewhere in Singapore. We visited a street near Little India that houses, side by side, both a Hindu Vaishnavite temple and a Kuan Yin temple. Outside the Hindu temple is a huge incense pot that, we were later informed, had been donated by Chinese devotees who wanted to burn incense to the Indian God Krishna. Similarly, in the Kuan Yin temple, we saw the occasional Indian praying to the Kuan Yin. Both Hinduism and Chinese folk religion (which is an eclectic mix of Taoism and Buddhism) are faiths in which God is worshipped in many forms. In Singapore, we find that this shared belief in the diversity of God's manifestation has in many cases facilitated a degree of mixing between the religious beliefs and practices of Indians and Chinese.

Arts

LaSalle-SIA College of the Arts. The LaSalle-SIA College of the Arts is a large, multidisciplinary school for fine and performing arts in Singapore. The institution's name reflects its mixed origins. It was founded in the 1980s by a retired member of the Catholic De La Salle order (the Institute of the Brothers of the Christian Schools), who was also a painter and sculptor, but a multimillion dollar grant from Singapore Airlines (SIA) facilitated its subsequent growth.[7] We met the principal, Mr. Govind, a native-born Singaporean of Indian descent who studied anthropology and sociology while at the National University of Singapore. He draws upon theories of both the social and the aesthetic to represent the practice of art as a form of critical reflection upon the social. He passes this vision on to his students, who represent a multicultural, multiethnic mix of young talent.

"In our school," he told us, "students try to understand each other's identities. They ask: 'What is it to be Singaporean? What are our roots?'" In the postcolonial context of Singapore, where "we learn British English and pay homage to the British in our schools ... hear American English on TV and speak Singlish [Singaporean English, a slang-like creole[8]] to each other," identity becomes a pressing question that Singaporeans need to explore. For Govind, ethnic identity is ever salient. Ethnicity, however, articulates with national identity in historically specific ways. He explained: "Indians were not really citizens in the sixties but we are today, 100 percent.... In the sixties, the Chinese schools were hotbeds of Chinese cultural nationalism, [but] today Singaporean Chinese would differentiate themselves from China Chinese.... [However,] since the nineties, we have been wanting to [re]articulate a relationship to China [as a nation-state for economic reasons]."

At the school, students employ art as a means to discover and express subjectivity: "Students recall and express dreams, [especially] of childhood. When they are disturbed, childhood objects become large in their art.... We don't have a culture of confession in Asia. Saving and losing face is a concern. Art provides an avenue to explore subjectivity without fear. Therapy came for one student, who had a terminal blood disease, through a rock band. Literature, such as Kafka, becomes a way to express angst."

Govind's intent is not to perpetuate blindly the cultural hegemony of the West, but rather to reflect boldly the syncretism that characterizes contemporary Asian culture—to "practice yoga while training in ballet." He mentioned Rabrindranath Tagore, whose school in West Bengal expressed this syncretic notion of identity. The dean of research, Mr. Suresh, also of Indian descent, later spoke to us in greater depth about LaSalle-SIA's vision: "Tagore thought of research as active, and we also promote [such] research [sometimes] in a traditional mode resulting in publication. [He showed us a large book[9] as an example.] Last Saturday, we had an inaugural project that mixed choreography, visual arts, theater, ethnomusicology, and writings related to the Mahabharata.... The Kauravas set a trap for the Pandavas ... but the Pandavas reversed the roles ... they did not become victims when the city burnt down. [Like them,] one has to continuously transform identities."

Suresh described several examples of the center's experiments in theater: "An example comes from Joyce Steel. Urban noises transform responses. Urbanites used to urban noises react irritably to nonurban noises such as the incessant chirping of birds. Such responses then are transformed into cinematography. One form expresses the sense of being watched, surveillance, being 'policed.' ... Another choreographs how we greet: we use eight or ten systems, so we bring eight dancers to put this into practice.... Another foregrounds faces: a dancer from Bali employs masks and places herself in various precincts then photographs people's responses.... The Singapore Arts Council is open to such continuous development of the production of knowledge." Such comments connect multicultural identities, national and transnational visions, the preservation of place, and the innovative expression of all of these through the arts.

Nanyang Academy of Fine Arts. We visited the Nanyang Academy of Fine Arts, an institution whose name is associated in Singapore with training in Chinese-influenced theater and the arts.[10] There we met Dr. Yang, one of its directors, in his office. Yang told us about the institution: "This academy was founded in 1938. It now offers diplomas in theater, dance and arts management, music, and all forms of Asian dance [including] modern and ballet with Asian influence. Its mission is to be worldwide."

Recently recruited to head the institution, Yang is a non-Singaporean. He is from mainland China but obtained his training and professional experience in theater in Germany and elsewhere. He mentioned the influences that have shaped his work, including Richard Schechner, Eugenio Barba, the Theatrum Mundi in Bologna, and Professor Sieghart Döhring in Bayreuth. His conversation revealed the international nature of his practice and its amazing adaptability: "If you are in theater, you can find identity anywhere: in the opera house in Prague, in English, German, or Mandarin. In Germany, there are 250 opera houses but you immediately [adapt] to each house. The psychology is physical and logical: you feel no different in each, you forget where you are. You get a contract in Verona and you go there. All you need to know is where is the car park, where is the supermarket. It helps [in my present appointment] that I have moved from practitioner to management before. I worked at Theater an der Ruhr with Roberto Ciulli. In Singapore, it took me only two days to set up. If I were in Germany, I [would] only require one day. Theater training has a curriculum, you are responsible for the product. I design not only from theory, but know what the industry expects and wants."

While we were talking, we could not help but notice a beautiful Chinese opera headdress carefully placed in a red, cloth-lined tray that sat prominently beside Dr. Yang's chair. Upon enquiring, we learned that the headdress was to be featured in an event at the institute that night to launch the biography of a famous Singaporean Chinese opera singer. Later in the evening, we attended the book launch. The singer turned out to be an imposing-looking lady nearly one hundred years old who sat on the podium, holding a cane in her bejeweled hands while attended by a young relative. Two students introduced the singer and the book written by a mainland Chinese writer, who was also present. The writer spoke about his work, fêting the singer in Mandarin to vigorous applause. The old lady stood up and delivered a talk in Mandarin in a strong and resounding voice while old-timers shuffled up and down the aisle with video cameras. In her speech, she thanked the Singaporean government for being a good government and one that supports the arts. She sang a short opera piece to thunderous approval from the mostly elderly ethnic Chinese audience, and then Dr. Yang presented the headgear to her. The event opened a window into a bygone world of popular Chinese culture when people sat in the open air watching Chinese opera shows (*wayang*), whose popular singers were truly stars with a die-hard following. This world, too, now belongs to Singapore's ethnic history, an echo from the past that reflects Singapore's changed Chinese culture.

Practice Performing Arts School. We found the Practice Performing Arts School in a business park cum industrial complex owned by a local software company. We were met at the entrance by Sastra, a Singaporean-born Indian and a well-regarded professional stage actor in Singapore. He now heads the school's unique three-year professional training program in contemporary theater, the Theatre Training and Research Programme (TTRP).[11] He told us that the school was founded in 1965 by local playwright and director Kuo Pao Kun, who also started TTRP in 2000.[12]

Sastra explained that the TTRP is based on Kuo's vision of arts as multilingual, multicultural, and critically engaged. Kuo thought that Singapore, as a place located at the intersection of several Asian cultures, was uniquely situated to render a multicultural contribution to the arts: "In the 1970s, Pao Kun saw a confluence of Chinese theater and Stanislavski. I joined him here. Our mission is to bring diversity to performing arts." TTRP celebrates intellectual and spiritual flexibility: "We are [the intellectual] descendants of the eunuch Admiral Cheng Ho: he was castrated and powerless yet commanded an armada, he came to Southeast Asia and India. At every port, he took the religion of that port. You must get context!"[13]

Based on this philosophy, the program admits students from different Asian countries and demands a great deal from them. "In our training," he told us, "we combine a variety of Asian performing art forms [such as] *Wayangwong* [Indonesian epic theater], *BharataNatyam* [Indian dance], *No* [Japanese theater], and Chinese opera. Like this, students find a bridge with the help of Stanislavski ... We create a liminal space."

Sastra continued: "I give the students lectures on the humanities: philosophy, aesthetics, cultural theory. Actors are not intellectual, so we teach about reason and desire as practice. What they feel and desire is as relevant as concepts. In the morning, the students do tai chi, meditation, then speech, movement, strength [training], and dance. After lunch, we work on the theater forms. The year is divided into two semesters of twenty weeks each, at the end of which they give a performance. After two years of training, they do a third year of public performances. Right now, the students are rehearsing Molière's *Tartuffe*. The field of studies [for the first semester] includes the self, autobiographical reflection, and ideology. In the second semester, they put the project in relation to the community. They do not attempt a synthesis. The results could be lots of rubbish but also sometimes gems."

Training one's feelings and desires to serve in the theater is difficult: "Students are constantly pushed into uncomfortable situations. They must find ways to work through." Those who succeed must be willing "to stretch" and must "dissolve the self."

The Substation: A Home for the Arts. The Substation occupies the premises of what used to be an old power station. We knew of it as an independent arts venue popular with the "alternative" crowd. What we did not know, until we visited it, was that it was also founded by Kuo Pao Kun.[14] On the grounds is a small café with outdoor seating, and we met there with the artistic co-director, Miss Wang, a young woman in her twenties. She told us how the Substation arose from Kuo's vision to create an open, civic space for the arts that "implements a Singapore Arts Council plan to transform buildings into places to do arts." "Young people," she said, "need these spaces to do art. Our approach is bottom up rather than top down. We support experiential work. We organize little festivals and an annual arts festival. Substation tries to support artists with vision. For them, we organize exhibitions and rehearsals. Themes straddle contemporary culture and our roots—Eurasian, Indian, Malay, Chinese."

She explained that the Substation selects several "associate artists" each year and gives them space and various forms of support for their work, with the goal of nurturing them to become full-time practitioners. She gave an example: "Zai Kuning is an artist, 40 years old or so. [He's a] sculptor who also did theater using highly physical genres, pop music, and updated *Butoh* [a Japanese dance form]. The Substation exhibited his work. He went on to exhibit in East Asia and Australia. His work focuses on sea nomads [Malay fishermen]. He is an inspiration for younger artists. Right now, he's in Japan."

Wang told us that she was first drawn to join the Substation because of her personal admiration for Kuo Pao Kun. The Substation, true to his vision, tries to create an open, civic, and experimental space for the arts in Singapore that is at the same time critically and socially engaged. Wang points to the wall surrounding the café. We see that it is full of colorful writings and drawings. A peace demonstration was held at the Substation in the wake of September 11. Demonstrators left their work on the wall. Wang explained: "This peace wall is to raise civic consciousness, [to show] that art is not separate from society. Even if art is abstract, the Substation is public. Since the 1990s, the government has encouraged people to speak up. The Substation is a place to meet, stage forums, discuss issues, and address postmodernist questions."

Psychologists

Jessica is Chinese, one of more than a dozen practitioners of transactional analysis (TA) in Singapore. She happened to have been examined in Chapel Hill, NC, by the well-known TA analyst Van Joines and referred to his book on types. Many of her clients are male—she says that men prefer TA—and she does family therapy. Her office is in a shopping mall. She invited us to hear her speak to an audience of several hundred managers who were meeting in a five-star hotel. She told them: "TA liberates customer services by applying psychology.... TA applies in family life and work life. How does it work? I size up a person. What state is that person in? Regardless of race, religion, or age, that person can be parent, adult, or child. You in turn can take either of these roles. Each state has two kinds of energy, positive and negative." She then asked the audience to score themselves. She told them: "Most Singaporeans are high on parent and low on child type, [they] do not permit themselves to be child[like]. British and Japanese [are] also low on child role. Jakartans are higher on child. Lighten up, let go! You can be different kinds of parents to customers and workers: critical parent, nitpicker, fault finder, rescuing parent. Interfere, bottlefeed, breastfeed your agent." The audience laughed, and she responded, "Free the child!"

We met in the canteen of the National University of Singapore with two other psychologists. Lee is a male counselor, originally Malaysian Chinese, who studies with a Jungian who visits from Australia and New Zealand. Jun, his female co-counselor, is a Singaporean Chinese. Lee told us: "Individuation is key, the developmental aspect. The group I study Jung with includes an art therapist, a journalist, and a social worker."

Jun offered an overview of the "Singapore psyche." There is a pervasive anxiety, she said, "because of the bond to Malaysia," which was severed prior to Singaporean independence. She continued: "You must distinguish surface and real identities. All [of us here] have different cultures: racial, colonial, and *peranakan* [a Malay word for those Chinese who adopted Malay customs, something like "Creole"], pseudo-Eurasian. Before World War II you wanted to be British, [then, during the war, to] be Japanese, [at other times, to] be Malay, follow the West, follow China. Then came Lee Kuan Yew … [and] different styles of Chinese leadership, not Confucian but based on fear." As she sees it, there is no single framework toward which Singaporeans can orient themselves. Perhaps she means to imply that in the past, fear was prompted by the tiny nation's desperate prospects for survival, and in the present is more likely to be prompted by the necessity of choice in the absence of Confucian or other "traditional" order: "'If you don't want this, you fight against it, if you want that, you must fight for it.' [The Singapore psyche is] different from Israel. Israel has one faith. Students wonder: 'What is it that will make me, me?'"

"[An] economic [perception] of the world," she concluded, "helped Singapore [realize] it could not be rigid, must be flexible." After an interruption from her colleague, she explained that flexibility has grown from generation to generation: "[Those in their] sixties and over are less open to diversity, [those aged] 40 to 60 are in between, [while those] 30 and below are used to multiculturalism, [they are] postmodern, pluralistic…. Today, puritanical demand has lessened, [and the culture is] more forgiving than in the 80s."

Note the convergence of the three psychologists, who reached a common conclusion despite their polar opposite orientations (TA and Jung): Singaporeans need to open up psychologically (or are opening up). They must accept the "inner child" or become more forgiving, a conventional posture of psychology, perhaps—that is, a therapeutic orientation. Yet it parallels some of the religious themes we have heard—acceptance, for example—and it is echoed in some of the arts practices we were shown, such as the self-reflection exercises (inward) and the opening up to various traditions (outward). One could correlate this with the evolution Chua and Kuo noted—Singapore's transition from a postindependence struggle to survive to a phase of exploring how, having survived and flourished, one can regain the self. Characteristic of Singapore, this latter quest has almost been mandated as a policy. With the struggle to build a prosperous society accomplished, now there is official encouragement of the arts. Although that focus is still motivated by economic pragmatism, nevertheless the result is a certain degree of explorative freedom within a framework of established yet evolving identity. The seeming convergence is at least a suggestive hint.

Comments

None of these interviewees are civil servants in any of the city-state's core bureaucracies, such as the law courts or central government. Each speaks as a practitioner or administrator of a certain practice—religion, arts, psychology—that expresses and transmits certain cultural perspectives. Several themes emerge. We see diversity, with major ethnic and religious varieties being represented. We find cross-cutting identities, including a Chinese woman's adherence to an Indian-based Tibetan guru and the coming together of a Singaporean Muslim and an Indonesian ex-Christian within a liminal Islamic sect. These examples blur ethnic and cultural distinctions that are often the fault lines of conflict in other societies. Cross-cutting occurs through meditation as well as transnational pilgrimage, study, and performance.

Government support for the arts and religion encourages self-expression and communion to the end of making Singapore a more attractive place to live and work. State patronage, however, discriminates: literature, art, and journalism considered dangerous are censored. Their distribution is limited, or their authors are subjected to civil suits, criminal charges, or detention without trial. Like all organizations, religious groups must register under the Societies Act. If registration is denied, anyone who allows the illegal society to meet, invites someone to join it, collects money for it, or publishes or distributes its materials may be fined and imprisoned (Mauzy and Milne 2002: chap. 10; Singapore Government 2006).

In this context, although Singaporeans take care not to criticize their government thoughtlessly, we heard representatives of religious institutions, arts organizations, and schools of psychology at times echo—and at times contradict—official policies such as multiracialism, meritocracy, and the need to be flexible. They reported public acts that ranged from enlisting government support to protest. The SARS *puja* was an initiative with the stamp of government approval. The Peace Wall is a civic demonstration that implicitly voices a critique of the Singapore state's pro-American policy.[15] Our interviewees' words bear witness to boldness, independence, and commitments to their own ideals and principles despite official censorship and sanction. Brown argues that "Singaporean national identity" is "partially weakened and undermined by the strategy of state intimidation," which results in "a society imbued with a permanent state of anxiety, such that many Singaporeans retreat from public political life into the private apolitical sphere, seeking security either in personal relationships or in such 'escapisms' as religion, consumerism, *kiasu*ism ["Hokkien for 'scared to lose' … anxious, anti-social selfishness"], or gambling" (Brown 2000: 104). Although this may be largely true, the people we spoke with have not hidden in a "private apolitical sphere." Instead, they have given their religious convictions and creative endeavors institutional expression. Although the state suppresses dissent, Singaporeans test and challenge limits, as Kuo Pao Kun's life shows.

We find in Singapore a sense of identity that is explicit for many, part of the cultural theories of the art schools and theater troupes and of the Jungian and TA psychologists alike. We find a relationship to conflict that is implicit (for example, in allusions to neighboring Malaysia) and sometimes explicit (for instance, in references to the Malay-Chinese conflicts of 1969). We find a relationship to history. We were present at a juncture of moments—post–September 11, long after the ethnic riots of the 1960s, with the threat of terrorism near at hand reinforcing an old sense of threat from the Islamic, non-Chinese nations that surround the island: Indonesia, Malaysia, south Thailand (which is a Muslim area), and the nearby south Philippines (also Muslim). Finally, we note that the theme of globalism is usually implicit, although sometimes explicit, as a guiding ideology, as it is for Sastra.

Space and Identity

Visiting Singapore's religious and cultural centers, we met representatives of its varied social identities. Returning to the landscape, we now locate these actors in the spaces they inhabit, following them to their neighborhoods and activities—at least far enough to sense how they move through dynamic locales.

Institutional spaces are defined by governmental and other bureaucratic spheres. Physically, they are located primarily in the skyscraper office buildings, hotels, and remodeled colonial historic areas fanning out from the center of town to bank branches and community centers, hospitals, universities, and schools. They include, first, religious spaces. Religious buildings built in the postcolonial period reflect the PAP government's policy of ethnic mixing within neighborhood communities. Churches, mosques, and temples are open to varied ethnicities, though of course they divide by religious orientation. Churches usually have separate services in different languages—Mandarin, English, sometimes Indonesian. Temples—Chinese or Hindu—emphasize the languages correlated with their religion, for example, with Buddhism, Taoism, or Hinduism. Mosques offer services to Muslims who are multiethnic: Malay, Indian, Arab, Pakistani.

Institutional spaces also include art spaces. Some performance venues and schools tend to be ethnically divided in their cultural foci—Indian, Chinese—but creatively cross over and beyond those boundaries in their casts of performers and their student bodies. Others, like LaSalle-SIA, are global. The government allocates unused civic spaces to artists, sponsoring the creation of studios and performance venues in old schools and factory buildings. Thus, we find the pursuit of aesthetic and creative activities in the concrete and functional space of order and discipline, surveillance and policing.

Such sites include still useful spaces of education—formerly streamed by ethnicity (Malay, Chinese, English), neighborhood schools are ostensibly multiethnic—and they include marketplaces. Singapore is a universal marketplace, featuring everything from local vegetables to global Japanese and American stores that mix tourists with residents, especially the ethnic Indians and Chinese, who are the primary merchants as well as customers (Chua 2003). Other sites include amusements. Consider two notable examples: Sentosa, formerly Belakang Mati, which now features an amusement park reached by cable car that receives visitors of all ethnicities; and the racetrack, patronized largely by Chinese. Many more watch television shows of horse races in several provinces of Malaysia. Finally, such sites include residential neighborhoods, which are now mainly government-managed high-rise apartments dotted by temples, markets, community centers, and schools. Slogans on signboards such as "Patchwork for the nation" and "Together we make a difference: PAP community foundation" reflect a planned effort to build integrated communities.

National spaces gain salience on special occasions. In celebration of independence, the Istana (national palace) and its grounds were opened during our visit, as is the custom annually. Inside the palace, gifts from other nations were on display. Outside were exhibits ranging from the statue of Queen Victoria (now tactfully placed at the lily pond instead of at the palace, but not toppled) to schoolchildren's creations. The groups wandering through were a cross-section of ethnicities. Parts of the National University of Singapore, its art museum, canteen, exhibit hall, and campus, are also open to many groups on a regular basis. The faculty, staff, and students are multiethnic and somewhat international.

Histories are exhibited officially at sites such as Sentosa and Changi Prison. Sentosa includes a sequence of exhibits and tableaus beginning with the founding of Singapore, showing the varied ethnic groups and their cultures, including crossovers such as *peranakan*. The story moves on to the invasion by the Japanese, the defeat of the British, the replacement of British colonial rule by the Japanese, and then to independence. Changi focuses on the Japanese invasion, then on the imprisonment of British and Australian soldiers.

Of special note is Singapore's treatment of its Muslim history, which is at once prominent and connected to surrounding Muslim nations and cultures, yet eclipsed and suppressed within Singapore itself as a predominantly Chinese, global, and non-Muslim society. During the late nineteenth and early twentieth centuries, Singapore was a point of convergence of Southeast Asian Muslims, as the records of associations, journals, schools, and organizations attest. Before that it was home to the great Arab families, Alsagoff, Aljunied, and Alkaff. The schools still exist, as does the sultan's mosque. The sultan's palace has been emptied, and the area is being turned into a cultural center, as is the Malay *kampong* (village) in Geylang, which is now a tourist exhibit of artifacts and scenes preserved from "traditional" Malay life. These are parts of Singapore that link it to its large, predominantly Muslim neighbor nations, Indonesia and Malaysia, and to the Muslim world of South Asia and the Middle East. Once the owners of the island, the Arabs have diminished in wealth and power, while the Malayo-Muslims are a somewhat impoverished minority. Both are perceived by some of the majority population, the Chinese, as a threatening link to Islamic terrorism, whether in the Arabic world or nearby in Indonesia, Malaysia, and the southern Philippines.

Within Singapore, the Muslim minority is assigned to an official category, and, like all other legally defined religious and racial groups, is "packaged" in several ways. Spatially, as part of urban growth and planning, the visible Muslim subculture is concentrated downtown in the Arab Street section, focused around Sultan Mosque; surrounding stores run by Pakistani, Arab, and Indian merchants; and the palace of the former Malay sultan, now remodeled, as noted, as a Malay cultural center. Governmentally, the Muslim subculture is incorporated into the broader governmental structure through an Islamic council, an Islamic court, and a ruling official, a mufti. Group representation constituencies (multimember districts for which each competing party must run a full slate) reserve slots for the minority ethnic groups, guaranteeing the presence of Malays in Parliament while limiting their independence. Muslims are allowed to send their children to Islamic primary schools (*madrasahs*), although these schools in the past have poorly prepared their students for secondary education (Mauzy and Milne 2002; Tan 2005).

At once elusive and obtrusive, governmental control pervades much. The precision of control is illustrated by a taxi driver whose friend ran into a tree and was fined for each tree ring that was damaged. A similar precision is suggested by caning—a certain number of strokes for a given offense. Milder symbols of control focus less on human wildness than on nature. Here we note the excellent botanical garden of Singapore and the more recent and commercial game park, which takes its customers on safaris in miniature jungles mirroring the larger jungles of the neighboring islands.[16] Acknowledging such control, while perhaps admiring as well as deploring some of its consequences, we are impressed nonetheless with the creative variety of identities and their cross-cutting interrelationships within this context. Crabgrass, like the even more fecund grasses of the jungles of Southeast Asia, is a resourceful force of nature.

Globalization, if one believes many who boost or fear it, destroys locale, and Singapore might appear to exemplify that destruction, leading to a placeless place—a crossroads, an airport and an Internet, an intersection for coming, going, and communicating. In fact, we have encountered people whose lives and identities do have locale and who struggle to sustain a sense of place in dynamic tension with global forces. Lily Kong, Rev. Nam, and Boi Sakti are among the many Singaporeans whose work and thought reflect the impact of globalization on place. Kong, a geographer and leader of the National University of Singapore, addresses the issue of preserving place in a global nation in her writing (e.g., Kong and Yeoh 1994). Nam's sermon on Smyrna is cited above. Boi Sakti, composer of *Reminiscing the Moon*, choreographs dances at the American Dance Festival in Durham, NC, in Singapore, and elsewhere. Dancers in the Singapore Dance Theatre, which focuses on ballet and modern dance, come from throughout Asia—the Philippines, Australia, New Zealand, Malaysia, Japan, and Hong Kong.[17] Boi Sakti, who works with them, deals with "lost space," with leaving villages for cities: "*Lost Space* impacts Singaporeans," says a dancer. "Boi speaks to me," comments the dance director.

"We need to develop a theater landscape," says Dr. Yang of the Nanyang Academy of Fine Arts. The Singapore Repertory Theatre[18] agrees, citing statistics: theater receives ten times as much public support in Denmark as in Singapore. Such place making engages symbol making, arts, audiences, tickets, grants. Richard Florida's (2002) thesis that culture and the arts are essential for social and economic development is affirmed by arts leaders as well as political leaders.

Dance embodies place. Dancer K. P. Bhaskar, director of Bhaskar's Arts Academy[19] and creator of the Nrityalaya Aesthetics Society, instructs yoga: "Breathe in, fill your lungs, hold 3–4 seconds, let the air out through the nose, then vomit out the air four times, do some jumps." He asserts: "Dance puts your feet on the ground." N. Charumathy, principal of a dance and music school the Singapore Indian Fine Arts Society,[20] states that Ganesh, the Hindu god of wisdom, removes obstacles and grants success for any undertaking. She practices yoga or meditation from 5 to 6 AM. When she wakes up, she chants mantras: "God talks to you." Recruited from India with no recommendations, she now has fourteen teachers. Her domain is ethnic—her craft sustains an Indian ethnic space. The point is that space/place undergirds culture and symbol making. The mind and body undergird place. Identity is mind/body/place. All of it is distilled by the arts, whether ethnically or globally envisioned.

Mr. Tan, a Chinese taxi driver, laments, "How can I feel attachment to Singapore if the place is constantly changing? Where I was born is a road. Memory is all that remains. We are now in the last days: thousands of years have passed since Moses and Jesus, but for God that is only an instant. I can only follow the Bible, I cannot interpret it." His point is that as space is being lost, history is about to end. Mr. Abdullah, a Malay taxi driver, 44 years old, mourns the loss of Malay landmarks: "Tan Sri School [a Malay school] was torn down. Streets in my neighborhood, formerly with Malay names, are now given Chinese names. In '69 my father narrowly missed being killed by a *parang* [machete] wielded by a Chinese. He fled on a bicycle. The Malay soldiers arrived just in time [he laughs]." As he speaks of lost spaces, he remembers a conflicted ethnic history: the riots of 1969, which pitted Chinese against Malays. Memories of place become memories of loss when the city is transformed and old places destroyed. These memories haunt places even as new memories are built upon and come to inhabit those transformed premises. A tense dialectic exists between the creative and the destructive forces unleashed in the process of nation building, a troublesome relationship between the creation of identity and its loss.

Crabgrass symbolizes an intrusion of wilderness into cultivated nature, a threat symbolized even more intensively for Singaporeans, especially Chinese and Indians, by the jungle on the nearby Malaya Peninsula. The jungle (*utan*) connotes Malays and even more primitive aborigines (*orang asli*) who inhabit it (Benjamin and Chou 2003). Malays, aborigines, and the jungles in turn harbor not only dangerous animals but also spirits who animate a world at once anchoring and challenging the civilization of urban Singapore. In a film made in Singapore, a group of students—led by Chinese but also including a Malay and an Englishman—sets out to explore the Malay jungle. One by one the students are killed by a spirit inhabiting that wilderness. Singapore controls nature in its botanical garden, safari park, and bird reserve. Spirits, too, are managed; for example, given space constraints, the dead are cremated and stored in small urns sold to families. But as the film suggests, roving spirits are at hand, just beyond the causeway.

Identity, then, is experienced locally, globally, and also eschatologically as part of history leading to the end of time. Identity is embodied in arts and religion, in culture transmigrated to a new place, in urban renewal and destruction associated at once with cosmic futures, ethnic pasts, and nearby natural, animistic habitats. Singaporean identity is located in all of these aspects; it constitutes a process that is also a place.

Conclusion: Singapore Identity and Singaporean Identities

Several themes confront us. We find cross-cutting identities in Singapore, flexible beyond received ethnic or religious categories. Singapore is a nation whose survival depends on its connection to the global economy. Singaporeans, especially in the educated and secular domains, are attuned to world events and international power relations. Global awareness is an important aspect of Singaporean identity, but there is also clearly a strong sense of national identity entailed in being a Singaporean. At the social level, it identifies one as a participant in a working system. At the level of civic history, it identifies one's citizenship in and sense of being part of the history of a self-created nation. And at the level of culture, it includes a special language, Singlish, as well as arts and culture seen as streaming toward a Singaporean synthesis—pan-Asian and global but converging locally.

We find, too, a dynamic sense of place where memories of the old and the demands of the new collide. New spaces are created on top of older ones. In one's own lifetime, remembered and cherished sites (neighborhoods, schools, churches, or mosques) are cross-cut with new ones that are urban and global reaching (the airport, the seaport, and, perhaps above all, Singapore Airlines, the glittering link to the world). Government policy is evident everywhere: beyond defending the nation and managing its economy, the PAP and the government attempt to shape society. But the identities cultivated by the state are enriched and made more complex by experiences that both reproduce and challenge official categories. Streams of spirituality, artistic creativity, psychological reflection, and quests enrich the externally structured lives of Singaporean individuals. The vignettes we have presented illustrate the richness in these streams—a richness unexpected, perhaps, by those who view only the external structure of the state.

What does the case of Singapore illustrate? Our interviewees describe concrete identities in action; the dynamic processes of these lives and endeavors are each part of an organic entity, Singapore. What is Singapore? In a global world, it is a small, bustling, prosperous, workable urban society that has intentionally constructed a pragmatic, meritocratic, multicultural national identity based on constitutional government and the rule of law, and which, aware of its geographic vulnerability and the powder keg its mix of religions and ethnicities might become, values stability more than democracy. This Singapore identity pervades Singaporean identities, yet these are independent, too. Individuals are creatively developing religiously meaningful and artistically expressive modes that reach beyond Singapore, not only through global economics and politics, but also through world culture.

An overriding tension exists between creating and sustaining a Singaporean identity and countervailing forces, which include loss of place as Singapore globalizes and otherwise changes, the special orientations of varied individuals, and oddities. Official policies and culture define a national identity, but the official symbols, even in so well controlled a nation as Singapore, harbor interesting wrinkles. Take, for example, the national anthem, "Maju Singapura" (Advance, Singapore). This is sung in Malay, a minority language; it would be roughly as though, in the United States, the so-called Negro national anthem "Lift Every Voice and Sing" were to replace "The Star-Spangled Banner." But this is an even more radical displacement, since most Singaporeans do not speak Malay. It would be as though the Negro national anthem were sung by all Americans in Gullah dialect.

History haunts. Singapore, a society with a Chinese majority and a Malayo-Muslim minority, is surrounded by nations with Malayo-Muslim majorities, within a region (Southeast Asia) overshadowed by another (East Asia) with a huge Chinese majority (China, Taiwan, and the overseas Chinese). In 1963, the senior author attended Singapore's celebration of independence allied with Malaya. In 1969, he was present in Malaysia when tear gas was shot at students to quell riots, part of conflicts between Chinese and Malays, and in Singapore at meetings of the Malay minority party and other Malay groups that were connected to conflicts within Singapore itself. That time of violence (noted above by the Malay taxi driver), the history of Singapore, and the geography of Asia are kept in mind by those who formulate policy and participate in the contemporary peaceful nation of Singapore. Threatening forces surround the city-state, most immediately terrorism. In July 2003, some Islamic terrorists were arrested in Singapore. The next month, bombings in Indonesia killed at least one Singaporean. Both Ahmadiya and the more orthodox Sultan Mosque on Arab Street in downtown Singapore have denied Islamic sponsorship of terrorism.

As one penetrates a bit into individual lives, exemplified by our vignettes, the gray officialdom and the more abstract visions melt into varied cross-cutting and particular identities, leading us back to the question: is there a salient larger identity, a Singaporean identity? The answer is arguably yes. The formal and informal layers and facets do unite to constitute a substantive core identity. Evidence for this is the fact that Singaporeans who leave the island sense a loss. Jessica, the TA psychologist, described this feeling when she traveled to Chapel Hill. She felt lonely, as if she had "left something behind." What is this thing left behind? Is it Singapore, the officially defined nation—the Merlion (the iconic lion-fish statue); the PAP; the hybrid, multicultural, multiracial "Patchwork for the nation"; the Padang? Is it that nation's rebels and critics? Is it a place and the memories tied to that place? Or is it just a particular set of attachments—familial, ethnic, religious, privately symbolic? Varied anchors help Singaporeans constitute their sense of who they are: the *sangha*, the child inside, the Tagore-inspired school, Changi Prison, and many others. All of this, so tangibly felt, so difficult for any single Singaporean to articulate, is part of what it means to be Singaporean.

The policy of Singapore's government is to instill in the citizenry a single, many-faceted identity. What is distinctive about Singapore's self-conscious construction of this national image? The metaphor that comes to mind is packaging. Singapore is a packaging operation. Nature, history, places, religions, and arts are efficiently packaged: wrapped up, offered, sold, sometimes, to tourists, visitors, or even natives. This is done elsewhere, of course, as heritage tourism, preservation, and patriotism. But it is especially evident in Singapore.

A huge port, Singapore is used to and adept at packaging and transporting. This very efficient city-state carefully controls its parts, and one way to control them is to package them in ethnic pieces, religious groupings, neighborhoods, theme parks, and historical museums. Where ethnicity and sectarian identities are involved, Singapore compresses ethnic diversities into a few official categories, notably "Chinese, Malay, Indian, and Others," or CMIO, and sectarian diversities into other official categories, such as Muslim, Buddhist, Hindu, and Christian. Each is then labeled and represented by certain languages, institutions, schools, neighborhoods, and cultural centers. In contrast to surrounding nations, such as Indonesia, Singapore appears to package safely, cleanly, and efficiently.

The result, some think, is a certain sterility, a flatness that develops as the cultural and historical energy, diversity, and experience are drained away or defined neatly into forms and structures acknowledged officially. One could suggest a loss of what Malays and Indonesians term *semangat* (spirit). *Semangat* is present in spirits themselves, a part of Malay (and Chinese or Indian) tradition. It is key too in Indonesian nationalist mythology as a romantic religious or quasi-religious feeling drawn from a Malay sense of spirits energizing the world, harnessed into a national identity fueled by the struggle (*berjuang*) for revolution. Singapore compensates for its comparative lack of spirit of these kinds with efficiency and control. *Semangat* is trapped, packaged, and fed into the bustling work activity that generates its own spirit, enthusiasm, and energy: it works, we work, we are alive. A sense of Singapore as a viable working nation comes also from officials at high levels of government and education. They speak of how they dealt with the SARS epidemic (efficiently), of a dialectic between control and autonomy, and of a realistic appraisal of conditions, recognizing that the population is small, and that the nation must cope with neighbors ranging from Indonesia to China. "We can do nothing about our geography," says Ms. Lim, an official in the Ministry of Education. But, she implies, if we cannot change where we are, we can control that environment.

Many Singaporeans who go away for study return for service and work, while others do not. Why choose to return? Loyalty to an entity identified as Singapore? Alternatively, feeling a connection to one another as a relatively small and tight-knit group of leaders and workers? Both? Why choose not to return? Longing for a less stressful, less constrained way of life? The desire to live in and contribute to the wide world that Singapore teaches its children to embrace? Do those who choose not to return still feel an identity with Singapore?

Among the cases presented in this book, Singapore is an exemplar of a rationalized, viable implementation of identity as contrasted to disruptive, volatile identities that rip societies apart. Among the nations born after World War II and at the end of European colonialism, Singapore is distinctive in size, prosperity, and stability. It is also noteworthy in its integration of identities—Muslim, Asian, and Western—that clash in the wider world. Admittedly, this integration is on a small scale and is organized bureaucratically. But it is also, as we have seen, organic and dynamic, bursting out like crabgrass in the manicured lawns and clean sidewalks of official Singapore.

Notes

The National University of Singapore, Department of Sociology and Professor Lily Kong greatly facilitated the fieldwork for this chapter. The analysis is, of course, the responsibility of the authors.

1. In fact, as far as we know, crabgrass is alien to Singapore, unlike the irrepressible subcultures we observed there, for which crabgrass serves us as a metaphor. In reality, the carefully maintained Padang shows no signs of weeds at all.
2. The Constitution recognized Malays as the "indigenous" population of the island and therefore granted free tuition to all Malay students in tertiary education. This policy has since been modified to benefit only those Malays deemed financially deserving.
3. See, for example, historical studies of the wider area by Day (2002) and Reid (1996), the survey by Mauzy and Milne (2002), and the assessment by National University of Singapore sociologist Khondker (2002: 41–42) that "judged by the penetration

of global capital, technology and the level of cultural interaction with the rest of the world, Singapore is ahead of most other Asian countries."

4. Information was obtained from the Metta Welfare Association's *Annual Report 2002*. See also the organization's Web site (http://www.metta.org.sg/). (Web sites are noted here as a supplement to our primary sources of information: on-site interviews and observations.)

5. Peacock did fieldwork among Muslims in Singapore, including Ahmadiya, from July to December 1969 under the auspices of the Institute for Southeast Asian Studies, National University of Singapore, and among Muslims in Indonesia, especially Muhammadiyah, from January to August 1970. For Peacock's earlier study of Muslims in Southeast Asia, see Peacock (1978).

6. Additional information on the Wesley Methodist Church was procured from its publication, *Wesley Tidings*, April–June 2003 issues, and from the church's Web site (http://www.wesleymc.org/).

7. See the Web site of the LaSalle-SIA College of the Arts (http://www.lasallesia.edu.sg/), which was accessed on 20 March 2006.

8. Singlish mixes words from Malay, Tamil, and a variety of South Chinese dialects into English, grafted onto a mainly Chinese grammatical structure.

9. Govind showed us Victor and Lingham's book, *An Equation of Vulnerability* (2002).

10. See "Nanyang Academy of Fine Arts: Different Talents, Unique Individuals" at the Web site of the Nanyang Academy of Fine Arts (http://www.nafa.edu.sg/), which was accessed on 20 March 2006.

11. Information was obtained from the Theatre Training and Research Programme publication, *Prospectus: Practice Performing Arts School*. The TTRP's Web site (http://www.ttrp.edu.sg/) was accessed on 20 March 2006.

12. Kuo, arguably the most influential figure in local theater, died in 2002, the year before our visit. He had a checkered career. He was detained without trial under the Internal Security Act for "alleged communist activities" from 1976 to 1980, and was stripped of his Singaporean citizenship, which was not restored until 1992. In his later years, he won official acclaim. He was awarded the Cultural Medallion for drama in 1990 and the Excellence for Singapore Award in 2002.

13. *Descendants of the Eunuch Admiral* is one of Kuo Pao Kun's best-known plays.

14. See "The Substation: A Home for the Arts" at the Substation's Web site (http://www.substation.org/), which was accessed on 20 March 2006.

15. Singapore is careful not to associate itself too closely with any single superpower. In the past, it has often opposed invasions of small nations (East Timor, Grenada, Cambodia, Afghanistan, and Kuwait) in the name of respect for national sovereignty, although it has contributed peacekeeping forces or observers to some of these conflicts. Since our visit, Singapore has contributed a police-training unit and material support to the war in Iraq (Mauzy and Milne 2002: 176; US Department of State 2005).

16. Marks's (1984) discussion of game parks as extensions of governmental control is suggestive.

17. The Singapore Dance Theatre Web site (http://www.singaporedancetheatre.com/) was accessed on 20 March 2006.

18. The mission of the Singapore Repertory Theatre, founded in 1993, is "to produce outstanding theatre with an Asian spirit and help Singapore take its place among the world's cultural capitals" (http://www.srt.com.sg/03/SRT.com.sg.html).

19. Information about Bhaskar's Arts Academy Ltd. can be found at its Web site (http://www.bhaskarsartsacademy.com/index.php). In 2003, the organization presented *Quest: A Mystic Arts Drama* at the Victoria Theatre in Singapore.

20. See the Singapore Indian Fine Arts Society Web site (http://www.sifas.org/).

References

Benjamin, Geoffrey, and Cynthia Chou. 2003. *Tribal Communities in the Malay World: Historical, Cultural, and Social Perspectives*. Singapore: Institute of Southeast Asian Studies; Amsterdam and Leiden: International Institute for Asian Studies.

Brown, David. 2000. *Contemporary Nationalism: Civic, Ethnocultural, and Multicultural Politics*. New York: Routledge.

Chua, Beng-Huat. 2003. *Life Is Not Complete without Shopping: Consumption Culture in Singapore*. Singapore: Singapore University Press.

Chua, Beng-Huat, and Eddie Kuo. 1998. "The Making of a New Nation: Cultural Construction and National Identity in Singapore." In *From Beijing to Port Moresby: The Politics of National Identity in Cultural Policies*, ed. Virginia R. Dominguez and David Y. H. Wu, 35–68. Amsterdam: Gordon and Breach, Overseas Publishers N.V.

Day, Tony. 2002. *Fluid Iron: State Formation in Southeast Asia*. Honolulu: University of Hawaii Press.

Florida, Richard. 2002. *The Rise of the Creative Class: And How It's Transforming Work, Leisure, Community, and Everyday Life*. New York: Basic Books.

Hill, Michael, and Lian Kwen Fee. 1995. *The Politics of Nation Building and Citizenship in Singapore*. London and New York: Routledge.

Khondker, Habibul H. 2002. "Globalisation in Asia: Current Trends and Future Challenges." *Commentary* (Special Issue on Globalisation) 18: 39–44. Published by the National University of Singapore Society.

Kong, Lily, and Brenda S. A. Yeoh. 1994. "Urban Conservation in Singapore: A Survey of State Policies and Popular Attitudes." *Urban Studies* 31: 247–265.

Marks, Stuart A. 1984. *The Imperial Lion: Human Dimensions of Wildlife Management in Central Africa*. Boulder, CO: Westview Press.

Mauzy, Diane K., and R. S. Milne. 2002. *Singapore Politics under the People's Action Party*. New York: Routledge.

Peacock, James L. 1978. *Muslim Puritans: Reformist Psychology in Southeast Asian Islam*. Berkeley: University of California Press.

Pendley, Charles. 1983. "Language Policy and Social Transformation in Contemporary Singapore." *Southeast Asian Journal of Social Science* 11: 46–58.

Purushotam, Nirmala. 1998. *Negotiating Language, Constructing Race: Disciplining Difference in Singapore*. Berlin: Mouton de Gruyter.

Reid, Anthony, ed. 1996. *Sojourners and Settlers: Histories of Southeast Asia and the Chinese*. Honolulu: University of Hawaii Press.

Singapore Government (Attorney General's Chambers). 2006. "Singapore Statutes Online," esp. chaps. 107 ("Films Act"), 143 ("Internal Security Act"), 206 ("Newspaper and Printing Presses Act"), 290 ("Sedition Act"), 311 ("Societies Act"), and 338 ("Undesirable Publications Act"). http://statutes.agc.gov.sg/ (accessed 4 April 2006).

Tan, Eugene K. B. 2005. "Multiracialism Engineered: The Limits of Electoral and Spatial Integration in Singapore." *Ethnopolitics* 4, no. 4: 413–428.

US Department of State (Bureau of East Asian and Pacific Affairs). 2005. "Background Note: Singapore." http://www.state.gov/r/pa/ei/bgn/2798.htm (accessed 3 April 2006).

Victor, Suzann, and Susie Lingham. 2002. *An Equation of Vulnerability: A Certain Thereness, Being*. Singapore: Contemporary Asian Arts Centre.

8

THE CASAMANCE SEPARATIST CONFLICT
From Identity to the Trap of "Identitism"

Hamadou Tidiane Sy

Two decades of deadly conflict between the government of Senegal, a West African nation on the shore of the Atlantic Ocean, and the separatist Mouvement des Forces Démocratiques de la Casamance (MFDC), based in its southern region, Casamance, have singled out Casamance and some of its inhabitants as different from the rest of the Senegalese nation. Although referred to generally as "the Casamance crisis," this separatist conflict pits the Senegalese government primarily against the Diola, one of the many ethnic groups in Casamance, which is among the most ethnically diverse regions of Senegal (Benoist 1984). Setting aside the sometimes biased generalizations of the media about the origins of the conflict, as well as the MFDC's claim to Casamance independence, it is worth asking whether there is any historically solid basis for the existence of an identity that is held in common either among the Diola or throughout Casamance, that is alien to other ethnic groups or regions of Senegal, and that serves as proof at once of the integral nature of the rebel group and of the impossibility of Senegal's assimilation of that group. Or, if such a historical Casamance identity does not exist, has a new Casamance or Diola identity (or identities) emerged and been framed—as I would suggest—by the conflict itself?

It is important to note that the type of identity discussed in this essay is social or group identity, and most specifically ethnic and regional identity, as opposed to civic national identity. The difference between civic national identity and social or group identity is in fact central to the Casamance conflict. Many studies in the fields of psychology, sociology, and other social sciences stress the obvious link between identity and conflict (see Azzi 1998; Druckman 1994). Very often, these analyses offer as a paradigm the causal relationship between the two, considering identity and its varying manifestations to be a root cause of conflict, whether those identities are "primordial" or "constructed." But I would like to explore another dimension of identity and the process of individual and collective identity formation in the context of an overt conflict. My question is this: What if conflict comes first? That is, what if conflict itself—whatever its economic, ethnic, political, religious, or other origins—shapes new individual and collective identities? Identity, and the feeling or obligation of loyalty inherent in it, becomes a sine qua non for every actor in the conflict area or situation, prompting individuals to ask themselves, "To which of the conflicting groups do I belong? How do I define myself in the current battle or war?" Defining one's individual and group identity then becomes an outcome of the conflict and at times a matter of life and death. When ordinary people become involved in a conflict, in short, they have to consider who they are and what common values they share with other people in the group with which they identify.

The process might begin with the individual, but the outcome is, perhaps, much more significant. When each of the conflicting groups attempts to use identity elements to prove the relevance of its cause, begins to justify its place in the conflict based upon identity, and tries to create and mobilize support to defend its identity, then conditions favorable to the emergence of new social or ethnic identities are in place. Being a member of the MFDC and fighting for the secession of Casamance from Senegal involves sharing some core values and practices with other members of the movement. It establishes new criteria in the definition of personal identity, and it may even have created an entirely new collective social identity that could only have emerged following the beginning of the conflict and may not have been possible without it. Equally, choosing to remain loyal to the Senegalese nation can also give birth to a new identity or to new criteria for defining some aspects of personal identity.

In conflict situations, moreover, we see what I refer to as "identitism," which I define as the overemphasis on, ideologization of, and politicization of the identity issue. Identitism can be witnessed in the tremendous efforts often undertaken by leaders or parties in a conflict situation to demonstrate their uniqueness, the social "distinctness" of their group (as the Québécois advocating secession from Canada might put it), which often leads to the generation of new symbols representing new groups, regardless of the original reason for the conflict.

A statement made by the president of the United States, George W. Bush, after the 11 September 2001 attacks against the World Trade Center and the Pentagon suggests how identitism comes into play in situations of conflict. Bush said: "Every nation, in every region, now has a decision to make. Either you are with us, or you are with the terrorists." In saying this, Bush appealed to other nations to add a new value to those they already used when defining their identities as nations. New identification criteria, he suggested, are made necessary by the context of a new war. Such criteria could lead nations to adopt totally new identities on the basis of whether or not they choose to join the United States in the "war on terror." Indeed, such a phenomenon is likely to occur in all conflicts, particularly when a conflict takes a violent turn, and it is more likely when a conflict persists, as is the case in Casamance. A vicious circle begins in which the definition, role, and defense of an individual or collective identity, whether or not the original cause of the conflict, become an integral part of the conflict itself. If we take the Bush case, those who will not join the United States become "enemies" simply because they have not signed on to the US war, although they might wish to define themselves as part of a third group or to assign themselves no category at all.

This chapter tackles the issue of identity formation and its relationship to conflict by reviewing and analyzing historical and contemporary events and discourses concerning the Casamance region, the Diola community, and the Casamance conflict from the perspective of theories about identity. My goal is to show how the Casamance crisis has helped generate totally different—and at times conflicting—identities within Casamance itself and within the wider national Senegalese society.

Triggering Incidents

It is generally believed that a march organized by a group of protesters on 26 December 1982 in Ziguinchor was the main triggering incident in what became the Casamance conflict. On that day in Ziguinchor, the largest city in the southern part of Senegal and at the time the capital of the administrative region of Casamance, residents woke up to find their city under siege after hundreds, maybe thousands, of secessionist protesters had attempted overnight to replace the green, yellow, and red national flag of the Senegalese with their own white flag. The response of the Senegalese security forces was firm and ferocious. Several people were killed, many others injured, and hundreds arrested.

There had certainly been earlier assertions of a separate Casamance identity. In 1980, a Senegalese priest, Augustin Diamacoune Senghor, a champion of Casamance traditions and culture who had worked as a radio producer for a local branch of the Senegalese state radio station, sent a letter to the president, Leopold Sedar Senghor, who was preparing to hand over power to his designated successor, Abdou Diouf.[1] In his letter to President Senghor, Father Diamacoune wrote that from now on, "Casamance intends to fly on its own" (*La Casamance entend voler de ses propres ailes*). Denouncing the "negative results" that "companionship" with Senegal had produced for Casamance at all levels (economic, political, social, cultural, and even moral), the priest presented the outline of a plan for the future of Casamance that included first "autonomy" and later "international sovereignty." At an August 1980 conference in Dakar, Diamacoune openly questioned the inclusion of Casamance within the new Senegalese state (Ndiaye 1999). In another letter written in

April 1981, he stated plainly that "the colonial power had not made of him a Senegalese" (*le colon n'a pas fait de moi un sénégalais*), and he claimed his "Casamance-ness" (*ma Casamancité*). Were Diamacoune's statements the spark that set the conflict ablaze?

Analysts and commentators have generally explained the upsurge of violence in Casamance as a result of the frustrations of the Diola community, whose members accused local civil servants of not treating them fairly and humanely and of failing to respect their cultural values. Indeed, Diamacoune himself once told me that the Senegalese civil servants were at times worse than the French colonialists whom they replaced. Speaking to an assembly of Catholic priests in 2001, a former president of the Ziguinchor region, Passcal Manga, declared that "the colonial development policy of Senegal has marginalized Casamance, and the independent Senegalese state has not fundamentally corrected these discrepancies." In attempting to pinpoint when the state's unjust treatment of them became too much for the Diola in Casamance to bear, some mention the January 1980 schoolboys' strike in Ziguinchor, during which one schoolboy was killed.

Ordinary people in Casamance often speak of yet another triggering incident: a football match in 1980 between Casa-sports, a Casamance local team, and Jeanne d'Arc de Dakar, the oldest of the Senegalese soccer squads in the capital city. The match ended in violence, leading to tough disciplinary sanctions against the Casa-sports players, who were charged with bad behavior in the presence of the highest Senegalese authorities. This event, and particularly the anger and frustration it provoked in the Casamance youth (anger that probably encompassed almost all Casamançais, mindful as they were of their new identity as supporters of the team that represented their region), was later used to mobilize support for secessionist ideas. The separatist leaders argued that the Casamançais as a whole were not treated fairly by the Senegalese government in Dakar and that the sanctions against the Casa-sports players were overly tough because the state treated Casamançais as second-class citizens at best.

Whichever of these events we consider to be the actual trigger of the Casamance conflict, it remains true that the identity issue—and identitism—were clearly present in the conflict from the beginning. Why this is the case is open to debate.

Rebellious Region?

To explain the cause of the current crisis in Casamance, many Senegalese—scholars and nonscholars alike—label the province a "rebellious" one by nature. Today, most people in Senegal generally refer to the natives of Casamance, and most particularly the Diola community, as "rebels." Any Diola is simply identified as a "rebel," regardless of whether she or he is a member or supporter of the secessionist MFDC.

The depiction of the south of Senegal as totally "ethnically and culturally" different from the rest of the country has its roots in the colonial period. Here, too, it seems that the colonial authorities' strong stress on ethnic identity—their identitism—was the result of conflict. The "rebellious" label is the result of the attempts of the French to understand why they could not peacefully establish their authority in the region of Casamance without being challenged. This conception of the Casamançais has carried over into the postcolonial period. In his master's thesis about the Casamance conflict, Pape Samba Ndiaye (1999) listed the "long tradition of rebelliousness of the Casamance region" (*la longue tradition d'insoumission de la Casamance*) as one of the causes of the conflict. Documenting his thesis with accounts and narratives written by French missionaries and colonial administrative authorities, Ndiaye illustrates the "rebellious" nature of Casamance's people by highlighting the many battles fought in Casamance against the colonial power. The French were ferociously fought in other parts of the country as well, but since independence in 1960, these parts of the country have not challenged the Senegalese authorities in their efforts to build a Senegalese nation and Senegalese civic identity. Therefore, their earlier demonstrations of a rebellious nature have been forgotten.

Other sources that reproduce the prejudices of French colonial writing portray the Diola as a group whose social structures and values—particularly their lack of centralized authority—differ totally from those of people in most of the rest of Senegal, and hence they suggest that the Diola tendency to enter into rebellion grows out of the structure of Diola society. But pointing out Diola individuality, or distinctness, as a cause of conflict makes little sense in the context of a nation formed of several different ethnic groups, where state structures and arbitrary territorial boundaries are a mere construction inherited from the colonial power. The same distinctness, or singularity, exists in all of Senegal's other ethnic groups: the Bassari in the extreme southeast, the Pulaar in the north, the Wolof in the west central part of the country, and so on. Most of these groups evolved separate political entities before merging into one Senegalese nation. Each one has, more or less, its own distinct language, its own cultural values, and its own history; if it did not, it would not be referred to as a distinct group (Diouf 1998).

In this context, the distinctness of the Diola seems insignificant. And indeed, in his study of Senegalese ethnic groups, Makhtar Diouf (1998) shows how several factors have shaped the formation of an integrated society in Senegal despite ethnic differences, which never produced violence until the Casamance conflict began. Canadian scholar Geneviève Gasser (2000) qualifies Diouf's opinion a bit, arguing that Senegalese society has been only "semi-harmonious" rather than perfectly integrated. Nonetheless, the work of both scholars acts to minimize the "distinctiveness" of the Diola. Though both Diouf and Gasser question the ethnic foundations of the Casamance crisis, issues of identity continually crop up in discussions of the existence of the conflict and explorations of its dynamics. Perhaps this is simply a manifestation of identitism:

explaining the conflict in terms of Diola ethnic identity provides a simple way of conceptualizing a complex issue.

Very recently, the actions of an individual Diola have strongly challenged common perceptions of the Diola people. To the general surprise of the Senegalese public, Sibiloumbaye Diedhiou, a traditional king from Oussouye, a city in the heartland of the Diola community, began speaking out, calling for peace in the region of Casamance and clearly stating that he is doing so as a traditional leader and spokesperson for other traditional leaders. He was later invited to attend peace talks and make a statement on behalf of his peers. For twenty years while the conflict simmered, no one ever heard of a Diola king or of any Diola authority who could play such a unifying role—apart from the leaders of the MFDC. Ironically, it seems that this king saved his own throne and those of many others when peace was at a premium while simultaneously contradicting with his very existence the generally admitted view that Diola society lacks central authority. And he is no fraud: scholars have proven that in each traditional Diola community there was a king whose power was religious and who was in charge of leading the community. Ndiaye (1999) acknowledges that the French were "misguided" (*trompé*) in their views of the Diola because of errors in a commissioned report they received in 1891. This was, according to Ndiaye, the starting point of the misunderstandings between the French colonial power and the Diola community in Casamance.

The point here is not to deny the existence of Diola identity but simply to show how through history and because of specific social and political conditions it has been trapped in a particular mold. The episode of the Diola king helps to emphasize the flaws and bias generated by identitism, pointing to how the symbols and history that help characterize and define collective identities—and these identities themselves—solidify in times of conflict. As a result of identitism, the notion of the "specificity" of Casamance has survived the colonial rulers and is now embraced by contemporary local leaders, analysts, politicians, Senegalese administrative authorities, and members of the MFDC. Each actor conceives of Casamance in this particular way to further personal interests and purposes.

A History of Ethnic Diversity

In the aftermath of the first scenes of violence in December 1982, an opinion piece by Boubacar Obeye Diop (1982), then a prominent member of Parliament, was published in the government-owned daily *Le Soleil*. Titled "Nation et spécificité régionale" (Nation and Regional Distinctness), it attempted to prove that Casamance and its inhabitants are a specific entity different from Senegal. The longer the conflict has lasted, the more that theories like Diop's have flourished. Their task has been made easier by the physical separation that exists between Casamance and the rest of Senegal: with the exception of its most eastern part, Casamance is cut off from the rest of Senegal by Gambia, another small West African nation that slices across and nearly bisects the territory of Senegal. Gambia was formerly colonized by the British, while the French administered Senegal. The geography and weather of Casamance are distinctive as well: while most of Senegal has a dry climate, with a rainy season of only three months, Casamance prides itself on its greenness and has abundant rains for half of the year.

Yet despite the obvious physical distinctness of Casamance, others insist that Senegal and Casamance have long been united. In an article written in *Le Soleil* in the aftermath of the violence of December 1982, Senegalese historian Iba Der Thiam (1984) indicated that Casamance was part of Senegal before the colonial era of the nineteenth century and that its peoples had for centuries been in "communion" and interaction with the rest of the Senegalese nation and people. Some historians, Thiam says, date the union of Casamance and Senegal back to two thousand years before colonial times; others, such as Cheikh Anta Diop, assume that it took place still further in the past. A closer look at the history of Casamance and its people helps to reconcile such different views, demonstrating how Casamance came into existence as an administrative territory and why this process did not create a single Casamance identity, despite assertions to the contrary.

Part of Casamance was under Portuguese control from 1645, when the Portuguese settled and built a commercial office in Ziguinchor (Thiam 1984). The Portuguese stayed in Ziguinchor until 1850. In the meantime, the French had settled in Carabane and Sédhiou in 1836 and 1837, and these two cities were administered from Gorée, an island off Dakar where the French had a naval base. Later, the Portuguese agreed to transfer Ziguinchor to the French. While most of the Senegalese territory came under French control, the French colonial administration faced multiple forms of resistance from the Diola until 1920 (Benoist 1984), and the whole of Casamance was not totally "pacified" until the early years of the twentieth century. Because of these ongoing battles and what some refer to as the "rebellious" nature of the populations in the region, three Casamance subentities called *cercles* (circles)—Ziguinchor, Kamobeuk, and Bignona—were administered by a military officer beginning in 1882 (Thiam 1984). Other sources indicate that it was not until 1886 that Ziguinchor was actually handed over from the Portuguese to the French after an agreement between the two colonial powers (Cissé 2002; Ndiaye 1999). By the end of the 1880s, in any case, the territory of modern Casamance was occupied by the French and administered as part of the larger colony of Senegal.

This version of events is commonly accepted among Senegalese and French historians. But the MFDC and, namely, its clerical leader, Augustin Diamacoune Senghor, have disputed it. According to Diamacoune, Casamance has never been part of Senegal, not before nor during the colonial era. In this view, the union of Casamance and Senegal was imposed by the French. In letters written in 1980 and 1981, Diamacoune maintained that a few years before independence, the leaders of the two "nations" of Senegal and Casamance agreed on a deal to walk together along the same path for a certain time. The Senegalese nationalists, fighting for their independence from the French colonial rulers, agreed with the Casamance leaders that Casamance would choose its own path and destiny at some point in the future. In an interview in November 2002, Diamacoune told me that he still strongly believed there has always been a separate Casamance nation. This is the historical argument upon which he and his movement rested their claim for independence and that led to the events of 26 December 1982, the spark of a conflict now more than twenty years old that has yet to be resolved.

The Senegalese authorities and the international community have been reluctant to accept Diamacoune's version of events. The scholars' outline of Casamance history given above is complicated, however, by the fact that it depicts only the history of the Diola-dominated area of Lower Casamance (Basse-Casamance), ignoring other parts of the region—namely, Upper Casamance and Mid-Casamance—that are dominated by the Peul and Mandingue (the "Mandingoes," in English-speaking Africa). Of course, interactions and population movements have blurred the lines between these subregions of Casamance somewhat, but the Mandingue and Peul nonetheless had their own history and interactions with the colonial power. Settling mainly in the Upper Casamance region, they originally lived in a traditional kingdom called Gabu, founded in the twelfth century by Mandingue warriors from Mali who enslaved or assimilated people from the first indigenous inhabitants, the Bainouk. The Bainouk, or Banun, who believed in one god, were pagans governed by an elders' assembly and a designated king. They depended mainly on rice production, and some believe they practiced ritual human sacrifice. They have become an almost insignificant minority in population size in Casamance today (Sow 1989).

According to B. S. Sow (1989), the Mandingue were divided into two subgroups: the pagan Mandingue (or Soninke) and the Muslim Mandingue. The Soninke subgroup performed "bloody" rituals and believed in the holy Jalan, symbolized by a giant tree where sacrifices and ritual ceremonies were held. The Soninke had a political system within which the king was the leader, but the "higher interests of the community" were in the hands of the elders' assembly. Both the pagan Mandingue and the Bainouk were eventually invaded and defeated by the Muslim Mandingue. The Muslim Mandingue also had a very stratified society, with an aristocracy, a huge class of "free men" (mostly farmers, who were neither aristocrats nor slaves), lower classes (castes), and slaves (ibid.). The Mandingue kingdom of Gabu was toppled by the Peul, who created their own kingdom, Fuladu (Ngaide 1998). The Bainouk, Mandingue, and Peul still live in Upper and Mid-Casamance, moving around within the region depending on the political and social circumstances. These ethnic groups are joined by the Balante and Mandjack, who fled Portuguese domination of Guinea-Bissau, located just to the south of Casamance, and settled near the Senegalese border. This migration phenomenon has created strong links between communities on both sides of the border.

The Diola ethnic group, which lives mainly in Lower Casamance, probably came from "the south," according to Joseph Roger de Benoist (1984), a specialist on Diola society. This community is composed of about ten subgroups scattered along the Casamance River and the shore of the Atlantic Ocean. The Diola may originally have come from Mali in the fourteenth century, fleeing the Mandingue warriors. They settled first in what is now Gambia before moving farther south to Casamance, where they assimilated and integrated a good part of the already weakened Bainouk group and settled in the fertile lands along the river and the coast.

To underscore the differences between the Diola and other groups in Senegal, authors and experts stress that within Diola culture there are no classes, caste systems, slaves, or griots (a caste of traditional singers, storytellers, and guardians of the heroic deeds of the ruling classes). Hence, the Diola communities lacked the type of social stratification and organization that was dominant in many West African societies, including those of their neighbors. The most stable social unit in the Diola community was the family or the neighborhood, according to Benoist. In many ethnological or anthropological studies, the lack of a strong central authority among the Diola has been considered the main reason for the existence of an incompatibility between the Diola community and local authorities appointed by the Senegalese government after independence, and thus as the reason for their separatist movement. Benoist (1984) acknowledges, however, that there were "kings" (*roi*) in the Diola communities who acted more like traditional priests than secular rulers: they were in charge of the rituals in the sacred forests that the spirits of the community were said to inhabit. Interestingly, however, Benoist also writes that "in some communities the king has clearly defined social and political responsibilities" (*dans certains groupes, il [le roi] a des responsabilités sociales et politiques bien définies*).

Knowledge of the Diola society's traditional kings gained wider acceptance with the recent high-profile appearance of the king of Oussouye. But why did it take so long for this knowledge to come to light? Perhaps for scholars to assess and accept the fact that Diola society is hierarchical would have required them to deny the perceived distinctiveness of Diola society and identity. Deeper research is needed into the reasons why analysts continue to use shortcuts to highlight the "absence" of authority and hierarchy in traditional Diola society. It is possible that ignoring the hierarchical structure makes it easier to argue that the Diola are strangers and totally hostile to the culture of authority that a modern state requires its citizens to observe and accept. Here again, the danger of identitism looms large.

It was only during the final years of French colonial rule and the early years of Senegalese independence that the territories of the Mandingue and Peul were merged with those of the Diola to create one administrative unit called "Casamance," named after the river that runs through the region. The separatist movement, which has never clearly defined the boundaries of its would-be territory, operates militarily in all parts of Casamance, but the fact remains that the MFDC began recruitment and its first military operations in Lower Casamance, the heartland of the Diola. As a result of the current conflict, administrative reforms in 1985 split the region in two, into Ziguinchor and Kolda. Although the name "Casamance" is still used, from a strictly administrative point of view, Casamance has ceased to exist.

Clashing Identities and New Identities

The preceding overview makes it clear that there has never been a unified historical Casamance identity, and it suggests the complexity of the context in which modern definitions of what it means to be Casamançais are emerging. "It is widely recognized," Peter Black (2003) writes, "that some of the most recalcitrant of deep rooted, fundamental conflicts are those between identity groups." He continues: "Much wisdom, both folk and scholarly, is organized around this truism; such terms as ethnocentrism, outgroup, prejudice, stereotype, xenophobia, racism, othering, and scapegoating, which appear in both scholarly and ordinary discourse on this topic, suggest a rather developed descriptive apparatus for talking about the role of social identity in conflict." Almost all of the terms Black mentions have been used to analyze the Casamance conflict and establish its root causes.

When discussing the issue of identity, there are at least three levels of social or group identity that need to be to taken into account. Because the MFDC claims to fight for the independence of Casamance, the first level falls along regional and territorial lines, encompassing the region of Casamance. Because it recruits mainly, though not exclusively, within the Diola community, the second level must be defined along ethnic lines, encompassing the Diola ethnicity. Third, we must consider Senegalese civic identity as the "other," or enemy group, being fought by the MFDC. Considering these three levels of identity allows us to question the existence of a Casamance identity—of *Casamancité*, as Diamacoune proudly called it in his letters. We can ask what criteria would be used to define or characterize such an identity. It also helps us to assess the idea that, in times of conflict, identities are transformed and new ones are generated through the trap of identitism.

After the trial of the Casamance separatist leader Diamacoune, who was arrested in 1982 and later sentenced to a five-year prison term for his involvement in the separatist cause, a Senegalese citizen, most likely a native of Casamance, expressed the dilemma he was facing in a way that almost certainly reflected the uncomfortable situation of many Senegalese citizens from Casamance. In a letter published by an opposition-owned Senegalese newspaper in January 1984, Poucet Mandiaby (1984) wrote that Dimacoune's trial "was enough to raise doubts and unease in people's minds" (*Il aura fallu ce procès pour que le doute et le malaise s'installent dans les esprits*). He added that he would not for a single moment have thought that Casamance could be separated from Senegal but that for him the trial of the separatists raised "many questions" (*des tas de questions*). As a Casamançais, Mandiaby—who clearly acknowledged in his letter that Senegal was "one and indivisible" (*un et indivisible*)—felt that he was an individual citizen caught between two stools: loyalty to his country, Senegal, the nation-state of which he was a citizen, and loyalty to Casamance, his native region, which was in the grip of a serious crisis. Mandiaby further wrote that Diamacoune was a hero who deserved praise equal to that bestowed on other Casamance heroes.

The double loyalty—and double identity—evident in Mandiaby's letter was also evident in the actions of the Association des Cadres Casamançais, an elite group that brings together natives of Casamance who are opposed to the armed struggle and the idea of independence for Casamance. The members of the association emphasize their Senegalese citizenship, but only to claim the need for better representation for Casamançais among the higher ranking members of the Senegalese civil service. Lebanon and the new Iraq both appoint government members along the lines of ethnic and sectarian affiliations; it is possible that such a model could be applied also to Senegal, an African country that aspires to be a modern democracy.

Taken at both the individual and collective level, these situations illustrate the complexity of Casamance nationalism, which appears to be a nationalism without nationalists—without actors who share values and practices that would unite them in a common cause for a common goal. Indeed, for a region such as Casamance—which has long been a land of interaction and diversity, and where several different ethnic groups have settled and lived in harmony for decades—to claim the existence of any common identity would be as artificial as it is for the Senegalese to claim the existence of a civic identity; thus, Casamance identity must be constructed. This is what the MFDC is attempting to do. The lack of a common vision and shared values among all the peoples and communities that have had their history enacted within the boundaries of the territorial region of Casamance has indeed been one of the main obstacles to the success of the separatist movement.

It is obvious that the level of support for the separation of Casamance from Senegal would be totally different if the Mandingue, Diola, Peul, Mandjack, Balante, Bainouk, and so forth agreed that the space they inhabited is one region and is their "nation," as opposed to a part of the Senegalese nation. Far from it, some ethnic groups in the region have developed the "Min-Tawaa-ka" concept to show their loyalty to the Senegalese state and claim Senegalese identity. "Min-Tawaa-ka" means "we were not there" or "we are not taking part" in the language of the Peul. As early as the beginning of the separatist movement, ethnic groups within Casamance, including the Peul, demonstrated their disagreement with the idea of a distinct Casamance nation without denying their heritage and identity as Casamançais by using the phrase "Min-Tawaa-ka" to describe themselves. Denouncing state policies that neglect their region, they have simply asked for better consideration in terms of economic and social development while totally rejecting any claims to independence.

But the bias of identitism has already shaped a common "Casamance identity" in opposition to the Senegalese civic identity, making their voices less influential in the wider world. Thus, we find at least two *Casamancités*—one paying allegiance to the nation-state and accepting Senegalese citizenship, and one fighting for independence and unable to operate within the nation-state. Is a common region.l identity the imagined community of the MFDC? If so, this implies the existence of a totally new Casamançais, beyond the simple boundaries of the territory within which decades of interaction have been unable to frame one unique Casamançais. What would be the common characteristics, the cultural and religious values, or the national symbols of this *Casamancité* that would allow or even justify the creation of a would-be nation of Casamance?

During a meeting in Ziguinchor in April 2003, Nouha Cissé, a history professor and analyst of the Casamance conflict, stated that the separatist fighters, in killing children and women, had "de-sacralized the sacred" (*désacralisé le sacré*). His point was that Diola traditions proscribe the killings of children and women, but members of the MFDC military wing had performed such normally outlawed acts. A thorough reading of this statement suggests that in the context of conflict, collective identities are transformed and new ones are generated. Diola loyalties are torn between traditional identifying values on the one hand and the need for the MFDC to demonstrate its strength by targeting men and women alike on the other. Can Diola who kill women and children still be identified as Diola? If they belonged to a religious order, they might be excommunicated or sanctioned for their actions. But being members of the MFDC affords them a new identity that does not proscribe these acts and so might exempt them from punishment, providing them with protection and support. The fighters need to show loyalty and commitment to their commanders and to the movement when they take up arms. But by doing so, they contradict the foundations, the shared values, and the beliefs of the community and culture they purport to defend. From the perspective of the other Senegalese citizens, the violent actions of the separatist movement reinforce the idea that the Diola are rebellious by nature.

Conclusion

Twenty years of conflict in Casamance have clearly generated new identities. The emergence of the MFDC as a guerilla movement has displaced loyalties in the Diola community from family and village to a totally new structure with new values and new goals. The Casamance regional identity has also been reshaped because of the conflict, with at least two new groups emerging: those who are willing to superimpose or merge their ethnic and regional identity with their

Senegalese identity and citizenship, and those who, like Diamacoune, believe that for historical reasons they are not and cannot be Senegalese citizens.

More worrisome than the conflict with the Senegalese authorities is the risk of interethnic or intergroup clashes between civilians from these two sides. What if some local political entrepreneurs use the split that has emerged during the last twenty years to mobilize support for, or to engage a war against, the MFDC? So far, the violence, which has mainly opposed the Senegalese Army and the MFDC guerilla fighters, has been restrained to a relatively low level. A senior Senegalese officer explained once why the army never launches severe strikes against the guerrilla fighters: "If we kill them, we're killing our own brothers; therefore, we try to avoid as much violence as we can, although we know where all their bases are." This officer may see the guerrilla fighters as his brothers, but it is doubtful that Senegalese citizenship and identity can be imposed on people who have willingly said that they do not want it.

Will the stereotypes generated or reinforced by the conflict be removed from the collective memory? Will most Senegalese's impressions of the Diola as rebellious or most Diola's perceptions of the Senegalese as arrogant occupiers vanish as quickly as those working for peace would wish? Such questions help us to reconceptualize the discussion of the issue of identity in times of conflict. Avoiding what I have termed "identitism," which oversimplifies complex and intricate issues, might be one way to provide opportunities for peace and reconciliation to come more quickly.

Note

1. Father Diamacoune showed copies of these letters to me. I do not know whether Senghor received them.

References

Azzi, Assaad E. 1998. "From Competitive Interests, Perceived Injustice, and Identity Needs to Collective Action: Psychological Mechanisms in Ethnic Nationalism." In *Nationalism and Violence*, ed. Christopher Dandeker, 73–138. New Brunswick, NJ: Transaction.

Benoist, Joseph Roger de. 1984. "Les Diolas de Casamance veulent être respectés." *Croissance des jeunes nations* 258 (February).

Black, Peter W. 2003. "Identities." In *Conflict: From Analysis to Intervention*, ed. Sandra Cheldelin, Daniel Druckman, and Larissa Fast, 120–139. New York: Continuum.

Cissé, Nouha. 2002. "Historique et déterminants de la crise Casamançaise." In *Vingt ans de conflit en Casamance*, Les cahiers du CONGAD no. 2. Dakar: CONGAD. 9–24.

Diop, Boubacar Obèye. 1982. "Nation et spécificité régionale." *Le Soleil*, 31 December.

Diouf, Makhtar. 1998. *Sénégal: Les ethnies et la nation*. Dakar: Nouvelles éditions africaines du Sénégal.

Druckman, Daniel. 1994. "Nationalism, Patriotism and Group Loyalty: A Social Psychological Perspective." *Mershon International Studies Review* 38, no. 2: 43–68.

Gasser, Geneviève. 2000. "Manger ou s'en aller: Le conflit ethno-régional sénégalais." PhD thesis, Department of Political Science, Université de Montréal.

Mandiaby, Poucet. 1984. "Autour d'une même table, bâtissons un Sénégal fort." *Takussan*, 6 January.

Ndiaye, Pape Samba. 1999. "Conflits ethniques et renforcement des acquis démocratiques en Afrique de l'Ouest: Le cas du conflit casamançais au Sénégal." MA thesis, Université Gaston Berger, Saint Louis, Senegal.

Ngaide, Abdarhamane. 1998. "Le royaume Peul du Fuladu de 1867 à 1936: L'esclave, le colon et le marabout." PhD thesis, Université Cheikh Anta Diop, Dakar.

Sow, Boubacar Sadio. 1989. "L'homme et la terre en Casamance: Ténure et pratique foncière dans quatre villages de la communauté rurale de Diende." MA thesis, Université Cheikh Anta Diop, Dakar.

Thiam, Iba Der. 1984. "La Casamance en question." *Le Soleil*, 9 January.

MANUFACTURING SECTARIAN DIVIDES
The Chinese State, Identities, and Collective Violence

Patricia M. Thornton

In the predawn hours of 24 April 1999, an unusual group slowly began assembling before Zhongnanhai, the highly guarded and gated compound that houses the elite national leaders of the Chinese party-state. Appearing to arrive nearly simultaneously in small bands from all corners of Beijing, they silently congregated before the compound gates and formed a neat grid only a few blocks from famed Tiananmen Square, the site of the massive student demonstrations that had been brutally suppressed almost exactly ten years earlier. By noon, the crowd had swelled to over ten thousand and occupied at least three streets surrounding the perimeter of the compound, with most participants silently standing in meditation or reading the written works of Li Hongzhi, the venerated founder and leader of the quasi-Buddhist movement commonly known as Falun Gong (Practitioners or Cultivators of the Wheel of Law). Many of the participants had packed food and water to sustain them during their long vigil, and some even vowed to spend the night.

Despite a week of unrest orchestrated by Falun Gong practitioners in nearby Tianjin, the Beijing police were caught off guard by the demonstration. After stationing uniformed police officers every six meters around the perimeter of the protesters' grid, police authorities took well over twelve hours to disperse the group. Most left voluntarily around 8:30 PM after police threatened to herd them all onto eighty buses waiting behind the nearby Great Hall of the People. Opting instead for public transportation, they disappeared peacefully into the crowds on Beijing's streets.[1]

Notes for this chapter are located on page 187.

The 24 April demonstration was striking for a number of reasons, including the size of the group, the silent and peaceful nature of the protest, and the strict discipline observed by the participants. During the protest, most of the petitioners refused to speak with nonparticipants; however, when a foreign reporter asked about their unusual organizational tactics, one participant purportedly responded: "We communicated by telephone and other networks from all over China, to gather here this morning" (Agence France-Press 1999). Several weeks later, when Master Li Hongzhi, the enigmatic founder and leader of the group, living in exile, was asked how the protestors had managed to pull off such a large-scale event without alerting Beijing's formidable public security network, he confirmed the importance of information technology to the group's tactics: "You know, there is the Internet; they learned about it from the Internet."[2]

Weeks later, Chinese party and state officials branded Falun Gong an "evil and heretical sect," and outlawed the group's meditative practices, the sale of Master Li's writings, and any public display of the movement's slogans or symbols. The organization's assets were confiscated, its offices and practice sites—including 39 branches nationwide, 1,900 subunits, and some 23,000 places where it purportedly held gatherings—were sealed and placed under heavy police surveillance (O'Neill and Lam 1999). A March 2000 Amnesty International report on the crackdown noted that in the months that followed, tens of thousands of Falun Gong practitioners were arbitrarily detained by police, some of them repeatedly, and put under extreme pressure to renounce their beliefs (Amnesty International 2000). Falun Gong sources based abroad claim that literally hundreds of practitioners in mainland China have been either tortured or beaten to death while imprisoned. More recently, evidence has surfaced that as many as six hundred practitioners are being held in specially constructed psychiatric hospitals, collectively known as Ankang (Peace and Health) facilities administered and run by the Ministry of Public Security, diagnosed with highly dubious "mental illnesses" (Munro 2000). Not surprisingly, those who have spoken out publicly about the persecution of practitioners since the ban have suffered harsh reprisals.

The treatment of Falun Gong and other *qigong* practitioners by Chinese officials raises several key questions about the nature of sectarian identity, social conflict, and the modern nation-state. The consensus view in the scholarly literature is that modern states seek to broaden popular support and therefore the legitimacy of those in power by engaging in a variety of nation-building activities, which are inclusive by design. Ethnic and sectarian tensions may become inflamed due to social dislocation, economic distress, or external pressures that undermine the allegiance of minority groups to the "imagined community" of the nation-state and threaten its continued survival by disentwining its internal cohesiveness. According to this view, subnational ethnic, sectarian, and cultural acts of violence are primarily antimodern, antistate, and anticivic expressions of aberrant and primordialist rage.

In this study, I adopt a different approach. Instead of assuming the interest of state elites in building social unity and consensus, I argue that the roots of ethnic and sectarian conflict lie in the foundation of physical violence that is part and parcel of the modern state-making process, which cordons off and claims specific strata of subject populations as legitimate targets for coercion and control. Through an analysis of Chinese legal documents and policy statements, I attempt to recover the elided history of exclusive nationalism and demonstrate that modern nation-states, when stripped of the pretense of civic inclusiveness, are at best little more than loosely organized machines of social violence that frequently resort to rituals of classification, coercion, and compulsion to better control their subject populations. Yet as Falun Gong's successful transition from spiritual group to outlawed cybersect shows, the information technologies that allow contemporary state officials to classify, surveil, and control their citizens can also be used by those same citizens to resist the incursions of the state. One key to the continued survival of groups accused of antistate agendas today may well be new information technologies, such as the Internet, cellular phones, and instant text messaging systems, which afford such groups some ability to evade the traditional controls and coercive measures of the state.

States and the Monopolization of Violence

The imbrication of modern state building with the overt expression of violence has figured prominently in political and social science theory at least as far back as Max Weber, whose definition of the modern state is now axiomatic in the field. It is "a compulsory political organization with continuous operations" in which an "administrative staff successfully upholds the claim to the monopoly of the legitimate use of physical force" within "a given territorial area" (Weber 1978: 54). More recently, Charles Tilly has argued that modern nation-states are first and foremost war machines. According to Tilly (1975, 1990), the bloody and brutal history of Western European state building involved, on the one hand, the elimination or subordination of internal political rivals and, on the other, the creation of differentiated, autonomous, centralized organizations designed to forcibly mobilize and extract resources for war. In the final analysis, Tilly (1985) concludes, the modern nation-state resembles nothing so much as a far-flung protection racket, which extorts resources—sometimes violently— from its subject populations in the name of protecting them against presumably even more dire and violent exploitation at the hands of external enemies.

Yet the protection provided in the name of citizenship is not extended to all who reside within the physical boundaries of the state. Rather, citizenship has most often been distributed on a preferential basis to the select few (Marx 2002: 106). As Bowman (2001: 31) has pointed out, the centralization of power inherent in the institutional architecture of the modern state strives to "enclose an 'I' or a 'we' and exclude—oft times violently—others." The some-times subtle distinctions between those included and those excluded from the nation's "imagined community" have been shown by Hobsbawm and others to be deliberately constructed categories, often based upon invented traditions that serve the shifting interests of those in positions of power at particular historical junctures (Hobsbawm 1983; cf. Berman 1998; Suny 2001). Partha Chatterjee has famously argued that the colonial state owes its existence as a modern regime of power in no small part to "the rule of colonial difference" based upon various socially constructed forms of exclusion tied to race, language, religion, class, and caste. The liberal-democratic ideology promulgated by the postcolonial Indian state was reinforced by an elaborate series of internal boundary-drawing exercises, separating the public from the private, and acknowledging some differences while simultaneously suppressing others. Yet the modern nation's proclaimed indifference to certain distinctions was "and continue[s] to be, overwhelmed and swamped by the history of the postcolonial state" (Chatterjee 1993: 10–11).

If we presume, as much of the political science literature on state-led nation building does,[3] that images of internal homogeneity and broad popular inclusion bolster domestic unity and therefore support for a regime, then why does modern nationalism so frequently resort to exclusivity? Anthony Marx proposes that exclusive nationalism may emerge when state elites attempt to strike bargains either to mend the slights and ruptures of the past or to avert threatened disunity among those viewed as members of a state's core constituency. In the process of state making, central leaders have rarely faced unified and internally homogeneous societies. Historically, state makers have confronted a complex series of nested challenges. Aspiring sovereigns have frequently adopted strategies designed to avert alliances between competing groups, often forging alliances with one group that are solidified by the deliberate exclusion of a rival group or groups (Marx 2002: 112). As Bowman noted, the historically successful strategy of divide and exclude

> culminates in the emergence of modern state formations wherein some agents of the state appropriate to themselves the power to perform violence against outsiders as well as against "deviant" forces within the society the state controls while others constrain and direct the non-deviant citizenry, so that it serves to perpetuate and reproduce the order characteristic of the state.... [H]enceforth "constructive" violence comes to be seen as pedagogy and conformity while repressive state violence appears as the legitimate expression of the "will of the people" ... [part of] the state's responsibility to protect the citizenry it represents from the illegitimate violence of the people's enemies (external enemies of the state, criminals, revolutionaries, mad persons, etc.). (Bowman 2001: 31)

The projection of the image of the internally coherent, united, and integrated nation-state constitutes an important resource of power for reigning central authorities, even as they continue to pursue strategies of internal fragmentation. As Philip Abrams once noted, the institutionalized forms of coercive power claimed by the agents of the modern state gradually become encoded, not as the expressions of coercive violence that they clearly are, but instead as the indispensable instruments of a unified, centralized social order: "[A]rmies and prisons ... as well as the whole process of fiscal exaction ... are all forceful enough. But it is their association with the idea of the state that silences protest, excuses force and convinces almost all of us that the fate of the victims is just and necessary" (Abrams 1988: 76–77).

Maoist Narratives of Inclusion and Exclusion

Official narratives of collective membership and segregation are therefore central to the processes of both state making and identity formation. The involvement of the state in identifying and repositioning subjects in narrative frameworks—of rendering them "legible" to the agents and designs of the political center (Scott 1998)—is central to the expression of modern political authority. The process by which identities are officially recognized typically involves not only the classification of groups and individuals into specific categories—racial, ethnic, religious or sectarian, professional or socioeconomic class-based—but also a determination regarding the political status of such groups. At minimum, newly recognized collectivities must be defined in relationship to the conceptual boundaries of the state, with those falling within those boundaries hailed as "citizens" and accorded the rights and responsibilities attendant with such status. But as Marx (1998: 5) notes: "[B]y specifying to whom citizenship applies, states also define those outside the community of citizens, who then live within the state as objects of domination."

How did the process of defining legitimate political subjects and separating them from in-dwelling objects of political domination unfold in post-revolutionary China? Official concerns about precisely who was to be counted among the people within the new People's Republic of China (PRC)—and who was to serve as an object of domination—date back to the official founding of the republic, which was constructed as "a state of the people's democratic dictatorship." In a 1950 speech, Chairman Mao Zedong asserted:

> The people's democratic dictatorship has two methods. Toward the enemy, it uses the method of dictatorship: namely, it does not allow them to take part in political activities for certain necessary periods; it compels them to obey the law of the people's government and compels them to work and remodel themselves into new men through labor. Toward the people, it is the opposite; it does not use compulsion, but democratic methods: namely, it does not compel them to do this or that but uses democratic methods in educating and persuading them. (Mao Zedong 1950: 25)

The fundamental distinction between the "people" on whose behalf the state would rule and the "enemies" who would be ruled underwent a series of permutations over the period of Mao's leadership. Reflecting back on the meaning of the "people" some forty years later, Chinese Communist Party (CCP) Central Committee member Bo Yibo noted:

> I think its meaning is quite obvious. "People" (*renmin*) is not the same as "nationals" (*guomin*). In the past, we generally used to say that "nationals" included the landlords and other antagonistic classes. In any case, persons (*ren*) living on the national soil are all [*sic*] "nationals" and are all called "nationals." Then there is another term, called "citizen" (*gongmin*). "Citizens" are different from "nationals" and from "People." Politically and legally there are such things as "citizen's rights," the most important of which are the right to vote and the right to be elected. So much for "citizens." With "People" it's different. For example, the People's Democratic Dictatorship with the worker-peasant alliance as its main body: here "People" includes workers, peasants, the urban poor, intellectuals, etc., but certainly not landlords and comprador bourgeois elements. (Schoenhals 1994: 1)

Nearly every successive mass mobilization campaign after the founding of the PRC state in 1949 interpellated a new class of objects for political domination. For example, in 1956, Mao readily identified five subcategories that would be targeted for struggle in future mass campaigns: "bandit chieftains, professional brigands, local tyrants, special agents, and leaders of reactionary secret societies." To these five he added another ten categories of political "non-people," collectively referred to as "other bad elements," who were designated by the Central Committee of the CCP as legitimate objects of political struggle by the people (Schoenhals 1994: 4). One study of CCP terminology of the early 1950s uncovered well over a hundred commonly used "keywords" associated with "enemies of the people" in New China, which regularly appeared in the state-run media. These early enemy labels designated targets of political struggle that tended to fall into five main categories: imperialists and their collaborators, feudal forces, bureaucratic capitalists, counterrevolutionaries, and unaffiliated adversaries, such as class enemies and "public opinion oppressors" (Wang Cheng-chih 2002: 85–87).

As the first decade of the new People's Republic neared its end, terms of political exclusion and approbation took on an increasingly dehumanized coloration, suggesting an intensifying level of political violence. Indeed, by the advent of the "Anti-Rightist Campaign" in New China, Chairman Mao had taken to hailing presumed enemies of the people as *yaomo guiguai* (evil spirits and monstrous freaks). The following year, this term of excoriation gave way in Mao's parlance to what would subsequently become a commonly invoked label of political abuse during the Great Proletarian Cultural Revolution—*niugui sheshen* (ox-monsters and snake-demons) (Schoenhals 1994: 6).

This trend continued throughout the convulsive onset of the Cultural Revolution in 1966. Schoenhals notes that then-president of the People's Republic, Liu Shaoqi, delivered a speech in which he expressed his hope that the emancipation brought about by Marxism might one day even include "landlord elements, rich-peasant elements, reactionary elements, and hooligans." President Liu's listeners promptly responded that such groups "count as human beings (*ren*) but not as people (*renmin*)." President Liu remonstrated with them, arguing: "They count as humans. They are not animals.... Humanity includes proletarian laborers as well as the sons and daughters of the exploiting classes and any [members of those classes] not executed.... Human beings not yet executed are still human beings" (Schoenhals 1994: 10). The hostile audience demanded an apology from the president; he was later forced to submit a written self-criticism recanting his error (a mistake of "putting the incidental before the fundamental"). Months later, he and his spouse were both detained, subjected to public criticism, and repeatedly harassed by a group of university and high-school students, who taunted him with his earlier comments. Deposed in disgrace, exiled, and imprisoned, he died not long after his confinement.

Mao's death in 1976 was followed by the return of the formerly deposed Deng Xiaoping, who called for an end to the Maoist pursuit of permanent class struggle. Yet even as the Dengist regime oversaw the rectification of literally thousands of cases of former "struggle objects" and their reintegration into the ranks of the citizenry, its policies created new classes of undesirable elements that would find themselves interpellated and repositioned by the center outside the margins of political inclusion. The overriding Mao-era concern with continuing class struggle was replaced by reform-era narratives with an interest in "seeking truth from facts" that valorized scientific inquiry over ideological purity. However, the vigorous pursuit of "scientific materialism" by the reform-era state ultimately served to create new categories of nonpersons, and the coercive machinery of the Chinese state once again reinvented itself as the will of the people.

From Reform to Spiritual Revival

The dismantling of key Mao-era institutions, the relaxation of centralized political control, and the opening of Chinese markets to foreign trade under Deng's rule all contributed to a proliferation of spiritual sects and popular quasi-religious practices in the years following Mao's death. Visitors to the Chinese countryside after 1978 noted the widespread revival of shrine building, temple fairs, geomancy, and rituals of exorcism. In the cities, a phenomenon known as *qigong re* (*qigong* fever) took hold in the 1980s, resulting in a popular fascination with traditional techniques of breath control, meditation, and healing. The Dengist state sponsored campaigns in 1980–1982 to eliminate fortune telling, witchcraft, and other "feudal superstitious activities" in rural Shaanxi, Hainan, and Anhui. Yet even as the state moved to stem the tide in rural areas, the 1980s nonetheless witnessed an explosion of interest in the paranormal among Chinese urbanites. New print media, testing the waters of relaxed censorship, eagerly competed for the attention of the reading public by seizing upon a succession of self-proclaimed *qigong* masters who "came down out of the mountains" to demonstrate their paranormal abilities and spread their teachings.

A rapid proliferation of new teachings—such as Daziran Zhongxin Gong (Nature-Centered Gong), Taiji Qigong (Taiji Gong), Bagua Qigong (Eight Trigrams Qigong), Guo Gong (National Gong), Xiang Gong (Fragrant Gong)—appeared, many of which drew upon either remembered or reconstructed traditions for inspiration, but were no less popular for their syncretic roots (Thornton 2003). Into this rich milieu of spiritual practices, one group emerged that focused their spiritual attention on what they called the Practice of the Dharma Wheel (Falun Gong), which interwove Buddhist, Daoist, and postrevolutionary themes and practices. Li Hongzhi, a worker at the Changchun Cereals and Oil Company with an interest in *qigong*, developed a unique system of five basic meditative exercises designed to assist in the removal of bad karma by visualizing a rotating dharma wheel in the abdomen. In 1991, Li retired from his factory job and began to teach his system to a receptive audience.

Yet Li's timing left much to be desired. Following the 1989 crackdown against the student movement, CCP and state leaders grew uneasy with the seemingly ceaseless parade of *qigong* masters and the huge audiences they drew on a near-nightly basis in China's major cities. Stringent new regulations were imposed on social organizations and large public gatherings, resulting in closer government surveillance of popular *qigong* sects. Some *qigong* leaders and their adherents chafed under the new regulatory regime: Falun Gong practitioners, who numbered nearly seventy million in mainland China at the movement's height, became increasingly defiant in the newly repressive atmosphere of the mid-1990s. When articles critical of Li Hongzhi and his teachings appeared in the press, Falun Gong practitioners responded by staging mass protests around the offices of media outlets that published or broadcast reports, sometimes involving more than a thousand participants per gathering. Some reporters and government officials complained of being harassed by phone calls from defiant practitioners; a few claimed that their residences were being targeted by Falun Gong activists for protests (Xia Ming and Hua Shiping 1999: 87–90). When a popular science magazine published in April 1999 an article that referred to Falun Gong as "sham *qigong*," literally thousands of loyal Falun Gong practitioners descended in protest upon the offices of both the magazine and the Tianjin municipal government, resulting in a spate of arrests. With several Tianjin practitioners still in police custody, a group of more than ten thousand Falun Gong activists gathered to stage the silent protest before the leadership compound in Beijing described in the opening paragraphs of this chapter. The official response was to ban Falun Gong and similar groups and to single out practitioners unwilling to renounce their beliefs with coercive measures designed to isolate them from the people.

Yet the implementation of such a ban was anything but simple. One problem faced by the regime was its own promotion during the reform era of the *qigong* movement as a healthy and positive social development. The popular enthusiasm for *qigong* sects was initially not only tolerated but even encouraged by CCP and PRC leaders. One Hong Kong periodical claimed that each of the "Eight Elders" of the Party's Central Committee during the late 1980s (including Deng Xiaoping himself) personally retained four to five *qigong* masters for regular specialized treatments and, in some cases, private soothsaying sessions. By the summer of 1990, over 200 *qigong* adepts were purportedly on the payroll at the Zhongnanhai leadership compound (Li Da 1990: 14–15). Thus, the process by which charismatic *qigong* masters and their masses of enthusiastic practitioners were excised from the Chinese body politic resembled an operation akin to delicate political surgery. The interpellation, stereotyping, and scapegoating of *qigong* practitioners necessarily invoked a series of complex internal boundaries that repositioned these subjects outside of the margins of the people and targeted them for special handling by the state.

Constructing the Cult

In an August 1999 statement, the "Ten-Thousand Word Letter to the Party Center," loyal Falun Gong practitioners argued that the process by which they were being systematically transformed from loyal and law-abiding Chinese citizens into deviant members of society began well before the formal ban imposed on the group at the end of July 1999. Citing the 1996 article published by the *Guangming Daily* that referred to Li Hongzhi's magnum opus, *Turning the Dharma Wheel* (Zhuan Falun), as "spurious science," and Falun Gong practitioners as "idiots," the followers charged: "It is well known that the *Guangming Daily* is the mouthpiece of the State Council, and that a signed commentary probably represents the opinions of certain people in the government." The "Ten-Thousand Word Letter" also charged that a notice circulated by the Public Security Bureau in 1998 "was labeling citizens as law-breakers and criminals before a conscientious investigation had been made or before any hard evidence had been obtained" (Xia Ming and Hua Shiping 1999: 73–74).

The 1998 circular was followed by an intensification of repressive activities surrounding the group, its members, and its texts. While reports on the *qigong* movement that appeared in the 1980s and early 1990s overwhelmingly lauded its leaders and adepts for pushing the boundaries of scientific knowledge by testing concepts and ideas loosely related to particle physics, by the mid-1990s, party and state authorities had clearly begun the process of introducing and policing new discursive boundaries that were gradually shifting the *qigong* movement to the margins of political credibility. By 1998, increasing numbers of newspaper and magazine articles were intimating that some branches of *qigong* were related to *wei kexue* (pseudo-science) or, perhaps even more ominously, to *fengjian mixin* (feudal superstitious beliefs).

The official announcement of the ban on Falun Gong on 22 July 1999 drew a series of linkages between the group and other organizations previously targeted for repression and elimination by the CCP. One legal and discursive strategy deployed by Chinese officials linked Falun Gong to other illegal and unauthorized social organizations, like those the regime claimed had been behind the 1989 unrest ("counterrevolutionary rebellion") centered in and around Tiananmen Square in Beijing. Following the crackdown, a wave of legislation required that all social organizations undergo a process of official review and registration. A decade later, the Ministry of Civil Affairs charged that Falun Gong failed to register "in accordance with the relevant stipulations of the Regulations and Management of Mass Organizations" established in 1989. Accordingly, a Ministry of Public Security notice published alongside the document prohibited "activities that support or publicize Falun Dafa (Falun Gong) such as holding gatherings, parades, or demonstrations in the form of sit-ins or appeals to higher authorities," as well as any "activities that incite disruption of public order by such means as creating fabrications and distorting facts, intentionally spreading rumors, or other means."[4] Two days later, an article appeared on the front page of *Fazhi Ribao* (Legal System Daily), outlining the legal basis of the state's case and listing no fewer than nine laws and regulations that the organization had already broken, effectively criminalizing the group and placing it outside of the bounds of state law.[5]

A second discursive and legal strategy employed in the ban accused the Research Society of Falun Gong, its founder Li Hongzhi, and key personnel with "propagating superstition and fallacies." The term "propagating superstition" recalled the various local-level campaigns to suppress "feudal superstitious activities" pursued in various provinces during the early and mid-1980s. The discursive linking of Falun Gong and related *qigong* groups with such organizations—including secret societies, sworn brotherhoods, and religious sects not recognized by the state—cast a pall that invoked memories of the campaign to suppress counterrevolutionaries of the early 1950s, and of the violent efforts of the ultra-leftist Red Guards to destroy the "Four Olds" during the Cultural Revolution.

With this legal and discursive groundwork in place, the delicate political surgery required to excise *qigong* practitioners from within the Chinese body politic proceeded apace, beginning with a purge of ranking officials. The first page of the 23 July 1999 issue of the *People's Daily* reprinted a circular from the CCP's Central Committee, explicitly forbidding members of the Communist Party of all ranks from practicing Falun Gong; also reprinted was a notice from the Ministry of Personnel forbidding state employees from doing the same. Employing nearly identical language, both documents enjoin party and state officials to "strictly observe policy demarcation lines" and engage in "study and education" activities designed to promulgate the new policies banning the organization and to bring about the conversion of Falun Gong practitioners within their ranks. The timing process by which these changes would be effected was to be "relatively concentrated," involving a round of meetings—"heart-to-heart talks" among party and state officials—to be followed by a round of criticism and self-criticism sessions.

The documents further outlined the delicate political microsurgery that would split targeted party and state officials into four categories. Those who participated in Falun Gong in a general manner were told to expect no repercussions provided they refrain from practicing Falun Gong of their own volition. "Core" members of Falun Gong who played roles of in the sect's organizational structure "of an ordinary nature" were ordered to provide an account of their participation and to publicly denounce the organization, after which they could expect to escape without punishment. "Core" members who participated in the organizational structure and propagandizing activities, on the other hand, were promised only administrative punishments if it were determined that they had made "serious mistakes" in the course of their participation. Finally, the documents noted the existence of a "very small minority of backstage personages who harbor political intentions and the planners and organizers who must be resolutely expelled" from the ranks of officialdom. The latter group would either be purged from the party and have their names stricken from the rolls or be released from government service (in the case of state officials) and subjected to serious punishment. Party and state officials who had participated in Falun Gong activities in the past and were willing to withdraw from the group but "for the time being, are unable to set things straight in their minds ... may be allowed a period of time to recognize matters and effect the ideological transition."[6]

One month later, another published circular outlined the manner in which "policy demarcation lines" would be set for Falun Gong practitioners among the general public. All work units and grassroots organizations were instructed to make the same fourfold distinctions among their members: general Falun Gong participants were expected to cease their participation; "core" members of an "ordinary nature" were instructed to report their activities to their work units or grassroots organizations, and denounce Falun Gong; "core" members who may have committed errors were expected to make a "conscientious confession of their participation" and "actively expose the inside story of the Falun Gong organization" before they could be promised leniency; and a "very small minority of core elements who have organized and plotted behind the scenes" would be charged with crimes and punished accordingly. Like those that preceded it, the circular advocated leniency but warned that those who refused to comply would find themselves designated "objects of political domination" and "struggle targets" by the People's Republic (Xia Ming and Hua Shiping 1999: 52–55).

An editorial published in the *People's Daily* on 27 October 1999, entitled "Falun Gong Is Nothing But a Cult," signaled a crucial turning point in the ban and ushered in a new phase of elevated political exclusion. Whereas the earlier published circulars and notices counseled leniency for the contrite under the rubric of "curing the illness to save the patient," the October editorial painted a far starker portrait of the group and its leader than had previously appeared in the official press. Noting that previous documents from party and state officials had already determined that Falun Gong was an "illegal organization" that had propagated "superstitions" and "fallacies," the new editorial further denounced the group as a "cult" or *xiejiao* (evil and heretical sect).

> [W]hen the fraudulent nature of Li Hongzhi's teachings was fully revealed, Falun Gong organizations fell apart, and the absolute majority of Falun Gong practitioners became determined to make a clear break with their past. However, a handful of practitioners, who were still deluded and entranced by Falun Gong's deceitful doctrines, and who refused to face the appalling facts of the tragedies that belief in it had caused, persisted in allowing themselves to be controlled by Li Hongzhi from afar.... How on earth can Falun Gong exert so strong an evil influence on its followers' minds? Only a cult exhibits such features. (*Renmin Ribao* 1999: 1)

The article listed six characteristics that define cults as a specific type of harmful and illegal organization—a tightly organized, hierarchical structure; a reliance on "mind control"; the fabrication of "heretical ideas to deceive and entrap the people"; participation in money-making schemes; a basic secrecy of association; and practices that endanger social order—and described how Falun Gong manifested each of the six traits. Likening the group to others around the globe, including Jim Jones's People's Temple, the Branch Davidians, and Aum Shinrikyo in Japan, the article placed the ban in a global context by comparing it to measures taken by other governments to suppress cultic activities among their citizens. In conclusion, the "policy demarcation lines" described in earlier articles were transformed into a hardened boundary, with readers being urged to pay "close attention to the applicable scope of relevant policies with a view to uniting the vast majority and isolating the tiny minority of diehards."

> The central government stressed shortly after this campaign started that different policies should be applied to different people so as to unite, educate, and convert the vast majority of practitioners, while at the same time isolating and cracking down on the tiny recusant minority. Those wire-pullers, organizers, and core members of the Falun Gong organization who refuse to mend their ways, follow Li Hongzhi, antagonize the people, and violate the law should be punished severely. The majority of practitioners, who were deceived and victimized due to a lack of knowledge about the heretical nature of Falun Gong have now broken with Falun Gong. Governments at all levels should help ... these people ... rather than confuse them with the diehard cult followers. (*Renmin Ribao* 1999: 1)

The editorial signaled the deepening of the "conflict discourse" against the designated sect, as evidenced by the stereotyping of the out-group's members and the dehumanization and scapegoating of its continuing practitioners. By portraying practitioners as a small group who had abandoned their own families and all semblance of reason so as to "antagonize the people and violate the law," the article attempted to unite the law-abiding people in a "grave, complicated and fierce struggle ... to eradicate the evil forces of Falun Gong" (*Renmin Ribao* 1999: 1).

State-Sanctioned Violence

There are few reliable statistics on the extent of the state-sponsored violence enacted against Falun Gong practitioners, as well as members of other similarly targeted groups on the Chinese mainland. However, one commentary dated 7 September 2003 lauded the success of the government's campaign to eradicate Falun Gong, initiated in July 1999 "by the urgent demands of the broad masses of the people, and carried out in accordance with the law." The commentator noted with satisfaction: "The entire country, from top to bottom, appears to have responded to the evil heretical organization Falun Gong, which scurries through the streets like rats being beaten by masses of screaming people.... We must exterminate the cult, and the evil must be totally eradicated."[7] Recent Amnesty International reports estimate a death toll of over seven hundred practitioners due to torture or ill-treatment at the hands of Chinese authorities (Amnesty International 2003). A Human Rights Watch Asia (2003) report noted that a localized crackdown on the prestigious Qinghua University campus in Beijing—often hailed as China's MIT—resulted in the detention of some three hundred staff and students suspected of being Falun Gong practitioners or sympathizers. In December, a Beijing court sentenced six academics to terms of up to twelve years for distributing Falun Gong materials. Another nineteen Falun Gong members were tried for hacking into television stations in the cities of Chongqing and Changchun to broadcast information about the organization; these individuals received sentences ranging between four and twenty years (Amnesty International 2003).

For its part, Falun Gong has been driven largely underground on the Chinese mainland, but scattered reports suggest that the organization continues to cling to a tenuous existence despite the ban. As overt state-sponsored violence against the sect continues, it is unclear what types of violent measures, if any, the group has been willing to deploy against the state and its agents. The best-known episode authored by alleged Falun Gong practitioners was corroborated by a CNN news crew based in Beijing: the self-immolation of a group of five alleged practitioners in Tiananmen Square on 23 January 2001. Timed to take place on the auspicious first day of the Chinese (lunar) New Year, a group of seven people, including a mother and her twelve-year-old daughter, made their way from the small city of Kaifeng in north-central China to Beijing. Once in the capital, the group appears to have wandered about the city for several hours before turning up in Tiananmen Square late in the evening, carrying soda bottles that were in fact filled with gasoline. One middle-aged man appeared to signal the group, and they took up various physical postures associated with the practice of Falun Gong after dousing themselves with the gasoline and then setting themselves alight. Two would-be members of the group, for whatever reason, were not successful in immolating themselves, but of the five that were, only the mother died at the scene. The other four were surrounded by police officers, who extinguished the fires and transported them to a local hospital for treatment. The twelve-year-old, who was filmed in the hospital and evoked a groundswell of horror and sympathy from the Chinese public, later died of her injuries. Falun Gong sources abroad have expressed skepticism about the incident, claiming that the participants were not in fact practitioners, and have furthermore made available on their Web site a video documentary purporting to show police officers clubbing to death the burning woman who expired on the scene. Falun Gong spokespersons argue that the incident was staged to discredit the group and incite popular support for the crackdown (Vermander 2001: 4–6).

Driven even further underground in the aftermath of the collective self-immolation incident, Falun Gong practitioners resorted to more technologically elaborate means of subverting the state's ban. In the months following Master Li Hongzhi's move to the United States in 1994, the Foreign Liaison Group of the Falun Dafa Research Society gradually shifted the brunt of their organizational work to virtual reality.[8] The movement developed an elaborate Web ring linking together approved Falun Gong sites, some with electronic bulletin boards and e-mail distribution lists, all in an impressive range of languages.

Falun Gong activists abroad have continued highly public forms of political activism, such as engaging in mass protest demonstrations and parades, and lobbying foreign governments for support. Mainland Chinese practitioners, by contrast, have resorted to a highly secretive cell-like structure, and continue to employ Web-based communication strategies. Using untraceable Web-based e-mail accounts accessed in Internet cafés, erecting firewalls that detect signals from computers attempting to identify particular users, and logging on to banned Web sites via proxy servers, some mainland practitioners have apparently managed to elude detection. The most technologically savvy among them use encryption programs and frequently switch Internet accounts, operating systems, hard-disk drives, and telephone lines to conceal their identities while disseminating information and texts to other believers. Several Falun Gong Web sites provide instructions on how to evade official surveillance by using proxy servers to log on in order to view or download banned information. Practitioners still in China continue to use the Internet to upload information on the ongoing crackdown to those abroad.

The initial response of Chinese authorities to Falun Gong's leap into cyberspace was the creation of a ring of anti–Falun Gong Web sites to broadcast the state's official view of the group. However, the effectiveness of this measure was uncertain at best, as it was unclear how many Internet users were actively seeking and visiting sites broadcasting anti–Falun Gong messages. More recently, Chinese officials have focused on controlling and surveilling Internet use. Throughout the 1990s, Ministry of State Security agents routinely visited the offices of Internet service providers to install updated monitoring devices in order to track e-mail and filter access to Web sites. The list of banned sites continues to grow and now even includes some search engines that permit users to view "cached" versions of documents without linking directly to specific sites. For two weeks in September 2002, officials blocked access to the search engine Google, diverting Internet traffic instead to sites providing officially approved content. When access to the search engine was restored, users reported selective blocking that was effected in part through use of "packet sniffers"—devices that are capable of scanning Internet transmissions to block text containing sensitive word combinations. Yahoo's China site escaped blockage when the company agreed, along with some three hundred others, to sign the "Public Pledge on Self-Discipline for the China Internet Industry." The signatories voluntarily remove information from their Web sites that might possibly jeopardize state security, disrupt social stability, or spread superstition (Human Rights Watch Asia 2003).[9] Yet such measures have not put an end to all Falun Gong Web traffic, and Chinese newspapers routinely carry news of individuals arrested and tried for uploading or downloading materials related to the group.

Conclusion: Exclusive Nationalism and Transnational Sectarianism

While many both inside and outside the scholarly community continue to see the modern nation-state as the unfortunate target of divisive and secessionist ethnic and sectarian conflict, I have attempted to demonstrate that episodes of collective violence can also arise directly from the larger state-making process. The forces of exclusive nationalism, by which state authorities define specific strata of subject populations as legitimate targets for coercion and control, can and do create racial and ethnic tensions that are used to divide and regulate the societies over which they preside. Anthony Marx (1998) demonstrated this process in his comparative study of the racial and ethnic categories used in the United States, South Africa, and Brazil. Gyan Pandey (1992) and Partha Chatterjee (1993) have both persuasively argued that the British colonial regime in India generated ethnic- and caste-based communalist discourses that were later used to legitimate exclusionary policies that supported elitist development.

Sectarian divides, too, can be created by state elites and then wielded by them for a wide variety of ends. Ussama Makdisi's (1996) study of postwar Lebanon has shown that "[w]hile the nation is projected as inclusive, stable and democratic, sectarianism is depicted as exclusionary, undemocratic and disordered.... 'Sectarianism,' however, is a neologism born in the age of nationalism to signify the antithesis of nation; its meaning is predicated on and constructed against a territorially bounded liberal nation-state.... In the modern reconstructed nation, sectarianism serves as a metaphor for the unwanted past."

As the case of Falun Gong demonstrates, a similar process involving exclusive nationalism and the invention of sectarianism is at work today in China.

Collective sectarian identities associated with specific *qigong* practices did not exist as such until the reform-era state created them. Legal and discursive strategies were used to create "sects" and then to transform them into dangerous antistate "cults" in 1999. At the heart of the mass campaign to eradicate "evil and heretical sects" was a state-sponsored and state-generated effort to delineate members of a target group and reposition them with respect to the political center: not as one with the people, on whose behalf the state claims to act, but instead as an in-dwelling group targeted for control, violence, and abuse, and as legitimate objects of political struggle. In so doing, central officials sought to bolster the state's image, not only as the legitimate representative of the collective interests and will of the people, but also as the repository for modern scientific rationalism in the face of resurgent "feudal superstitions" and "pseudo-scientific fallacies." The violence that has since ensued, overwhelmingly originated by the agents of the state, has sought out practitioners and their sympathizers as its primary targets.

This violence and repression have produced a unique hybrid form of politico-religious mobilization that I have referred to here and elsewhere as cybersectarianism. Targeted groups like Falun Gong use extensive Web-based strategies of text distribution, recruitment, and information sharing to fashion transnational media campaigns with the goal of maintaining pressure on the Chinese state. Partially funded by overseas Chinese communities in nations where they operate more openly, some groups have pooled resources to lobby international authorities for support. One result of this dynamic has been the creation of small groups of practitioners who remain highly dispersed and largely anonymous within the larger social context and who operate in relative secrecy while still linked remotely to a larger global network. Overseas supporters provide funding, while domestic practitioners distribute tracts, participate in acts of resistance, and share information on the internal situation with outsiders. In the case of Falun Gong, a reliance on the Internet and other high-tech resources has created a viable virtual community that transcends political borders, allowing members to engage in collective study via e-mail and to use online chat rooms and Web-based message boards to pursue their collective spiritual goals. However, some cybersects, including Aum Shinrikyo in Japan and the apparently wide-ranging al Qaeda, do engage in what some refer to as "repertoires of electronic contention," using Web sites and e-mail to mobilize participants for protest and contention, as well as "hactivism" (acts of electronic disruption) and even cyber-terrorism (acts of physical harm caused by the disruption of power grids, traffic control, and other systems of resource delivery and public safety) (Costanza-Chock 2003).

This is not to suggest that the Internet has ushered in a brave new epoch of organizational freedom across the globe, or that the advent of the information era spells the beginning of the end of traditionally repressive state structures. Ronald Reagan's 1989 prediction that "the Goliath of totalitarianism will be brought down by the David of the microchip" has certainly not come to pass, and the Web has done little, as of yet, to measurably weaken authoritarianism—in China or elsewhere (Kalathil and Boas 2003). Yet what the case of Falun Gong and other cybersects suggests instead is that new technologies have provided new opportunities, both for state authorities who seek enhanced control over their subject populations and for those who seek to subvert them.

Notes

1. Numerous accounts of the protest appeared in the foreign press. In addition to Agence France-Press (1999), see Deutsche Presse-Agentur, "China Cabinet Says Cult Protest Resolved through Persuasion," 26 April 1999; Anthony Kuhn, Maggie Farley, and Henry Chu, *Los Angeles Times*, "10,000 Protest in Beijing: Members Demand Government Officially Recognize Sect," 26 April 1999, A8; and Deutsche Presse-Agentur, "Religious Group Protests in Chinese Capital," 25 April 1999.
2. See "Falun Dafa and the Internet: A Marriage Made in Web Heaven," *Virtual China*, 30 July 1999 (http://www.virtual-china.org/archive/infotech/perspectives/perspective-073099.html, accessed March 23, 2003).
3. A classic work in the field in this vein is Gellner (1994). Widely read studies on the concept of citizenship, including those by T. H. Marshall (1991) and Reinhard Bendix (1964), agree that citizenship rights may be allocated preferentially to certain individuals or groups, and that the extension of universal citizenship may experience various delays and lags, but that the trend toward universal inclusion is the norm, and permanent and deliberate exclusion the exception to the rule.
4. Both documents were published in *Renmin Ribao* (People's Daily), overseas edition, 23 July 1999, 1.
5. "Qudi 'Falun Gong' you fa keyi" (The Ban on "Falun Gong" Has Legal Basis), *Fazhi Ribao* (Legal System Daily), 25 July 1999, 1. However, as one recent article propounded, the state's deployment of law in its crackdown "is rooted in its historical preference for an 'instrumentalist' approach to law and social control ... and the regime's response ... has adversely affected internal debates concerning the importance of judicial independence and the substitution of judicial interpretation for legislative responsibility in the justice system" (Keith and Lin 2003: 627).
6. The CCP circular appears on the first page and the Ministry of Personnel notice on the third page of *Renmin Ribao* (People's Daily), overseas edition, 23 July 1999.
7. Xinhuashe (New China News Agency), "Qudi 'Falun Gong' Sinian Shuping" (A Commentary on the Four-Year Ban against Falun Gong), 7 September 2003 (accessed at http://big5.xinhuanet.com).
8. Foreign Liaison Group of the Falun Dafa Research Society, "Falun Dafa's Transmission of Internet Notice," 15 June 1997 (accessed at http://www.falundafa.org/fldfbb/gonggao970615.htm).
9. In 2006, as this essay goes to press, Google, Yahoo, and other Internet-based firms are being roundly criticized for their willingness to cooperate with Chinese censors.

References

Abrams, Philip. 1988. "Notes on the Difficulty of Studying the State." *Journal of Historical Sociology* 1, no. 1: 76–77.

Agence France-Press. 1999. "Largest Demonstration Since Tiananmen in Beijing." 27 April.

Amnesty International. 2000. "People's Republic of China: The Crackdown on Falungong and Other So-Called 'Heretical Organizations.'" (ASA 17/11/00), 23 March.

_____. 2003. "People's Republic of China: Continuing Abuses under a New Leadership—Summary of Human Rights Concerns." (ASA 17/035/2003), October.

Bendix, Reinhard. 1964. *Nation-Building and Citizenship*. Berkeley: University of California Press.

Berman, Bruce J. 1998. "Ethnicity, Patronage, and the African State: The Politics of Uncivil Nationalism." *African Affairs* 97, no. 388: 305–336.

Bowman, Glenn. 2001. "The Violence in Identity." In *Anthropology of Violence and Conflict*, ed. Bettina E. Schmidt and Ingo W. Schröder, 25–46. New York: Routledge.

Chatterjee, Partha. 1993. *The Nation and Its Fragments: Colonial and Postcolonial Histories*. Princeton: Princeton University Press.

Costanza-Chock, Sasha. 2003. "Mapping the Repertoire of Electronic Contention." In *Representing Resistance: Media, Civil Disobedience and the Global Justice Movement*, ed. Andrew Opel and Donnalyn Pompper, 173–191. New York: Greenwood.

Gellner, Ernest. 1994. *Encounters with Nationalism*. Oxford: Blackwell.

Hobsbawm, Eric. 1983. "Introduction: Inventing Tradition." In *The Invention of Tradition*, ed. Eric Hobsbawm and Terence Ranger, 1–14. Cambridge: Cambridge University Press.

Human Rights Watch Asia. 2003. "China and Tibet." In *Human Rights Watch World Report 2003: Events of 2002: November 2001–November 2002*, 216–229. New York: Human Rights Watch.

Kalathil, Shanthi, and Taylor C. Boas. 2003. *Open Networks, Closed Regimes: The Impact of the Internet on Authoritarian Rule*. Washington, DC: Carnegie Endowment for International Peace.

Keith, Ronald C., and Zhiqiu Lin. 2003. "The 'Falun Gong Problem': Politics and the Struggle for the Rule of Law in China." *China Quarterly* 175: 623–642.

Li Da. 1990. "Zhonggong qingli 'qigong dang'" [Party Central Purges 'Qigong Party']. *Dangdai shishi zhoukan* [The Current Age Weekly], 25 August, 14–15.

Makdisi, Ussama. 1996. "The Modernity of Sectarianism in Lebanon." *Middle East Report* 200 (Summer): 23–26.

Mao Zedong. 1950. "Chairman Mao's Closing Speech" [abridged text]. *People's China* 2, no. 1: 25.

Marshall, T. H. 1991. *Citizenship and Social Class*. London: Pluto.

Marx, Anthony W. 1998. *Making Race and Nation: A Comparison of South Africa, the United States and Brazil*. Cambridge: Cambridge University Press.

_____. 2002. "The Nation-State and Its Exclusions." *Political Science Quarterly* 117: 103–126.

Munro, Robin J. 2000. "Judicial Psychiatry in China and Its Political Abuses." *Columbia Journal of Asian Law* 14, no. 1: 6–8.

O'Neill, Mark, and Willy Wo-Lap Lam. 1999. "Mainland Outlaws Falun Gong." *China Morning Post*, 23 July.

Pandey, Gyan. 1992. *The Construction of Communalism in Colonial North India*. Delhi and London: Oxford University Press.

Renmin Ribao [People's Daily]. 1999. "Falun Gong jiushi xiejiao" [Falun Gong Is Nothing But a Cult], 28 October, 1.

Schoenhals, Michael. 1994. "'Non-People' in the People's Republic of China: A Chronicle of Terminological Ambiguity." Indiana University Working Paper Series on Language and Politics in Modern China, No. 4, Summer 1994.

Scott, James C. 1998. *Seeing Like a State: How Certain Schemes to Improve the Human Condition Have Failed.* New Haven, CT, and London: Yale University Press.

Suny, Grigor. 2001. "Constructing Primordialism: Old Histories for New Nations." *Journal of Modern History* 73: 862–896.

Thornton, Patricia M. 2003. "The New Cybersects: Resistance and Repression in the Reform Era." In *Chinese Society: Change, Conflict and Resistance,* 2nd ed., Elizabeth Perry and Mark Selden, 247–270. London and New York: Routledge.

Tilly, Charles, ed. 1975. *The Formation of National States in Western Europe.* Princeton, NJ: Princeton University Press.

_____. 1985. "War Making and State Making as Organized Crime." In *Bringing the State Back In,* ed. Peter B. Evans, Dietrich Rueschmeyer, and Theda Skocpol, 169–191. Cambridge: Cambridge University Press.

_____. 1990. *Coercion, Capital and European States, AD 990–1992.* Cambridge, MA: Blackwell.

Vermander, Benoit. 2001. "Looking at China Through the Mirror of Falun Gong." *China Perspectives* 35 (May–June): 4–13.

Wang Cheng-chih. 2002. *Words Kill: Calling for the Destruction of "Class Enemies" in China, 1949–1953.* London: Routledge.

Weber, Max. 1978. *Economy and Society.* Vol. 1. Ed. Guenther Roth and Clause Wittich. Berkeley and Los Angeles: University of California Press.

Xia Ming and Hua Shiping. 1999. "The Falun Gong: *Qigong,* Code of Ethics and Religion." *Chinese Law and Government* 32, no. 6 (November–December).

ISLAM AND THE WEST
A Perspective from Pakistan

Mohammad Waseem

Since 11 September 2001, a lot has been written on the emerging relationship between Islam and the West, represented respectively by Muslim states and nonstate actors and the capitals of the Atlantic community. Intellectual debate first framed this relationship in terms of terrorism and then, increasingly, in the context of a war against terrorism led by the United States.

As is well known, the US reacted to the events of 9/11 by seeking to destroy the infrastructure of terrorism. The global consensus that supported the initial stages of the US response quickly disintegrated into a controversy that continues to split Western societies and Muslim communities. In the West, opinion polls and media reports indicated growing opposition to the "war on terror," a trend that seemed to begin among the citizens of France and Germany and was given voice by those nations' governments. Muslims worldwide felt progressively alienated as the fighting moved beyond Afghanistan in 2001 to Iraq in 2003 and as US policy, which at first seemed a pragmatic response to an act of terrorism by a nonstate actor, seemed to shift to an intellectual onslaught against Islam.

Pakistan has acted at the heart of the controversy in contradictory ways. It cooperated for years with the Taliban, drawing criticism from the diplomatic community, which held it partly responsible by association for its northwestern neighbor's human rights violations and terrorist activities. Yet when the war against Afghanistan's rulers began in 2001, the Pakistani government enlisted as an ally of the US. More than geopolitical opportunism prompted this change in policy. As we will see, in Pakistan sectarian division co-exists

References for this chapter are located on page 204.

with institutions that could resolve or defuse it. Those institutions have gained strength in the first half-decade of the new century.

The present study outlines the evolving pattern of relationship between Islam and the West.[1] It focuses on Pakistan for the following analytical purposes:

- Pakistan is strategically located at the meeting point of three regions: South Asia, the Middle East, and Central Asia. It has displayed several characteristics respectively ascribed to these geographical and cultural zones, such as a political system emergent from the British imperial tradition; an overriding commitment to Muslim destiny tugged at by the vortex of the continuing Arab-Israeli conflict; and spillovers of the conflicts in and beyond Afghanistan.

- Pakistan, as a legatee of British imperialism, is potentially one of the most democratic countries in the Muslim world. While Turkey and Malaysia have enjoyed longer periods of formal rule by public representatives, Pakistan displays a sustained constitutional tradition derived from the Westminster model, a detailed schema of electoral politics, and British Common Law as a source of legitimacy for the rule of law. Constitution-alism has bounced back after each stint of military rule.

- Pakistan is a model of monumental and momentous change in policy. Its conversion from a supporter of Taliban in the late 1990s to an ally in the US war against terrorism in 2001 demonstrates that strategic, diplomatic, and economic incentives can prompt the transformation of regional commitments in favor of a global agenda.

- Pakistan is a laboratory for emerging relations between Islamism and the state. For example, following the October 2002 elections, Muttahida Majlis Amal (MMA), a proto-Taliban group of political parties, ruled two provinces, the North Western Frontier Province (NWFP) and Balu-chistan. After the elections, the pro-US Musharraf government engaged in constitutional negotiations with the professedly anti-US MMA to the exclusion of mainstream liberal and modernist forces for more than a year. This points to a major theme of this chapter: the modern state elite has often felt obliged to Islamize the polity. Whenever constitutional sources of legitimacy rooted in the mass mandate have posed a challenge to its predominant position in the constellation of powers ruling Paki-stan, the elite has chosen to tap divine sources of legitimacy, strengthen-ing the Islamic establishment by default.

Sponsored, crystallized, and projected by interlocutors claiming allegiance to either side, a dichotomous worldview depicting Islam and the West as adversaries plays a key role in the political idiom of Pakistan and other Mus-lim countries as well as in the West. To explain policies pursued in Washington and Islamabad, we must understand and contrast two opposing stereotypes: the multiple frames of reference that underpin Western statements on Islam, and the collective visions through which Muslims see themselves.

Western Statements on Islam

Analyses currently popular in the West consider Islam problematic per se, akin to fascism, promoting violence and antimodernism—in sum, the antithesis of Western rationality (Pipes 1983; Schwartz 2003). Islam is considered deficient in human rights (Mayer 1998), democracy (Halpern 1963), modernity (Lewis 1976), and tolerance, especially in its Wahhabist incarnation (Fuller 2003). What are perceived to be Islamic values and norms vis-à-vis women, music, art, and sculpture contribute to the religion's peculiar profile. However, the alarm with which Western media and academia characterize contemporary Islamic movements has another source: dashed optimism, the result of a complacent belief that the end of the Cold War would lead forthwith to a peaceful new world order and the "end of history" (Fukuyama 1989). After the first Gulf War in 1991 and ethnic cleansing and civil war in Yugoslavia, the West came to expect that future wars would be fought across identity-based fault lines. This concern expressed itself in a paradigm of the clash of civilizations (Huntington 1996), a theory that is fast becoming a self-fulfilling prophecy.

In this context, we can outline four major patterns in Western scholarship on Islam that distort understanding and promote stereotyping: a discourse of difference, a focus on text rather than context, the conflation of religion and politics, and the assertion that Islam is a primordial force.

Discourse of Difference

A Western intellectual tradition derived from neoclassical Orientalism essentializes Islam. It reifies stereotypes of the religion and disregards the living reality of Muslim practices, both sacred and mundane. Threads of meaning and truth are lost in the scholarly pursuit of sophistication and style and in attempts to epitomize Islam and its symbols. For example, Islam is described as monotheism with a tribal face, and Muslim countries are characterized by the opposition of strong societal networks to weak state systems (Gellner 1992).

The transcultural dynamics of the discourse of difference have helped define two essentialisms—"the West" and "Islam," each of which operates as a cognitive modality for identity formation. The paradigm suggests two opposing cultural universes. The West is characterized by rationality, civil society, and development, while Muslim societies are the realm of subjectivity, terrorism, and stasis.

There are both epistemological and empirical problems with this dichotomous model. Epistemologically, one can argue that by imagining a generic Islam as the "other," the West reimagines itself as distinct and distant from that other (Turner 1997). That distance reflects, generally, the lack of potential for intersubjectivity in an era of unequal relationships largely shaped by the colonial encounter. For centuries, the West has defined its own civility as the antithesis of Oriental despotism. For this reason, an understanding of Islam has been crucial for Western self-perception.

On the other hand, empirically speaking, it is the West that has critically shaped the Islamic east as well as the rest of the non-Western world during the last three hundred years. European conquest, trade, and cultural exchange transplanted ideas, norms, and institutions, bringing about revolutionary changes in the way Muslims lived their social, economic, and political lives. Muslim societies, directly ruled or indirectly influenced by Western powers, internalized a variety of attitudinal and institutional patterns, such as territorial nationalism, individual property rights, the rule of law, the juridical equality of citizens, the dynamics of capitalism, rational-legal bureaucracy, tutelary democracy, constitutionalism, federalism, parliamentarism, popular sovereignty, international law, international organization, and, in the last century, international regimes governing the environment, nuclear nonproliferation, human rights, child labor, drug trafficking, and many other nontraditional aspects of security. The Westernization of Asia over the last three centuries can be considered the most comprehensive intercivilizational borrowing known to history (Darling 1979). With so much in common, it can be argued that there is only a difference of degree, not kind, between the West and Islam. That is to say, at the heart of the problem lies the dichotomy between the West on the one hand and a politically, socially, culturally, and economically Westernized Islam on the other.

Text Rather Than Context

The essentialization of Islam in Western thought depends crucially on the selective reading of classical Islamic texts. Text, rather than context and scriptural literature, and its contrived meaning, rather than the social experience and its cultural projection in the contemporary Muslim world, shape influential Western statements on Islam. This practice has its roots in the medieval construction of inwardness carried out by Western Christianity and Islam alike. Each sought to exclude the rival faith from a universal consensus. European scholars collected and selected "original" sources to support their analyses, and because they influenced the societies that came to dominate the world, their interpretation shaped the idiom of transcultural understanding. As Oriental philology grew, it became a differentiating enterprise, a conversion belt that transformed early Islamic texts into well-constructed idea systems for consumption in Western universities and libraries (Said 1978). Today, much of the post-Christian West still sees the contemporary Muslim world through the prism of what can be figuratively called pre-Reformation Islam.

Emancipation from the hermeneutics of the text has been a principle of religious studies in the West for more than a century. Scholars who accept this challenge attempt to understand the inner realm of faith through the values and norms expressed in ritual and in everyday life (Salvatore 1997). A flurry of post-9/11 research on Islam abandoned this approach. It focused instead on Qur'anic teachings and on the jihadist literature of contemporary Islamic movements. Its findings provide a text-based profile of an undisciplined, medievalist, and irrational force, inherently disruptive to modern civilization. This shift to logocentric interpretation is justified by the argument that Islam is a different kind of religion and by the fact that Islamic scholars themselves attach a deterministic value to the Qur'anic text. However, asserting Islam's uniqueness begs the question. Using ahistorical textual analysis to explain the basic nature of a present-day Muslim society is problematic and misleading. If one wishes to sketch the role of Islam in today's world, one should examine instead the contemporary social and cultural context, shaped as it is by values and practices both traditional and modern.

Conflating Religion and Politics

A third pervasive trend in Western scholarship holds that Islamic civilization fuses religion and politics. This is a manifestation of an overly intellectual attitude toward Islam that mistakes values for facts, norms for practices, and vision for reality. In part, this approach can be traced back to the ideas of classical Muslim thinkers under the Umayyad and Abbasid dynasties—to political philosophers who viewed the state as a mechanism through which the rule of Islamic law could be established. However, one is obliged to read Islamic history upside down to find actual conflation between religion and politics. There are present-day Islamic movements in several Muslim countries, including Pakistan, that were seldom if ever governed by or through Muslim clerics in the premodern age. Separation of church and state, always alien to the political doctrine of Islam, has been the practice in most Islamic societies for the greater part of the last fifteen hundred years.

Resembling somewhat the duality of Caesar (or the Holy Roman Emperor or a king by divine right) and the pope, the caliph-sultan duo typifies the dynamics of power in Islamic history. Rulers in Muslim countries throughout history have sought ideational sanctions from the Islamic establishment. In the last several decades, ruling elites have appealed more and more often for the support of the clergy in their struggles to retain power in the face of grave challenges rooted in populist politics.

Primordialism

The roots of radical Islam, Orientalists argue, lie in the faith itself rather than in Muslims' complex relations with the non-Islamic world. In this view, Islamic militancy is a self-propelling mechanism, primordial loyalties and identities are determining variables in the realm of politics, and the innate mobilizing strength of God's word is emphasized. Pakistan's history and politics point in a different direction (Malik 1996). In the Pakistani context, Islamic ideology seems more a tool of persuasion than a set of primordial beliefs—a social construct sponsored by certain elite groups in pursuit of their political agenda

(Brass 1991). Islamism here as elsewhere is rooted in modernism inasmuch as it serves as an instrument of policy. It has been used to thwart the ascendancy of democratic forces in the context of civil-military crises (in Pakistan), to create and sustain a resistance movement against occupiers (in Afghanistan in the 1980s and in Palestine since the 1970s), and to provide legitimacy to dictatorial and monarchical regimes (for example, in Saudi Arabia).

The analytical distinction between Western modernity and Islamic tradition is unsustainable in the political context of Pakistan. Instead, Islamic ideology serves Pakistan's modern elite as an instrument of policy at the national and international levels.

Muslim Collective Visions

Pakistan has been a crossroads for Islamic thought for at least the last 150 years, both as a successor of Muslim India in colonial times and as an independent country after 1947. This means we can trace the origins and patterns of development of the three major contemporary Muslim worldviews in successive phases of modern Pakistani history. The first phase covers the pre-independence period (the late nineteenth to mid-twentieth centuries), while the second and third phases correspond to the two generations who came to adulthood after independence.

Neoclassical Reformism

From the late nineteenth to mid-twentieth century, three generations of Muslim scholars responded to and adapted the discourse of modernity that accompanied Western political, economic, and cultural domination over the world. The neoclassical reformers of the first generation—Afghani, Abduh, and Rida in the Arab world; the Jadidis in Turkish-speaking Asia; Sir Syed, Amir Ali, and Iqbal in the Indian environment; and many others—indulged in brooding over the destiny of Muslims. These writers and teachers, largely deconflationists, focused on the need for modernizing institutions and thought patterns along Western lines. In the models of modernity that they developed, encompassing major fields of social, economic, and cultural activity, society was central—more so than the mosque or the state—and, for the most part, religion and politics played separable roles.

A dominant part of the state elite in the contemporary Muslim world still thinks in these terms. Archly pragmatic in its approach to the contemporary world and often holding the political initiative, it advocates pan-Islamic models of Muslim unity through such initiatives as the Organization of Islamic Countries (OIC) and seeks to mediate between tradition and modernity at home and Islam and the West abroad. In Pakistan, leaders in this mold (Jinnah in the

1940s, Ayub in the 1960s, Zulfikar Ali Bhutto in the 1970s, and Musharraf since 1999) have been protagonists of "enlightened moderation" in Islamic politics since the nation's founding.

Islamic Legalism

Pakistan's Islamic intelligentsia focused on the state as a means to its ends in the second half of the twentieth century—the postwar and early postcolonial period. It called on the state to establish the rule of *Shariat* (religious law), to lead the country down a path of moral and material development, and to enhance national security against perceived challenges from atheist communism on the one hand and godless capitalism on the other. Modoodi in Pakistan, like Syed Qutab in Egypt, was a state-based Islamic nationalist within the framework of pan-Islamism. These were conflationists par excellence. Their domestic politics had two goals: to make Islam the country's most potent source of political legitimacy (a nonrevolutionary strategy to capture state power) and to develop alternative Islamic legal codes. Abroad, their ideas contributed to the emergence of a dichotomous worldview, the "world of Islam," which envisions a smaller world that is home to believers and exists within the larger world.

Since World War II, largely inspired by "Islamic causes," Muslim societies throughout the Middle East, South Asia, and Southeast Asia have increasingly thought of themselves as separate from the non-Muslim world. The grand shaper of this worldview has been the Palestinian issue, which has kept alive a sense of us-versus-them for more than half a century. Events in Kashmir, Afghanistan, Bosnia, Chechnya, Kosovo, and Iraq have at various times inspired similar support, leading Muslims to perceive themselves as underdogs in the larger world.

Radical Islam

In Pakistan, the decade that began with the 1947 partition of India and ended with the 1956 Suez Crisis witnessed the transition from neoclassical reformism to Islamic legalism (described by contemporary writers on Islam as "essentialism" or "fundamentalism") under the leadership of Modoodi and his party Jamat Islami. A third wave of Islamists emerged in the decade from the 1979 Iranian revolution to the 1991 Gulf War, as a generation of populists, activists, revolutionaries, and militants came to dominate the streets, bazaars, and *madrasah*s. Many of their names are well known: Khomeini in Iran, Osama bin Laden and Mullah Omar in Afghanistan, Sheikh Omar Abdel-Rahman in the United States. In Pakistan, the influence of the third wave was felt within certain local sectarian groups, such as Sipah Sahaba, Lashkar Jhangvi, and Sipah Mohammad, and within the Islamic parties that provided support for the anti-Soviet resistance in Afghanistan, such as Jamat Islami and the two factions of Jamiat Ulema Islam.

The radical Islamists, like the legalists, saw the world in terms of Islamic causes. For example, Palestine's fate provoked anti-Zionist and anti-American feelings in both generations. The decade-long US-sponsored war against the Soviet Union's Red Army in Afghanistan created a sense of pride in and among the *mujahideen* fighters, developed their technological capabilities, and led to the establishment of transnational Islamic networks, which provided recruits and logistical support. The previous generation had come out of the world of learning (many of its members were based in colleges and universities) and influenced events through publications or by accepting positions in government. The third wave, by contrast, communicated through sermons in the mosques and through word on the street, making both the written and oral traditions their own.

Upon the demise of the USSR, the transition from bipolar to unipolar superpower politics helped this new generation of Islamists shed its confusion and further crystallize its dichotomous worldview. As if to confirm it, since 1989, gulfs have widened between Islamic nations and the West, between state and society within the Muslim world, and between Western societies and the Muslim minorities who live within them. Pakistan typifies these aspects of the growing tension within and between Islam and the West.

Western scholars tend to argue that the roots of Islamic terrorism lie within the Muslim world, and that core of the problem is Islam-in-movement, exacerbated by the faith-based agenda that dominates public policy in Muslim countries. Muslim thinkers, by contrast, for the most part locate the roots of radicalism outside the Muslim world in the domain of its relations with the West. Islam is under siege, they believe, and Western policies have caused the gross alienation of Muslim societies from their governments and from the ideas and nations of the West (Samad forthcoming). Each of these prevailing interpretations suggests that the two sides are moving informally, grudgingly, and openly toward a clash of civilizations.

Pakistan as a Complex, Westernizing Muslim Society

The discussion thus far has introduced several contradictory, often narrow, and sometimes false-to-fact assumptions with which Western scholarship has tended to frame the subject of contemporary Islam and with which Muslim thinkers have attempted to explain the West. A common, mistaken premise of these opposed yet similar conventional wisdoms is that Islam and the West have little in common. With this in mind, the second half of this essay explores the interplay of Islamic and European institutions and ideals in Pakistan.

An effort will be required to overcome the problem of intersubjectivity and to see Pakistani society in its own terms rather than simply as an Islamic cause, an American ally, or a battleground. In a polarized conflict we tend to define ourselves in contradistinction to our enemies, oversimplifying both who we are and who they are. For example, current debates in both the West and the Muslim world equate religion and tradition in Islamic countries. This is grossly misleading. Religion is only one component of social and cultural life. Other social forces are at work in Pakistan, including tribal, ethnic, and clan exchange networks that operate as security mechanisms at the local level. The structural and operational dynamics of a Muslim society are better understood in terms of the patterns of growth of a variety of citizen orientations in comparison with other societies, including Western ones.

There is considerable variation among Muslim societies, ranging from Turkey and Pakistan to Somalia, Sudan, and Yemen. However, I believe it is possible to construct a typology of a Muslim society that is heuristically useful. The simple framework presented here to summarize the competing identities within Pakistan might be applied to other Islamic countries.

The social fabric in Pakistan is knit together largely by an intricate network of patron-client relations driven by community-oriented values and norms. Major anthropological studies of exchange networks within Indian society, and their subsequent development in Pakistan, demonstrate that local life is dominated by the politics of patronage (Alavi 1973; Bailey 1970; Srinivas 1967). The network shapes the nature of culture, codes of ethics, customary law, factional groupings, electoral alliances, and patterns of adversarial politics, all of which are subsumed by politics at the provincial and national level. The complex attitudes exhibited in the country's elections can be described in terms of four idealized voters, each with a different relationship to patronage networks: clients, those who are economically dependent on a landlord-politician who controls their votes; mavericks, those who vote for the candidate who provides the best patronage either for themselves or for their communities; civic voters, those who hold a partisan opinion on issues and may identify with a political party; and primary voters, those whose vote reflects their ethnic or sectarian identity. Most voters exhibit a combination of these attitudes and allegiances (Waseem 1994). The importance of patronage networks in politics is one force behind an informal but widely accepted division between religion and state on the ground. This belies the assertions of the *ulema*, of conservative intellectuals in Pakistan, and of Western scholars that religion and politics are one and the same in Islamic countries.

Because of the history of its founding and the institutions it inherited from Britain, Pakistan stands out as one of the Muslim world's most serious candidates for democracy. A persistent crisis in civil-military relations has hindered fulfillment of this promise. The army, forced to choose between two rival sources of legitimacy—Islam and the mass mandate—has repeatedly chosen Islam. One can argue that the phenomenon of political Islam emerged in Pakistan when the governing elite, led by military leaders, chose to close the doors on the masses under generals Yahya in 1969–1971, Ziaul Haq in 1977–1988, and Musharraf since 1999. As a result, after the 2002 elections, Pakistan was caught in an anomalous situation: a modernizing, pro-US, forward-looking army leadership had aligned itself with an ortho-dox, anti-US, essentialist Islamic establishment in order to keep mainstream democratic forces at bay.

Public Policy: Issues and Recommendations

If this picture of Pakistan as a model Islamic country holds true, what public policies seem likeliest to promote democratic rule, to bind the society together so that sectarian violence is less likely, and to preserve and deepen respect for a pluralistic public sphere? We have questioned several ideas, deeply held by both Western scholars and Muslim intellectuals, about what it means for Paki-stan to be an Islamic country. It has been argued that there is distance—not difference—between Islam and the West, that social context rather than clas-sical texts best explain Islamic militancy, and that democratic politicians in Muslim countries typically do not conflate religion and politics. In Pakistan, a modernizing ruling elite—composed of the army and its civilian partners in the bureaucracy, the judiciary, and the business community—engages, mobi-lizes, promotes, co-opts, and strengthens the religious establishment to the detriment of liberal forces. Palestine and other epic Islamic causes—"unre-solved conflicts" in which Muslims seem to fight forever without a final victory or defeat—inspire radicalism, not the body of ideas represented by the faith.

We have outlined how Muslims' collective vision for the future in South Asia as elsewhere shifted from a relatively open-ended agenda of modern-ization with the West as its model in the late nineteenth and early twentieth centuries to a state-centered Islamic legalism that held sway for three decades, and shifted again to a populist anti-Western upsurge transcending national boundaries at the turn of the twenty-first century. This seemed to suggest the validity of the grim scenario of a clash of civilizations between Islam and the West—a confrontation that has the potential to destabilize the international system. This phenomenon is often defined by either side as a religious conflict, and solutions to it are sought through interfaith dialogue.

When the actual dynamics of Pakistan and Muslim societies are under-stood, it becomes clear that this is not, at its roots, an international religious war. Instead, it is a political conflict within Muslim countries as well as between these countries and the West. What is required, within Muslim societies and in the West, is not a policy on Islam but rather a policy on the politics of Muslim countries addressing their domestic and regional issues.

The "politics of Islam" varies with social, economic, and political conditions within and outside a Muslim country, making any attempt to choose among progressive, liberal, and conservative Islam a short-lived and futile exercise in patronage. The effort to co-opt certain Islamic groups on the basis of the ends they seek today leads to further empowerment of the religious establishment and helps keep the politics of a Muslim country such as Pakistan unstable and unpredictable. On the basis of these observations, we suggest the following policy measures in the context of Pakistan.

The Central Role of Civil Society

First, it is necessary to dampen the political volatility that causes Pakistanis to perceive the actions of their government as unpredictable. For that purpose, we need to go beyond the state with its predominant control function to the society at large. Pakistan functions as an "hourglass society," for which the prototypical case is Russia (Rose 1995). In such a society, authority flows one way, from top to bottom, with no significant institutional input from below.

This authoritarian arrangement emerged despite the efforts of the classical reformers, who provided the new country with a democratic political framework in the years leading up to independence and authored subsequent liberal constitutional reforms. The ruling elite provides government funding to Islamic institutions, especially *madrasah*s (religious schools), while professional associations, trade unions, nongovernmental women's organizations, chambers of commerce and industry, student organizations, and human rights organizations must fend for themselves. State bias in favor of Muslim institutions and the emergence of transnational Islamic networks has altered the shape of civil society in Pakistan. NGOs financed by the international donor community could help restore balance, but they focus for the most part on vulnerable groups and impoverished regions, not on what should be central institutions.

Civil society must expand from the margins of Pakistani politics to take its place in the main stream. Local nongovernmental organizations need leverage to overcome the essentialism that dominates certain areas of public policy in Pakistan and to wean the government away from its reliance on the influence of radical Islam. One way the organs of civil society can strengthen themselves is by establishing links with their counterparts in the US and other Western countries. Active support from the latter can help create a vibrant, internationalized civil society in Pakistan with the potential to counter religious radicalism and terrorism.

The prerequisites for a dynamic civil society are the rule of law, representative government, and guarantees of civil liberty and political freedom for all citizens. Unfortunately, the United States' on-again, off-again support of Pakistani Islamic groups and its more or less stable alliance with the country's army have been detrimental to the cause of democracy. Recently, some Western leaders have repudiated this policy. The more consistently Western foreign policy toward Pakistan and other Muslim countries supports democratic institutions rather than actors who subvert those institutions, the more likely it is to foster the establishment or re-establishment of balanced civil societies within which Islamic radicalism is likely to be a minority voice rather than a dominant political orientation.

Revitalizing the Public Sector

The liberal democratic political paradigm, based on private enterprise, limited government, and open competition, has limited applicability to Pakistan and other Muslim countries. In Pakistan, as in many postcolonial societies, a relatively overdeveloped state exercises near monopolistic control over much of the economy and sets limits on political debate. The state is the largest employer, the best guarantor of life and property, and the most potent link with the outside world. Its power limits the scope of private initiatives, which seldom succeed and are often frustrated, discredited, and, in the end, scuttled.

Before private efforts to improve the daily life of Pakistanis can hope to succeed, the public sector must be revitalized. Two cases in point are the education and health care systems.

Education. The vast network of public-sector schools has been neglected and allowed to deteriorate. The middle class is now obliged to enroll its children in expensive private-sector school systems, increasing the economic and social tensions that promote corruption and elitism. Low-income families are constrained to send their children to the *madrasahs*, which provide free boarding and lodging. There have been misplaced attempts to "reform" the *madrasahs* by supplying them with better textbooks and physical infrastructure in exchange for prospects of reduced militancy. This is Alice in Wonderland. Essentialist goals and modern technological and financial means represent a confusing mixture of vision and style. Instead, the government school system must be reinvigorated. Its funding must be restored, and it should be encouraged to establish institutional connections with school systems in other countries. As improvements in government schools are publicized, attracting students back from both the private academies and the *madrasahs*, the state bureaucracy's vigilance over education can reassert itself, protecting children from radical indoctrination.

Health Care. Government hospitals are becoming less efficient and less accessible to the public at large. Private hospitals, clinics, and nursing homes attract those who can pay away from the state-run medical system. The decline in available health care has led to cynicism, suicide, superstition, supernatural practices including reliance on *pirs* and shrines, and crime. Filling a need, Islamic parties such as Jamat Islami run mobile clinics on the model of Ikwanul Muslimin of Egypt. If the state hospital system were strengthened, expanded, and technologically better equipped, and the majority of Pakistanis were no longer deprived of access to medical care, both public health and public confidence would rebound.

As things stand, public-sector medical services are severely limited, yet only a fraction of the population can afford to pay for private medical care. A parallel crisis exists in education. One percent of GDP is spent on public health care and 3 percent on private health care, while 2.6 percent of GDP is spent on public education and 1.8 percent on private education. Income levels severely limit the scope for private initiative in the health and education sectors: 13.4 percent of the population lives on less than one dollar a day, while 65.6 percent makes less than two dollars a day. However, public-sector investment in health and education shows promise. Public financing has provided 62 percent of the population with sustainable access to modern sanitation, has supplied 90 percent with safe water, and has immunized 67 percent of children against tuberculosis and 57 percent against measles.

A Vision for the Future

When Pakistan became independent, its leaders planned for the country's economy and political institutions to develop along Western lines. Enthusiasm for this development agenda was lost over decades as inequality between classes, regions, and sectors increased. The national imagination has been largely unmoved by global programs directed at helping the Third World: debt relief, poverty alleviation, environmental protection, literacy campaigns, women's emancipation, and commodity pricing reform, protectionism, and regional trade zones. Cynicism is rampant. Development's failure has helped salvation, as projected by the radical Islamic movement, become an appealing mode of thought (Collier et al. 2003). Past has replaced future as the center point of the intellectual discourse.

What is needed is to cultivate the spirit of developmentalism with credible programs, attainable goals, short-term successes, and a vision for a better national life in the foreseeable future. Only a pragmatic and visible process of development combined with a viable public sector can turn the tide of public imagination in favor of civic behavior and constitutional forms of public activity. Globalization and development go hand in hand. Pakistani teachers, doctors, bureaucrats, entrepreneurs, and activists must work with partners throughout the world to repair the country's social and economic infrastructure and its political institutions.

The concept of the clash of civilizations has become a curse of our times. Several Western leaders and a generation of Islamic radicals imagine that the West is at war with the rest of the world and that the Muslim world is at war with the West. We need to dismantle the idea of the dichotomy of Islam and the West so that it no longer dominates the worldviews of both Pakistan (and other Muslim countries) and the US (and other Western countries). States, not civilizations, are actors on the world stage, albeit with an increasing input from nonstate actors. Instead of imagining civilizations to be agents for the projection of specific, interest-based identities and ideologies, we should cultivate the idea of a civilization as an end in itself, as an agent for the expression, crystallization, and articulation of ideas and norms across the globe.

Conclusion

We have seen that both Western scholarship on Islam and Islamic collective vision exaggerate the distinctions between the West and Islam. Emphasis on sacred texts and inattention to social context help either side sustain its stereotypes. The assertion that Islam is a political religion defies the de facto separation of religion and state that is the norm, not the exception, in Muslim history. Similarly, the idea that Islamic faith is an immutable primordial identity and, as such, a determinant of terrorist activity provides a poorer explanation for actual militancy than the world of Islam perspective.

Three successive waves of Muslim collective vision emerged in the last century and made themselves felt in Pakistani politics time and again: neoclassical reformers adopted Western models of development with no role for religion in government; Islamic legalists sought state adoption of *Shariat* (religious law); radical Islamists fought for (and elsewhere, founded) theocracies. All three worldviews co-exist. Yet it is a recurrent pattern in the contemporary Muslim world for an existing or aspiring political elite to transform Islam into a political ideology in order to claim divine sources of legitimacy.

Muslim countries are plural societies, not mere states. If their internal polarization is to be avoided, the organizations of civil society that are nascent in these countries should be promoted, directly with aid from their foreign counterparts and indirectly via support for the re-establishment of democratic institutions. The educational, health care, and other social welfare systems operating in the public sector must be safeguarded from further degeneration, if the public imagination is to be reshaped along peaceful, nonviolent lines of thought and action. A realistic agenda for development that earns the people's faith with tangible and enduring results and that rewards their efforts and ingenuity is needed to defeat rampant cynicism. An appreciation for the uniqueness of Pakistani society and the importance within it of Western, Islamic, and other elements must displace the idea of a clash of civilizations, in the minds of Pakistanis and in the minds of foreign policymakers worldwide.

Note

1. The author appreciates the comments of other Fulbright New Century Scholars on an earlier version of this essay in 2003 and the comments of the members of a colloquium in 2004 at the Fondation pour l'innovation politique in Paris on a related working paper, "Islam, Terrorism, and the West."

References

Alavi, Hamza. 1973. "Peasant Classes and Primordial Loyalties." *Journal of Peasant Studies* 1, no. 1: 23–62.

Bailey, F. G. 1970. *Politics and Social Change*. Berkeley: University of California Press.

Brass, Paul. 1991. *Ethnicity and Nationalism*. Delhi: Sage.

Collier, Paul, V. L. Elliott, Håvard Hegre, Anke Hoeffler, Marta Reynal-Querol, and Nicholas Sambanis. 2003. *Breaking the Conflict Trap: Civil War and Development Policy: A World Bank Policy Research Report*. Washington, DC: The World Bank.

Darling, Frank C. 1979. *The Westernization of Asia*. Boston: G. K. Hall and Co.; Cambridge, MA: Schenkman Publishing.

Fukuyama, Francis. 1989. "The End of History?" *The National Interest* 16 (Summer): 3–18.

Fuller, Graham. 2003. *The Future of Political Islam*. New York: Palgrave Macmillan.

Gellner, Ernest. 1992. *Postmodernism, Reason and Religion*. London: Routledge.

Halpern, Manfred. 1963. *The Politics of Social Change in the Middle East and North Africa*. Princeton, NJ: Princeton University Press.

Huntington, Samuel. 1996. *The Clash of Civilizations and the Remaking of World Order*. London: Simon and Schuster.

Lewis, Bernard. 1976. "The Return of Islam." *Commentary* 61, no. 1: 39–49.

Malik, Jamal. 1996. *Colonialization of Islam: Dissolution of Traditional Institutions in Pakistan*. Lahore: Vanguard Books.

Mayer, Ann Elizabeth. 1998. *Islam and Human Rights: Tradition and Politics*. Boulder, CO: Westview Press.

Pipes, Daniel. 1983. *In the Path of God: Islam and Political Power*. New York: Basic Books.

Rose, Richard. 1995. "Russia as an Hourglass Society: A Constitution without Citizens." *East European Constitutional Review* 4, no. 3: 34–42.

Said, Edward. 1978. *Orientalism*. London and Henley: Routledge and Kegan Paul.

Salvatore, Armando. 1997. *Islam and the Political Discourse of Modernity*. Reading, UK: Garnet Publishing.

Samad, Yunas. Forthcoming. *Fatal Attraction: Jihadi Islam, United States and Pakistan*.

Schwartz, Stephan. 2003. "Interviews: The Real Islam." *Atlantic Unbound*, March. http://www.theatlantic.com/doc/200303u/int2003-03-20 (accessed summer 2003).

Srinivas, M. N. 1967. *Social Change in Modern India*. Berkeley: University of California Press.

Turner, Bryan. 1997. *Orientalism, Postmodernism and Globalism*. London and New York: Routledge.

Waseem, Mohammad. 1994. *The 1993 Elections in Pakistan*. Lahore: Vanguard.

CONCLUSION
Ethnic and Sectarian as Ideal Types

Patrick B. Inman and James L. Peacock

The conveners of the 2002–2003 Fulbright New Century Scholars Program sought to understand the causes of ethnic and sectarian violence in order to aid in its prevention and amelioration. "Ethnic" and "sectarian" define marginal groups with nonhegemonic identities. A successful ethnicity is a nation; a successful sect, a religion. The proposal to study ethnicities and sects implied the perspective of outsiders, neither ethnic nor sectarian but somehow objective or ecumenical, above the fray.

In history, this is a point of view most often claimed by the representatives of empires, whether temporal, spiritual, or scientific. However, objective observers, impartial referees, imperial arbiters, or spiritual authorities can seldom resolve conflicts between cultures, because what is considered objective, impartial, arbitrary, or authoritative differs from culture to culture. Some means of understanding cultural conflict from the inside, from the viewpoints of the parties involved, is required.

Identity

Let us suppose, instead, that (1) it is human nature to identify with one or more moral communities; that (2) what is considered sacred, right, and good varies considerably between moral communities, making cultural conflict unavoidable; and that (3) the terms "ethnic" and "sectarian" define two polar opposites of social identity, two sets of constitutive principles for human

Notes for this section begin on page 230.

moral communities, two ideal types that provide a basis for comparing real-world identities.

The first two points have been developed by Charles Taylor in his philosophical account of the development of identity in the West from ancient Greece to modern times (Taylor 1989: esp. part 1 and chap. 25). In place of the social psychological definition of social identity—"those aspects of the self-concept that derive from an individual's knowledge and feelings about the group memberships that the person shares with others" (Pettigrew this volume, chap. 2)—Taylor proposes a notion of individual identity, or dignity, based on the "inescapable" "orientation" of each human self toward the good, within a "framework" of meaning that relates "three dimensions of our moral life": first, fame, honor, the respect we command from others, and the duties we owe others; second, self-mastery or the transformation of the will; and third, self-expression or creativity. Individuals become oriented to the good as they learn to communicate. As a person acquires language skills and attains articulate personhood, he or she is expected to "answer for himself or herself," to be able to state where he or she stands. Both the development of an orientation toward the good and the expression of it take place in communication with others. One's identity can change in the course of a lifetime but only within the moral space maintained by one's interactions with other people.

Worldwide and across cultures there is a large degree of agreement about what constitutes the good. For example, the modern "affirmation of ordinary life," Taylor says, is evident in the near-universal respect accorded to the protection of innocent life from harm or suffering. Respect for individual freedom of conscience is nearly as widespread, although often honored only in the letter of law and religious doctrine in societies and communities that repress dissent or even inhibit freely chosen assent to their rules. But paths to the good—frameworks that make sense of human life—are multiple, particular, and precious to those who rely on them for orientation. One cannot divorce the norms upheld by a duty to God, a sense of obligation to kin, or an ethic of honesty or decency or bravery or genius from the sources that maintain the narratives that teach those values and the relationships within which they are practiced and given life.

Ethnic, religious, and cultural groups cohere in part because of what they have in common. Among other possibilities, a group may share proximity, history, ancestors, economic roles, religious practices and beliefs, games, marriage markets, child-rearing practices, family structures, or a language or dialect. What Taylor's argument suggests is a deeper commonality: shared cultures include sources of moral frameworks, elements that enable members of the group to orient themselves toward the good. This may hold true for the most marginal of cases, for groups with nothing in common but a pattern of treatment or (dis)regard by another group; for example, outcasts may develop a shared culture composed of strategies that have evolved to help them cope with ill-treatment. Any group, including the exiled, defeated, delinquent, enslaved, and dehumanized, may define itself from within. No group's identity is ascribed only from the outside.

Taylor's goal is to describe the characteristics and genesis of "the modern identity" as it has emerged in the West, where, he explains, since the seventeenth century, problematic, multiple, shifting moral frameworks have displaced the authority of tradition. We are no longer confronted by the old "existential predicament ... which dominated most previous cultures and still defines the lives of other people today." It was

> a predicament in which an unchallengeable framework makes imperious demands which we fear being unable to meet. [This is] the prospect of irretrievable condemnation or exile, of being marked down in obloquy forever, or being sent to damnation irrevocably, or being relegated to a lower order through countless future lives. The pressure is potentially immense and inescapable, and we may crack under it. The form of the danger here is utterly different from that which threatens the modern seeker, which is something close to the opposite: the world loses altogether its spiritual contour, nothing is worth doing, the fear is of a terrifying emptiness, a kind of vertigo, or even a fracturing of our world and bodyspace. (Taylor 1989: 18)

Identity powerfully shapes the aspirations and horizons of human lives. The great transformation Taylor describes, the transition from unquestioned to problematic frameworks, from obedience (to avoid being cast out) to seeking meaning (in a context of anomie), has not changed that. And although Taylor believes his analysis applies only to the cultural and spiritual descendants of ancient Greece and Rome, Judaism and Christianity, and the European Enlightenment, there are two reasons to adopt his terms for crosscultural comparisons.

First of all, cultures in the distant past and throughout the world can be found spread along the spectrum between the two extremes that Taylor describes (Douglas [1970] 1996: 17–20): unquestioning acceptance of a ritual framework, on the one hand, and skepticism and moral confusion, on the other. Even if this were not so, all cultures are now to some degree global and to some extent westernized, as several accounts in this volume attest. All moral frameworks face questioning, and adherents of every religion and ideology and members of every tribe and nation must cope with the "modern" challenge of meaninglessness, as well as the "traditional" danger of ostracism for failing to fulfill prescribed roles and duties.

Second, and more important, Taylor self-consciously draws on the history and symbols of his own culture—his own identity—to try to imagine, in general terms, how identities function. How else could it be? The terms chosen would be different if they were the outcome of a different culture, a different confluence of traditions. Humility is advisable when one attempts to understand the deepest differences between peoples. Using

Taylor's ideas as a stepping-off point, rather than some set of purportedly objective, culturally transcendent categories, should remind us to be humble in our conclusions.[1]

Taylor's self-reflection also reminds us that cultural conflict is his heritage and ours, and that therefore we should have language and concepts at hand to describe its characteristics. The early modern and modern history of the West includes religious war and civil war, the expulsion or execution of dissenters, forced conversions, genocide, slavery, and the suppression of languages, religious practices, and ways of life, often in the name of enlightenment or national unity. Principles such as "toleration" and "equal protection of the laws" are scant centuries old in law and uncertain decades old in practice. No matter how much we might wish it otherwise, we did not leave violence against outsiders behind us as our nations became modern and democratic. Institutionalized indifference to marginal groups provides the most pervasive evidence that it is still with us (Herzfeld 1992). The forces of identity are at work in every society.

To summarize, Taylor's description of individual identity as a moral orientation, comprising duties to others, spiritual disciplines, and notions of what constitutes a good life, allows us to appreciate better the importance of social identity. Orientation to the good is a necessary attribute of any human being. It comes into existence through a person's relationships with others and is defined and limited by the language, rituals, and customs one shares with one's family, kin, co-religionists, or others with whom one lives, works, plays, or worships.

These moral frameworks can differ both in their content—the rules they prescribe and the values they endorse—and in their sources—what they hold sacred and how they embody orientation to good in symbols. So it is only to be expected that identities will clash. That discord could take place within the hearts and minds of individuals who can claim—or are claimed by—more than one group identity, within each group over differences in how members understand and interpret their shared values and symbols, and between groups. Assuming, as Taylor does, that respect for innocent human life is a near-universal value, one would expect cultural conflict to turn violent under three circumstances, which might sometimes overlap: first, when identity requires violent expression (that is, when violence itself means something or has symbolic value for the group that enacts the violence); second, when group members act in self-defense to protect what is sacred from being ignored or despoiled, either intentionally or unintentionally, and violence seems most likely to be effective (in most cases, this would imply that the targets of the violence are not innocent); and, third, when a group acts in a way that is not seen as violent from within its own moral framework but is understood as violent from other perspectives. (This begs the question of incommensurability—the possibility that two cultures may be unable to communicate their values and what they hold sacred to each other.)

Nomological and Idiographic Analyses of Cultural Conflict

Max Weber (1962) categorized the sciences along two axes: nomological-idiographic and natural-sociocultural. A nomological science seeks to determine the norm, to specify general laws, to explain trends. Idiographic science seeks to explain the sequence of cause and effect of a particular, concrete event. Natural science studies the behavior of the physical world to explain its regularities and to record its idiosyncrasies and attempt to explain them in terms of general laws. Sociocultural science studies human conduct to the same ends, but can grasp the particularities of a specific instance of human behavior in a way that is not possible for the physical scientist. As well as describing patterns, it can attempt to understand the motivation and "inner experience" of the actors as intervening factors, as part of the causes of an outcome (McLemore 1984).

Nomological explanations of ethnic and sectarian conflict abound. Communities large and small create and maintain moral frameworks of their own, adapting the language and norms of the societies that intersect within them. Examples include the families or institutions children grow up in, religious communities, military units, sports teams, fraternities, political parties, street gangs, knitting circles, Internet chat rooms, prison cellblocks, corner bars, secret organizations, marketplaces, and parliaments. Each has been studied by social scientists in order to deduce rules of group behavior that apply regardless of identity, or that break identity down into factors subject to explanation. Such efforts include the decades of research on the general laws of prejudice that build on the work of Gordon Allport (Pettigrew this volume, chap. 5), a recent World Bank study that factored out other variables to show that resource distribution was the root cause of recent civil wars (Collier et al. 2003), recent attempts to determine societal risk factors for genocide (Harff 2003), and the work of the self-labeled cultural theorists, a group of (mostly) political scientists and policy analysts who, starting with grid-group theory (Douglas [1970] 2003), came to explain the dynamics of cultural disputes in terms of five poles: fatalism, hierarchy, individualism, egalitarianism, and autonomy (Ellis and Thompson 1997; Thompson, Ellis, and Wildavsky 1990; Thompson, Grendstad, and Selle 1999). Another example is the typology of ethnocultural, multiculturalist, and civic nationalisms discussed by David Brown in our first chapter.

Ethnicity and sectarianism have often been understood as factors to be controlled and suppressed in order to avoid intergroup violence. Empires have incorporated conquered peoples into their own social structures, sometimes respecting their religions and customs, sometimes suppressing them. The religions of Islam, Christianity, and Buddhism each call upon their disciples to treat other human beings as kindred, as a larger family. Economists and political scientists can factor ethnicity and sect out of their models, arguing, for example, that if resources are distributed justly, ethnic tensions will subside and the threat of civil war will decrease (Collier et al. 2003). In the preceding chapters, some basic general rules have been suggested. Thomas Pettigrew argued that living and working arrangements that permit certain kinds of social interactions between members of different groups decrease intergroup prejudice. Brown explained that if the contradictory aspirations of different groups are intertwined, confusion can keep potential opponents from squaring off. Several other contributors to this volume drew general conclusions about how identity groups evolve and behave.

The value and lure of the nomological approach is obvious. Policymakers, theologians, and social scientists all aspire to formulate general laws that predict events by explaining the factors or variables that combine to bring them about. Their goal is to control or make sense of events through knowledge of these general laws. Often the application is simplistic: if we can establish that when conditions A, B, and C occur, conflict will occur, then we can stifle A, B, or C and thereby stifle conflict, nipping it in the bud because we know that the bud will flower only if fertilizer, rain, and soil (A, B, and C) are present.

But the nature of cultural conflict limits the usefulness of general laws. When one's own neighborhood or city or region or country explodes or seems about to explode in violence, it does little good to know the odds or the trends. Such knowledge may even make the situation worse. Those most likely to make a difference in the outcome are often those best equipped to flee. Only when the knowledge of probable outcomes is accompanied by insight into the situation and possible interventions, providing an opportunity to have a voice in how things turn out and a sense of efficacy that can buttress loyalty, is it likely that the most capable members of a threatened group will take action rather than flight (Hirschman 1970).

To approach the problem nomologically is to think as outsiders. In our analogy we experiment with cultural conflict, controlling all of the important factors as a botanist or gardener applies measured amounts of sunlight, nutrients, and weed killer. We are not the budding plant, though we are sympathetic to it. Push the analogy further. What if we are not the gardener but the plant, or, if not exactly that, a plant of the same species, a fellow entity subject to the same laws that we are trying to deduce? As we move toward an insider status—or perhaps toward the status of one who is similar, one who can identify with the insider—objectivity merges with subjectivity but is not entirely submerged into it. We still want to explain, to discern patterns and regularities, but we also want to understand, to experience the situation as it is understood by those within it.

Such considerations led Weber to two interrelated concepts, *Verstehen* and "ideal types." *Verstehen* is a distinctive kind of understanding in which one interprets action by grasping the viewpoint of the actor. Ideal types are a way of generalizing from such an understanding without losing its particularity and distinctive subjectivity.

For example, Weber tried to understand the capitalist who was also a Calvinist by grasping the viewpoint, economic and theological, of such a person. One opportunity to do so occurred when Weber visited his mother's first cousin in Mt. Airy, NC, in 1904. He saw a man baptized in icy water and asked his cousin why the man had subjected himself to that. His cousin replied, "He is opening a bank" (Weber 1952: 304–305; cf. Weber 1975: 296–300). This experience helped Weber envision a relationship between business and religion. Out of many such understandings of particulars, Weber imagined the ideal type described in *The Protestant Ethic and the Spirit of Capitalism* ([1930] 1992). In that book, he drew general conclusions about the logic of the Calvinist-capitalist perspective and illustrated his generalizations with figures drawn from history, such as Benjamin Franklin.[2]

An ideal type is grounded in particulars and is intended to illuminate further particulars. How does it do this? By simplifying, by exaggerating the logic of the pattern so that it can be more easily grasped, the way that a caricature exaggerates the memorable features of an individual's face. Ideal types are pure; concrete social reality seldom is. For example, a Calvinist capitalist is likely to be motivated by ideas and principles, physical and emotional urges, and social pressures other than predestination (or providentialism), asceticism, and a drive to make money. It is to be expected that the patterns of actual human lives will be more muddy, more complicated, and less apparent than ideal types suggest (Jacob and Kadane 2003).

In short, ideal types are a tool to help extend the insights of case analysis to other cases. The psychology behind the transfer of case-based *Verstehen* to further case-based *Verstehen*, thus allowing the application of local knowledge in a new locale, is important. Weber wrote that "[t]he ideal-typical concept will help to develop our skill in imputation in research ... it offers guidance to the construction of hypotheses. It is not a description of reality, but it aims to give unambiguous means of expression to such a description" (quoted in Burger 1987: 120–121). This works the way clinical experience works. Doctors come to understand diseases by diagnosing many instances. Detectives identify the likely authors of crimes by comparing the traces left at the scene. Art historians determine the provenance of a painting by first studying many other paintings and then taking into account all the idiosyncrasies that went into this composition. In each profession, practitioners learn which details are significant from repeated experience. This is a heuristic approach, not a simple, deductive one (Ginzburg 1989). Identities are richly complex subjectivities that give rise to both predictable and surprising behavior. Any cut-and-dried explanation of how identities function discards the elements of surprise and idiosyncrasy—why would a banker get baptized?—and can only explain, not attempt to understand, the phenomenon. Our goal is to retain in our analytical tools some of the richness of subjective understanding that can result from the close study of a particular cultural conflict.

Ethnic and Sectarian as Ideal Types of Social Identity

We start by recognizing that the terms "ethnic" and "sectarian" have pejorative connotations. The phrase "ethnic and sectarian conflict" implies that if those involved would only set aside their irrational attachments to their blood kin or fictive kin and simply discard divisive, marginal religious attitudes and adopt modern, live-and-let-live practices of tolerance, ethnic and religious violence would cease. If we define the phenomena in this way, we place ourselves outside it.

Instead, let us suppose that "ethnic" and "sectarian" define two ideal types of identity, two moral frameworks, two orientations toward good. As polar opposites, together they provide two points of perspective—neither in principle being better than the other—against which we can compare what we understand about the identities of groups that are at odds. It seems extremely unlikely that any actual human group exhibits all of the characteristics we will attribute to either extreme, but many if not all group identities can be described and compared by reference to these two ideal types.

A few of the ways in which we would like to be able to compare the ethnic and sectarian ideal types of identity require definition. Taylor describes identity as an orientation to good, analogous to orientation in physical space. A key aspect of good for a group is the continued existence of the sources it uses to orient itself, allowing it to survive as a culture and a way of life. A key element of cultural conflict is the extent to which contact with other groups threatens or reinforces identity. We can say that a group, subgroup, or individual with a particular identity may be extinct, annihilated, persecuted, marginal, tolerated, integrated, dominant, or universal. The goal of an individual or a group regarding its own identity—usually, to protect, expand, or purify it—is accomplished by maintaining one of these states of being or by achieving a better one, possibly by inducing another identity to change its state. In general, an identity group's aspirations, horizons, and ability to command respect might be categorized as shown in figure 11.1, using categories drawn from the social science literature on immigration and war.

Transitions along this spectrum of goals may not occur in the sequence shown in figure 11.1. One could express them in a different sequence or as a circle or as a star. Nevertheless, it is useful to think of these goals as states, like states of matter, and identities and holders of identities as seeking to transition from one state to the other, or to maintain a state. Identities and holders of identities may also be forced to change state or to remain in an undesired state.

Identities interact with each other and can be damaged or nourished as a result. Any symbolic system can be at once an expression of identity, a means of renewing and reproducing it, and a point of contact and possible interpenetration between cultures. Levels of cultural contact are venues for respect, connection, and conflict. Some examples are shown in figure 11.2.

Marginality often varies with the level of cultural contact. An outcast group may dominate the street or certain sectors of the economy. A church or school or sporting event may be integrated, while workplaces and neighborhoods are

FIGURE 11.1 How Horizons and Respect Vary with Aspirations in Identity Groups

		Aspirations			
	Survival	**Isolation/ ghetto** (negative integration)	**Integration**	**Dominance**	**Exclusivity** (ethnic cleansing or total conversion)
Horizons (limit of group's vision for itself)	Will we live to see tomorrow?	Our children will live to see a better day.	We're OK. We have our role in the world.	We are on top. Others exist to serve us.	We are the universe. Others are damned (or do not exist).
Respect (what the group wants from others)	Leave us alone.	Allow us to live in our own way.	Treat us just as well as anyone else.	Accept our ways as the norm.	Fear us (or join us).

Marginal ◄─────────────────► Central

Note: Placing conflicting groups in the appropriate columns on this chart will help determine each group's limits for compromise.

segregated. At any level, one group may exploit another, silence it, deny it dignity, or, alternatively, demonstrate respect. Taboos (things groups cannot think about) and totems (things group members must revere) differ. Rudeness, desecration, blasphemy, and what is perceived by the victim as a wholesale attack on a culture can result simply from indifference to (or ignorance of) a group's hang-ups or limits. One of the important tasks of idiographic social science is to discover hidden conflict and make it understandable through interviews, ethnography, documentary studies, and safe centers for collaboration.

With the dimensions of the aspirations, horizons (limits to vision), and self-respect of identity-based groups in mind, and some notion of the multiple levels at which cultures come into contact, we can proceed. The distinction between ethnic and sectarian has suggested two types of identity-based groups—one particularistic, the other universalizing. As an example of the contrast, note that what constitutes "survival" for an ethnic group is very different from what a sect requires. Marginality or ghettoization can preserve an ethnic group, but it frustrates a proselytizing sect. To avoid being excluded, the carriers of transcendent ideas may readily discard outward signs of difference. As they assimilate, their ideas penetrate their adoptive society.[3]

The ethnic and sectarian ideal types are multidimensional polar opposites. They are most easily visualized in chart format, as shown in figure 11.3.

There are other characteristics of identity, or what psychologists call "social identity," that may reward examination in light of these ideal types. One may want to keep an identity sharply defined or to infuse it into a larger identity. The Christian admonition to be "the salt of the earth" expresses this sort of goal. Identities may be more or less permeable.

Identities need space in which to define themselves and exist. Sometimes the space is physical, geographic, as with nation-states, towns, parishes, neighborhoods,

FIGURE 11.2 Some Levels of Cultural Contact

Level of Cultural Contact	Examples
Manners (Spanish *educación*) or protocol	Both Tibetans and Singapore Malays consider ethnic Chinese rude.
Education (German *Bildung*)	Education and similar institutions (like armies). The Karen of Burma in the British Army and civil service and in missionary schools, and later in their own army and refugee camp schools. Monastic education in Tibet, Burma, and Thailand.
Art (visual, literary, drama, music, dance, etc.)	*Mein Kampf*, *Uncle Tom's Cabin*, *Guernica*, samizdat, Singaporean theater.
Courtship, marriage, and divorce	The bride in *Beowulf*, "mixed marriages" in general.
Family relationships, kinship	The Senegalese officer who said, "If we kill them, we're killing our own brothers; therefore, we try to avoid as much violence as we can, although we know where all [the MFDC] bases are."
Adoption and fostering	Tibetan students in Chinese boarding schools. Karen nationalist San C. Po of Burma (educated in missionary schools and then by missionaries who fostered him in the US) wrote: "[T]he Karens . . . owe what progress and advancement they have made, to the missionaries whom they affectionately call their 'Mother' under the protection of the British government whom they rightly call their 'Father.'"
Care and relations of dependence (nursing)	Servants and nannies, teachers, doctors.
Exchange, consumption, and markets	Local stores and markets, catalogs, phone sales people. A counterpart to Islam in Pakistan.
Work, business, and labor markets	Collegiality, teamwork, hiring, unions, bosses, business associations, extortion, debt peonage, slavery—all the relationships of the workplace.
Face-to-face contact	Neighbors, bus riders, representatives, users of a well. Stereotypes flourish without this.
Friendship	Contact theory as explained by Pettigrew. The source of Hitler's complaint that every German knew one good Jew.
Social networks	The "grids" that bring groups together, or the "groups" within which different worldviews meet.
Sports	Olympics, city sports leagues. A soccer game may have triggered the Casamance conflict.
Religious ceremonies and practices	Praying together, using the same practices when apart. Falun Gong exercises—and Internet sites.
Bilingualism and symbol literacy	The ability to understand one's own language and that of another group and to translate between them, bridging the gap.
Sublimation and reification	Games can replace war. Striving for worldly success, fueled by longing for salvation, may displace that longing. Symbolic conflict can take the place of physical violence or lead to it. Sacrifices. Scapegoats.

or the "territories" of trading companies or urban gangs. More often, the territory is symbolic. Perhaps the most basic example of the space in which identity can exist is in embryo and infancy: the womb, the breast, the lap. Psychoanalyst D. W. Winnicott (1971) defined "potential space" as the space that opens up when an infant loses contact with its parent. If the loss is not too abrupt, violent, or enduring, the infant experiences both loss and expectation. To manage the fear that comes with the loss, it creates a "transitional object" in which to invest its feelings in the absence of its mother. The classic transitional object is the teddy bear. This suggests that for human individuals and social groups, new identities may emerge when the old ones are lost or fade, as long as the circumstances of the loss are not too threatening.

FIGURE 11.3 Two Ideal Types of Group Identity

	Ethnic	Sectarian
Time	Past, common history	Future, utopia, afterlife
Scope	Particular	Universal
Social organization	Clan, caste, class	Egalitarian or monarchical: "Equal before God"
Geographic ties to	Homeland	Sacred sites (Transcendental religions deny ties to places but often treat certain sites or relics as sacred: Mecca is not sacred, but the Haj is, for example.)
Internal ties	Blood kin	Fictive kinship
Attitude toward outsiders	Oppositional, closed	Inclusive, open
Style	Defensive	Creative
Relations with outsiders	Trade, conquest	Conversion or exclusion
If marginal, can assimilate into other identities via	Intermarriage, intermingling of histories	Insulation ("render unto Caesar") or infiltration ("the long march through the institutions"). Either fits pattern of "salt of the earth," which mixes in yet remains pure.
If dominant, can assimilate other identities via	Conquest, or alliance versus a common enemy	Adoption and transformation of pagan customs
Language	Particular to group	Universal as either (a) sacred language of clerics or (b) scripture, available to all (egalitarian) or to the elect who intercede with God for all (monarchical, hierarchy)
Ontology	Immanent	Transcendent
Membership	Involuntary	Voluntary
Time	Circle (cyclical)	Arrow (progress)
Time frame	Generations, eternal	Individual lifetime, millenarian
Social obligations	Dependency, duty, obligation (Kittay 1999; Tronto 1993)	Independence, freedom, free will (Hobbes [1651] 1998; Pateman [1979] 1985)
Corresponding social roles	Homemaker, mother, farmer	Migrant, teacher, soldier
Broadest aspiration	Nation, nation-state, master race	Established religion, its beliefs and practices universally shared
Corruption means	Disloyalty, abandonment	Lack of principle, venality
Survival means saving	Group's history and bloodline	Sect's beliefs and practices
Exclusion requires	Pure bloodline (Proscribe intermarriage.)	Pure practices (Heresy is mistaken practices.)
Isolation or ghettoization …	Preserves an ethnic group. Mixture with other groups destroys the group. "Ethnic networks" can be virtual ghettos.	Incubates a sect's practices. A sectarian ghetto is a monastery. Practices spread by leaving the ghetto; the sect grows as a result. (Luther: "Every man a monk, the whole world a monastery.")

FIGURE 11.3 Two Ideal Types of Group Identity (*cont.*)

	Ethnic	Sectarian
Kuhn's schema[1]	Normal science	Revolutionary science
Douglas's schema[2]	Group	Grid
Smith's schema[3]	Perennialism	Modernism
Social emotions and the status of women	Honor and shame. Women bear the tribe's shame, which must be protected. Shame can only be lost, never recovered. Male honor rests on the foundation of female shame and cannot replace it (Gilmore 1987; Peristiany 1966; Wikan 2002).	Guilt, repentance, and grace. All are equally guilty; all may receive grace. Women are potentially equal to men. Any hierarchy is justified only insofar as it carries out the will of the deity.
Triggers for conflict	Violate boundaries. Symbolic triggers may be buried in history. Classic trigger: rape.	Disrupt practices. Triggers evident in doctrine. Classic trigger: defilement.
Healing from trauma	Complex. Like the violated boundaries, the keys to healing are found in the group's unconscious, that is, in its history. Rape (the classic trigger) cannot be undone (Volkan 1997: esp. 36–80).	Straightforward. Reinstitute the practice. Rituals provide for healing. Defilement (the classic trigger) can be healed through grace, blessing, divine intervention. This is an ordinary function of religion.
Corollary #1	To heal ethnic conflict …	… find a shared religious framework.
Corollary #2		To end religious conflict, restore disrupted practices.
Corollary #3	One can also end ethnic strife …	… if it can be transformed into sectarian conflict. This echoes an idea of Freud: "The goal of psychoanalysis is the transformation of neurotic misery into common unhappiness."
Resources for conflict	Limited to the group and its allies	Potentially unlimited, because of ability to gain new converts.
Resources in defeat	Memory. The group can survive in history until memory fades. Defeat can be total.	Belief and practice. Either the ideas survive or they do not. Defeat is not possible.
Resources for compromise	Numerous, because the group seeks particular goals. However, it cannot compromise "blood and soil."	Few. The group may make less of a claim on the material world, but any compromise in its practices may cause a schism over purity.

[1] "Normal science" is textbook science or, rather, the pursuit of evidence to support an accepted cosmology. "Revolutionary science" is the consideration of alternative cosmologies when the evidence no longer fits an accepted worldview (Kuhn [1962] 1996).

[2] "Grid" is a "system of shared classifications"—a set of rules or principles, a doctrine, a conceptual map of the world imparted through education that transcends local knowledge and may link people from completely different backgrounds, so that all they have in common are symbols, tools for thinking and communicating that shape their worldview. "Group" consists of social obligation, loyalty, kinship, dependence, domination—the seemingly inalienable ties that bind us to others because we are of the same family, clan, nation, or fictive kin. The reductionism explicit in these definitions of "group" and "grid" is appropriate to ideal types. Douglas ([1970] 1996) further developed these terms in a nomothetic direction in her later works.

[3] Smith (1998: esp. 21–24) begins his analysis of theories of nationalism with two ideal types that resemble ours. We encountered his book long after this essay was first written and this chart was constructed.

FIGURE 11.3 Two Ideal Types of Group Identity (*cont.*)

	Ethnic	Sectarian
Examples: (These are intentionally chosen to provoke questions about the ideal types, as reminders of the best and worst examples of each tendency. These examples were categorized by the principle that ethnic groups have particularistic aspirations and sectarian groups have universalistic aspirations.)	Calvinism (the Elect) Judaism (the Chosen people) the (US) South Serbia Shintoism communitarianism patriarchy feudalism the family Senegalese Malays Russians and Tartars ethnocultural & multicultural nationalisms regionalism Karen in Thailand Pakistani civil society Islam as an instrumental identity	Christianity in general Islam in general Nazism (as a *Sammlungspartei*)[4] socialism Buddhism liberalism the Enlightenment nationalism in general the state Casamance rebels Singapore civic nationalism European Union Karen in Burma the Burman and Thai states Pakistani developmentalism Falun Gong and the Chinese state

Where would Tibetan identity fit?
How about Singaporean cross-cutting?
Where does the "intertwining" of logically incompatible identities fit?

[4] A *Sammlungspartei* is a "catch-all party." The ideal of the German nation that Hitler presented transcended family, clan, and class, so we place it in the "Sectarian" column. Racism has both an ethnic aspect (looking backward to a common history and ancestry) and a sectarian one (looking forward to a race to be created, in this case, of Aryan supermen). Hitler's political strategy was more than an attempt to unite the elite opponents of socialism, as Miquel, von Bülow, and Bismarck did with their original *Sammlungspolitik* of 1897. His goal was to bring together the mass of Germans, eliminating all other parties and political and spiritual allegiances, into "one iron-hard *Volkskörper*" (body of the people) which would conquer Europe and thereby gain the territory it needed for growth. Nazi ideology, built on "insolent lies" and inconsistent ideals, pretended at times to champion a return to a mythic past, but resembles more a proselytizing religion than a reinstatement of traditional kinship ties (Craig 1978: 274–276, 546–553, 676–677; cf. Szelényi forthcoming)

One can picture social identity—that is, the capacity for associating—as an ability that broadens with maturity, expanding from the lap to the sandbox, the neighborhood, the nation, the region, the globe and then, possibly, contracting in old age to the house, the sickbed, the grave. Or, alternatively, like the dying king, one's sense of identity may become more transcendent with the wisdom that accompanies an awareness of mortality.

One can imagine conflict among competing identities at any scale: among children in a family or nursery, among gangs in a neighborhood, among ethnic groups in a city or clans or tribes within a country, among religions, among nations, between the genders, among generations, among social classes, castes, or other strata. It complicates things that individuals may claim or be claimed by more than one identity and may find themselves both allied and at odds. The particular horror of civil war may pit one against one's own kin.

To the degree that an identity defines itself as universal, it finds itself in conflict with other identities that seek to use the same physical or symbolic space. Thus, the identity of France as republican and secular is threatened if an Islamic Frenchwoman wears a head scarf to school, indicating her submission to the rules of God before those of the state. Note that both France and Islam have universal aspirations: in our ideal typology, this is a conflict between sects. Or one could say this is a case of an ethnic identity (French) using religion (secularity) as a proxy identity.

Identities can define themselves in terms of other identities, held by or ascribed to members of the group or to outsiders. Thus, certain Christian sects define themselves in part by the precept that "wives submit to husbands." Armies may define themselves by dehumanizing their enemies. The notion of the scapegoat fits here. Nazism defined itself as seeking purification of German identity by eliminating others.

All things being equal, unless violence is part of what defines an identity, one assumes that strategies for establishing and maintaining an identity that avoid violence, or at least the risk of violence to one's own group, are more attractive. The available options depend on one's own goals, the goals of other identities, and the available resources.

In prehistoric Europe, and in European literature, groups defended their identities and conquered others through war. They established peace through marriage and built ties through trade that made war less desirable. Literally and in metaphor, conquest and defense, on the one hand, and marriage and exchange, on the other, are alternative means of maintaining identities. The first two establish boundaries. The second two cut across existing boundaries, at once tying groups together and distinguishing them in new ways made possible through distinct social roles, items of exchange, or language and customs. Rules of patrilocality or matrilocality and the degree of assimilation expected of a new bride or groom determine how much identities that cross-cut through intermarriage might change or come to resemble each other as a result. The marriages of kings and queens are one thing, but in everyday marriages, the concord between partners is balanced by the conflict of interests between in-laws.

In modern times, it was hoped that the sublimation of human passion into rational interest would reduce violence. Many proponents of capitalism believed that this would occur (Hirschman 1977), an outcome that would have been a triumph of "grid" over "group." But the twentieth century showed that sometimes human ties provide a sanctuary, communities in which alternative principles can survive the massive destruction—of peoples, cultures, ecosystems—that only rational systems could carry out.

One can think of identities in relationship to time. For example, an identity might have one set of characteristics before a conflict, another during the conflict, and yet another afterward, especially in an aftermath of defeat. One can also think of identities in relation to their goals. How different was it to be a Zionist before Israel existed, during the conquest of the former Palestine, and once the state of Israel was established? One can imagine identities that fade once their goal is achieved, identities based primarily on shared oppression. One can also imagine the disintegration of defeated identities.

Identity-based groups may contain cross-cutters, people willing to cross over into other identities. They may also contain integrators, who attract cross-cutters from other groups. Shakespeare's Romeo and Juliet were cross-cutters. Mercutio, the Nurse, and the Friar were integrators.[4]

One thing that is absent from many discussions of ethnic and sectarian conflict is the notion of freedom. Competing identities provide human beings with choices, and choices create opportunities for loss. When the loss is small enough and the individual or group is safe enough, he, she, or we may reimagine the groups we might belong to and the grids of principle we might align ourselves with. Religions whose histories we know emerged in this way. So have most national traditions.

A sense of play may mark the creation of new identities or the adaptation of old ones. Sometimes societies provide ritual space "between" identities for this activity. The theater has often served this purpose in Western societies, as it does today in otherwise tightly regulated Singapore. Crafts and folk arts have sheltered identities in distress: recall, for example, the many ways in which African cultures survived among slaves in the United States in song, story, and the fabrication of household goods. Published writers have remade their societies by scripting new identities later made flesh. Lincoln called Harriet Beecher Stowe "the little lady who started" the American Civil War by identifying slavery as the enemy and the North as the rescuers of people suffering as Christ had. Hitler's *Mein Kampf* cast Germans as sufferers who must rescue themselves by enslaving others. The salons in which the discussions that embodied the Enlightenment took place were "private" spaces, free from some of the rules governing public behavior.

One kind of "play" with identities, already mentioned, is cross-cutting. Identity-based conflict is always concerned with purity, with exclusion or conversion.

Cross-cutting is potentially creative: as one moves across categories or types, one creates something new that is neither here nor there. This sort of pregnant interaction between identities contrasts with the poverty of so-called identity politics in which, as Jean Bethke Elshtain (1995: esp. chap. 3) astutely argues, civic responsibility is exhausted when the participant affirms an identity, finding a slot and fitting the self like a peg into a hole. Claim membership in a gender or sexual orientation, in a political, racial, ethnic, or religious group or category, and that's it: you have flown the flag, revealed yourself as red state or blue state, Chinese or Malay, Christian or Muslim. Thence kicks in Freud's "narcissism of minor differences": all that is left to do is to obsess about, defend, and attack differences of identity. Cross-cutting rescues society from this impoverished level of conflict by sending ambassadors abroad or across the lines, carrying not the identity flag but rather the white flag, signifying surrender or willingness to negotiate with the enemy.

Although all societies, regardless of their forms of government, face the challenge of negotiating conflict between identities, the starkest challenge emerges in moments of democracy, "moments of commonality" when in "a free society composed of diversities ... through public deliberations, collective power is used to protect the well-being of the collectivity" and "ordinary citizens ... [discover] common concerns and ... modes of action for realizing them" (Wolin 1996: 31). When ordinary people momentarily hold power—to elect a Hitler or a Lincoln; to nonviolently resist (persist in the truth) in the face of colonial rule in India, segregation in the US South, apartheid in South Africa, or the dictatorship of the Communist Party (successfully in Eastern Europe, tragically in Tiananmen Square); to take up arms in defense of a way of life, as the Karen and Casamance rebels have, as the Burmese who allied with the Japanese to win independence from Britain did, as the anti-Semitic thugs of Nazi Germany's Kristallnacht and the lynch mobs of the American South did, as have both sides in civil wars ranging from Europe in the sixteenth century to England in the seventeenth to the United States in the nineteenth to China, Spain, and so many others in the twentieth—when ordinary people momentarily hold power, they claim new identities; confirm, adapt, or abandon shared moral frameworks; and cement intergroup enmity or harmony.

The potential for creative or inimical recognition exists in everyday encounters between individuals as well as in moments of collective engagement. The "distant, cool, and indirect" modern forms of subtle prejudice described by Pettigrew in chapter 2 may conceal the same depth of mistrust and misunderstanding—the same lack of *Verstehen*—as the blatant "close, hot, and direct" traditional expressions of racial, religious, or ideological hatred. Conversely—and harder to imagine, in the context of reductionistic identity politics—a rich, creative mix that can promote art, economic innovation, and public good is possible if the holders of radically distinct identities "operate from a stance of goodwill and an acceptance of the backdrop of democratic constitutional guarantees, as well as democratic habits and dispositions" and are "committed to rough-and-ready parity, an energetic desire to forge at least provisional agreements on highly controversial issues or remain committed to the centrality of dialogue and debate to [a] shared way of life" (Elshtain 1995: 67; cf. Pateman 1989; Yoshino 2006).

"Rough-and-ready parity" is not relativism. It is an acceptance of several facts of human life. Identities—moral frameworks—differ. Identities are sacred to their holders. The sources of those identities—texts and customs and practices—are also sacred. Happily, in our interconnected world most moral frameworks affirm the same basic ideas: respect for innocent human life, freedom of conscience and thought, an abhorrence of slavery and oppression. Unhappily, in that same interconnected world we are each confronted daily with the fact that we do not—cannot—agree about the source of those ideas. Can we live with the discomfort of knowing that our neighbors arrive by different paths to an orientation to the good?

Pessimistic answers to this question have a long pedigree. Hobbes ([1651] 1998), who survived the English civil war and knew violent religious intolerance firsthand, believed the only way to escape the "war of all against all" was obedience to an absolute ruler.[5] With the substitution of different ideals in different countries, Hobbes's vision is embodied in the leviathan of the modern state. The state has successfully imposed standards of tolerance—think of the integration of the public schools and public accommodations in the United States, the creation of a multiethnic society in Tito's Yugoslavia, or the official multiculturalism of Singapore or Burma or China—and of intolerance—think of indigenous peoples almost everywhere, the American South and South Africa until recently, the noncitizen status of the descendants of foreign workers in many countries, and, at the extreme, the state-organized holocausts of the twentieth century, for which Nazi Germany remains the too-often imitated prototype.

The state can act to ease prejudice, as Pettigrew explains in the conclusion to chapter 5, by arranging public life so that intergroup friendships are more likely. But the real work of avoiding intergroup violence requires the participation of citizens in meaningful, cross-cutting relationships.

What does it help to know in order to do one's part on the front lines where cultures meet? Our research suggests some rules of thumb. Identity-based groups do not act like nations or diplomats. The behavior of ethnic groups, sects, and other culturally bound communities more closely resembles that of families and kin groups. Negotiating the boundaries between identities is like fording a stream. In the short run, one adapts to each culture as it is, seeking points of common understanding and respecting the force of the current. Cultural conflict is like sharing a bed: intimate, uncomfortable, risky, and potentially fruitful. Think of marriage. Think of miscegenation. Think of divorce. Just as no two marriages are exactly alike, each combination of cultures in conflict has its own rules.

What else? Sometimes, ideals held in common can overcome difference. Identities that are more sectarian can transcend ethnic ones. The often-cited classic example is Christianity. As John Baggett (2005) illustrates in depth,

Jesus violated or transcended ethnic boundaries again and again. The parable of the Good Samaritan upheld an ethical over an ethnic principle; it was the detested ethnic, the Samaritan, not the ritually and ethnically pure Pharisee, who rescued the stranger. In James Peacock and Wee Teng Soh's study on Singapore (chap. 7, this volume), Chinese Buddhists show a similar transcending of their ethnicity, which famously equals that of Jews in its sharpness of boundaries, loyalty to kin groups and dialect groups, and sense of being "the chosen people." Likewise, the Hindu woman, Sita, abandons her priestly caste, Brahmin, to convert to Christianity—analogous to such a conversion for a Pharisee. Another Chinese Singaporean, Tan (later Talib), converts to the heretical Islamic sect, Ahmadiya, confounding his family.

These instances illustrate individuals who cross ethnic identities to affirm sect identities. What further potential lies in this ethnic-to-sect transition? Can this work for groups, for nations, for international bodies? More fundamentally, can it lead past identity itself, or does identity matter so much that each transcendence creates an identity?

Theorists have explored both questions. Weber is again fundamental. He shows how the transition from charisma to routinized organization is at once inevitable, necessary, and challenging to identity. This process of creating the machinery of government for any group threatens to sterilize the spirit that has energized its identity (Weber [1930] 1992: 180–183; 1978: 241–254, 1111–1157).

Sectarian or universalistic identities pose problems as well as solutions. As the example of Christianity and the memory of the many wars fought by Christians suggests, as "Buddhist" military rule of Burma shows, as the sectarian appeal of Nazism and Neo-Nazism demonstrates, and as is revealed by different degrees of state repression in the name of communism in China, republicanism in France, or democracy at some points in the history of the United States, the establishment of a common identity can act to redirect violence to those on its margins.

The promise of a universalistic identity, Brown suggested in different terms in chapter 1, may be that it permits confusion, that it allows those whose moral frameworks are logically incompatible nonetheless to see connections or compatibilities. Alternatively, when the instrumentality of the state is supposed to be in neutral hands, when a common vision for society has been abstracted from the personalistic or particularistic qualities of any one leader or group, each group can believe that its vision is coming to pass.

To us, "universal brotherhood" seems likely to be as transitory as the peace Tito brought to Yugoslavia. The passage of time, during which intergroup friendships can form, is always valuable. But identities may remain under the surface for generations, preserved in the culture's practices, not very noticeable to outsiders or insiders. Only in-depth understanding of one's own roots and those of one's neighbors can uncover and, through communication and mutual recognition, defuse the beliefs that could someday again fuel intergroup violence. If we want enduring peace in a multicultural world, we must make great efforts to understand each other's moral frameworks, to see how the divergent sources of different faiths (including belief systems that deny they are religions) provide foundations for lives worth living.

This is a challenge to the viability of society itself, especially in a globalizing world. Globalization entails interconnection—economic, political, military, cultural—through electronic media, immigration, tourism, trade, diplomacy, and war. One effect is the transmission of what Weber termed "rationalization" and Parsons described as the spread of specialized systems, for example, systems of education, government, economics. Each is rationalizing: society, thought, and existence itself are locally and globally mobilized and oriented toward the goals of such systems—profit, knowledge, civil society, etc. This general process is often described by particular terms, such as "Westernization," "the spread of capitalism," or "democratization," but the overall logic transcends any of these, hence the utility of the general term "rationalization."

Weber offered a further great insight, a paradox: rationalization requires irrationality, a sect identity. His example was the Protestant ethic spurring the spirit of capitalism, an example often misunderstood by those who fail to see the larger point—that the process of rationalization undermines identities. The lost identities must be replaced. Of course, irrationalities can also result from sect identity, as with any other identity, because identity is not governed by the logic of rationality or rationalization. It is governed instead by a need to identify: to belong to a category, to believe in a larger entity, to connect individuality and collectivity, biography and myth, the immanent and the transcendent. Identity matters greatly, and so does rationalization. The challenge is to sustain both.

This is where Weber's vision and Taylor's refinement of it can guide us. Weber spoke eloquently of modern society as "an iron cage," disenchanted, losing spirit, but functioning anyway, kept in motion by the systemic imperatives it had created. The larger thrust of his thesis was that not only did identity matter in creating a revolutionary process such as modernization through capitalism but that it continued to matter in sustaining the resulting system or process. The iron cage is not enough. Identities—the moral frameworks and meaningful narratives that provide the context for any human life worth living—reassert themselves.

As social scientists, like the representatives of powerful empires, like "the West," we are accustomed to think of ourselves as rational, and if we are not careful, to think of some of those we study as less than rational. "Ethnic and sectarian conflict," as we said to begin with, can be code for "irrational attachments" to blood kin and divisive, premodern religious attitudes. To avoid this trap, we have turned these pejorative terms into ideal types of social identity that can be used to compare actual identities. We assume that all moral frameworks have rational and irrational elements. Our own identities and those of the reader are as susceptible to this sort of comparison as those described in the cases in this book.

To understand identities in conflict, judgment must be postponed but not discarded. One must take the risk of according another way of life provisional respect and interact with it in order to learn whether those who share it aspire to be left alone, to integrate, or to dominate; to perceive the ways in which its manners, symbols, and taboos differ from one's own; and to assess the numerous dimensions along which moral frameworks differ, as suggested by our ideal types. Also crucial are the self-respect to assess one's own allegiances, convictions, and customs in the same light and the courage to judge how porous one's own and the other identities are and whether interplay between them is possible.

If we are aware of the competing and seemingly incommensurable moral frameworks that surround us, we can at least compare the costs of tolerance and co-existence, on the one hand, with violent confrontation, on the other. Then we can decide whether the former at least promises isolation or survival, or whether, as an individual and as a moral community, the only options are flight or fight (for an example of extended reasoning in this vein, see Wikan 2002).

We share a world where distances seem shorter and shorter; the movement of people and ideas across borders is unrelenting; and our neighbors may have histories, traditions, and beliefs very different from our own. If, as we believe, the roots of ethnic and sectarian violence must at least in part be understood idiographically, the best advice we can give the reader is to pay attention. We offer clues, suggested rules of thumb, and a method for applying insights from one situation to another.

Looking at the Cases in This Book in Light of the Ideal Types

In what senses, then, does identity matter? Locally and particularistically, identity matters for specific ethnic groups. Somewhat more abstractly but nonetheless passionately, identity matters for sects. Does identity matter in still more abstract or "rationalized" systems, for example, national, international, or global ones? If so, with what does one identify—with the national or international civic society, with humankind, with God or goodness? Or with some detached theoretical position, such as postmodernism or postcolonialism, or with an ideology, such as neoconservatism or liberalism?

Our authors go beyond simplistic partial answers to explore such questions in concrete instances, to consider sects and world religions in different contexts. Islam is shown to be not simply a sect entirely distinct from other sects, such as Christianity, or other civilizations, such as the West, or other ethnic groups, such as the Chinese or the Europeans. It is an identity that takes on different meanings in different contexts. In Pakistan, it interacts with both ethnic and civic orientations. In Singapore, it is part of being a minority. In Ukraine, it is a marker of a heritage of tolerance and a badge that distinguishes Tartars from Russians or Ukrainians. Buddhism can be emancipating for the

Chinese in Singapore, oppressive to the Karen in predominantly Buddhist Burma or Thailand, and a nearly lost heritage to the people of Han-occupied Tibet. Christianity, crossing ethnic lines, may free Brahmins from elitism, yet identification with it also sets Singapore against the neighboring Islamic nations, feared as sources of terrorism.

Consider ethnicity. Samuel Huntington (1996) portrayed a post–Cold War world in which civilizations, notably Asia, the West, and Islam, would clash, global powers would be supplanted by regional ones, and successful alliances between nation-states would require a common culture. Later events have conformed to his predictions, to a degree. Our case studies confirm the larger point—that identity matters—but in a context of flexibility, cross-overs, and counterpoints, varying with contexts. Neoconservative and fundamentalist analyses rigidly distinguish such identities in "for" and "against" categories. While acknowledging harsh realities, our analyses also show creative possibilities for relationships that interlace over the long term.

Singapore, for example, contains in microcosm the Western, Muslim, and Asian identities seen by Huntington and many others as key combatants macrocosmically, on the world stage. The city-state, a British colony until 1963, still embodies many Western values, including schooling, a work ethic, and the English language. It is Asian by location and predominant ethnicity (Chinese) and also by announced identity, neo-Confucian. Its largest minority is Muslim, and it is surrounded by Muslim nations, Indonesia and Malaysia. How do Western, Muslim, and Asian identities get along in Singapore? So far, so good, on the whole, setting aside violence between Muslims and Chinese in 1969, which spilled over from much more serious incidents in neighboring Malaysia. Nor is the seeming harmony simply the result of government control or a cultural façade, as chapter 7 illustrates with vignettes of individuals who bridge ethnic and sectarian divides. In Singapore, ethnic and sectarian orientations persist, with the characteristics associated with our ideal types. But our case analysis demonstrates how these types spring into action in individually motivated, contextualized quests, experiences, and group work. To be sure, both "hot" and "cold" prejudice exist in Singapore as elsewhere, and color lines and racism mar this officially multicultural society. However, creative efforts to overcome these divisions have both official sanction and variegated organic roots.

Mohammad Waseem, in his chapter on Pakistan, analyzes similar players on a larger stage. Several orientations—including Islam, a civil society of British parliamentary heritage, ethnic groups, and lively exchange networks—represent, again, the ideal types in action. Islam, a sectarian identity, is shown to have defined itself in part in dialogue with two related sectarian identities, Christianity and the West. In the last century, different generations within Islam have had different visions: one hoped Islam would adopt elements of Western identity, another called for it to set itself apart as a community whose laws embodied its submission to God, a third demanded that believers rise up in the name of justice to Muslims. In Pakistan, these distinctions matter little to an elite that seeks to maintain power by appealing to a reified Islamic identity—to the religious estab-lishment—rather than to a democratic process, in which these actual Islamic identities and the other currents of Pakistani society would have a voice.

This is the same sort of identity politics Elshtain and others have criticized in the United States, but with a twist. In Waseem's analysis, its perpetrators are not the possessors of reductionist identities, but politicians who short-circuit the political process by using Islam as a marker to reduce the complex interplay of several citizen orientations within the consciences of Pakistanis—in the give and take of their civil society, and as part of the potentially free debates of their parliamentary system—to the "you are with us or you are against us" formula so many of our authors mention in different contexts. To defend themselves against political opposition from citizens who expect the government to fulfill its promises of development, Pakistan's rulers have time and again accentuated the country's distinctively Islamic identity by, for example, supporting *madrasahs*, the Qur'anic schools that in Pakistan as elsewhere (including Singapore, by the way) instill Islamic, sometimes radical Islamic, commitments, not civic ones.

Singapore is intentionally multicultural and, both because of and in spite of official efforts, also home to organic cross-cutters who create new identities from their society's rich mix. Pakistan, which is in many ways officially monocultural, is a hybrid of several orientations that may yet overcome linguistic and tribal divisions to combine creatively. In these two examples, and the other cases in this volume, we see that the "clash of civilizations" on a small stage can be more complex than that suggested by Huntington's vision of a multipolar world. The global reach of cultures, ideologies, and migration streams has brought cultural conflict to every society. Nation-states around the world are confronted with the challenge of making that encounter constructive rather than violent.

Because the identities in conflict in any locale are unique amalgams of global currents of religion, ethnicity, and culture and of specific histories of isolated development, interrelationship, and cross-pollination, the broad substantive types proposed by Huntington to analyze world politics require refinement. We have suggested, instead, a pair of polar-opposite ideal types as a simple heuristic tool for understanding identities in conflict. Is this group more oriented toward the future (or eternity) or the past (or a cyclical view of time)? Does a competing group thrive in isolation or through assimilation? What is sacred to each side? Who speaks both languages? Imagining different identities in any culture as variants of "ethnic" or "sectarian" may help reveal where compromise is possible, what the likely triggers of violence are, and how possibilities for understanding and cross-cutting friendships may emerge.

Buddhism, rather than Islam, is the dominant faith in both Burma and Thailand, and the minority groups in question are hill tribes, the Karen, whose animistic traditions are sometimes overlaid with Christianity, sometimes with Buddhism. Here sect and ethnic orientations are double-edged. Buddhism, a sect transformed into a world religion, is institutionalized as the *sangha*, the Buddhist order represented by monks and monasteries. This order is buttressed in Thailand by a monarchy (the king and queen are the longest reigning, rivaling Queen Elizabeth) and by a parliamentary government, and its authority has been claimed for decades by Burma's military rulers. Buddhism supports and is supported by lowland-dwelling, traditionally wet-rice-growing majority populations, Thai or Burman, who reside in villages or cities and follow a bilateral kinship system that eschews clans and hence is open to governance by a national state. Here, ethnicity, ecology, and sect converge in the dominant nation-states.

In counterpoint, the hill tribes, represented by the Karen, traditionally follow a shifting cultivation pattern, live within a unilineal kinship system based on clans, and resist governance by a national state. Conversion to a sect, Christianity, gives an additional sense of difference from the Thai or Burmese majority, fueling millennial and revolutionary ideas that are nascent in tribal vision, as Edmund Leach (1954) notes in his classic study, *Political Systems of Highland Burma*, and Thomas Kirsch and others develop more broadly. Here sect and ethnic types conflict, and also one combination of sect and ethnicity conflicts with another. Southeast Asia provides a laboratory for comparison in that the mainland (Thailand, Burma, Cambodia, Laos) has a majority that is Buddhist, ruling over tribes that are not, while the peninsula and islands (Malaysia, Indonesia) have Muslim majorities in conflict with tribes that are not. Broadly speaking, the dynamics are similar in arraying minority against majority, with the majority a bilateral, lowland-dwelling, non-clan-based, world-religion-embracing group and the minority a unilineal, highland- or forest-dwelling, animist or, later, Christian group. The majorities merge the sectarian and ethnic ideal types by identifying an established religious order (Buddhist or Muslim) with a majority ethnic group (Thai, Burmese, Malay, Indonesian), while the minorities merge ethnic identities with tribal identities and clan kinship. Should we bring into the picture Vietnam and the Philippines, much would be similar except that Confucian (and recently communist) civilization is dominant for the first, Catholic Christianity for the second, and each has never succeeded in converting its hill or forest tribal groups.

We learn from this exercise that our ideal types can spur analysis, but that one must be astute in applying them to real-world situations, which are always complex. Ideal types combined with a case-study approach can help us grasp nuances, in contrast to a substantive generalization approach as advocated by Huntington, who demarcates three major civilizations (and some less major ones) that clash. We name two types of identity that can be applied, if one is discerning, in a range of conflict situations that array against each other a variety of cultural orientations, including those named by Huntington. Our method lends itself to the analysis of particular potential or actual conflicts by guiding attention to clues that often accompany triggers for violence and to possibilities for constructive contact between opposing identities.[6]

What if, however, Paul Collier is right, and the key factors predicting or controlling conflict are not identities at all but are economic—mainly, resources?

This returns us to our analogy of the plant and the ingredients that grow it: soil, water, and nutrients. Like the gardener, identity is a shaper, defining the way that resources are mobilized and directed. Matter is not all that matters. "Intelligent design" may be debatable in the natural sciences, but not in political economy, when the design is by humans (cf. Scott 1998).

Identities catalyze situations or facilitate their crystallization. The Karen "fit" with the British because the two peoples' mythologies were similar. They did not "fit" in the same way with the Thai kings, and as a result their relationship with their Thai rulers was more distant and less beneficial. Burmans did not "fit" in the same way with the British. Partly as a result, the Karen aided the British in subduing and ruling Burma, and in the process developed a sense of ruling themselves that propels a movement for independence. The French considered the Casamance region rebellious; it certainly did not "fit" easily into colonial rule. Or did it? Just as the Karen developed a reputation as fighters by working with their rulers, the Diola developed a similar reputation by resisting. Like the Karen, many Diola converted to Christianity, finding a counteridentity to that of the majority.

Falun Gong and the Tibetan people seem as different as two minority groups within China could be. What they have in common is the state, which marginalizes them. Falun Gong gave identity nonviolent expression until the state suppressed it. Left alone, was Falun Gong dangerous to the state? The ancient threat posed by mystic cults is that by bringing people together separate from the state, they might become an army—able to give voice to its wishes or to withdraw from the state or to incite violence. But here it is the state's reaction, not the group's actions, that seems most likely to cause an explosion. Tibet, on the other hand, has seen its way of life displaced and its dreams deferred. Everyone expects violence. China is ignoring Tibet to death with a pretended respect that permits local stores, crafts, and workers to be run out of business by a flood of Chinese imports and immigrants. Native foods, clothes, manners, and the Tibetan language are supplanted. In the countryside, especially, people remember their old way of life. Will the anger that Badeng Nima found, and that the Chinese disregard, explode?

Ethnic and sectarian conflict challenges everyone involved—minorities, majorities, those who control the state and the institutions of civil society. To find ways to resolve such conflicts, it is necessary for all to react creatively, to understand what is at stake for each identity, and to create new identities that bridge yet respect the old, lest mutual distance fuel prejudice and violence.

The politics of ethnic and sectarian groups is not a zero-sum game, not simply an exercise in resource redistribution, because different identities have different aspirations. In Crimea, Russian history would predict a winner-take-all battle for ethnic dominance, while based on the Ottoman tradition, one would expect compromise and power sharing in a multiethnic, multireligious state. In Germany, those who do not wish to see German identity subsumed in European identity are also those most unwilling to accept Muslims or southern Europeans as fellow citizens.[7] It is not that Ottoman practice was necessarily better than Russian, or that the bonds of "constitutional patriotism" will necessarily provoke stronger ties between Germans than a common language, a sense of common history, and a sense of duty to fellow Christians (or a sense of Christian duty) has. But where identities differ, hopes, expectations, visions of the good, and understandings of what is sacred and profane differ. "Render to Caesar the things that are Caesar's, and to God the things that are God's," said Jesus in three of the Gospels. The coin of the realm of identity varies from moral framework to moral framework.

What, in sum, have we learned? We have approached identity in several steps. At the most general level, guided by Taylor, we explored why identity matters for all humans in any situation. We then considered nomothetic and idiographic approaches to conflict involving ethnic and sectarian identities. At the nomothetic level, we noted efforts, including those of our authors, to define laws or general features of ethnic or sectarian conflict and modes of resolution.[8]

We faced a paradox of sorts. A nomothetic generalization led us to an idiographic approach, resulting in another generalization: globalization throws identities into unavoidable contact. The complexity of the multiple relationships that this creates and the numerous opportunities for violent or productive conflict between moral frameworks it opens up demand an idiographic response, attentive to the particular nuances of each encounter.

How might we bridge the nomothetic and the idiographic? Our strategy was to return to the terms "ethnic" and "sectarian" and delineate the dimensions of each as a Weberian "ideal type." We constructed caricatures of actual identities, turning the pejorative connotations of "ethnicity" and "sect" to a useful purpose, creating a pair of extreme, well-defined, multidimensional polar opposites. Their utility is that they can be used as benchmarks against which to compare actual social identities, which should fall somewhere between the two extremes.

Finally, since the purpose of the ideal types is not to represent reality but rather to facilitate comparisons, we applied them, illustratively, to the cases presented by our authors. We saw that the types at least act as reminders for features to look for, but also, as Weber intended, that we must be alert to deviations from the types and to consider the implications of such variations.

"Identity matters" is a pun that juxtaposes two messages. With "matters" as a verb, the phrase asserts that identity makes a difference, that it carries energy, force, and impact. With "matters" as a noun, the phrase refers to substances and issues that affect identity, the stuff of life. The verb reminds us that social conflict occurs between and within moral frameworks as well as between economies and polities and within societies. Identities really do matter: we must respect their energy and force. The noun tells us that social identities have substantive qualities, and we must attend to these also. Identities must be grasped in their particulars, the symbols and social patterns in which moral frameworks are rooted. The verb directs us outward, toward the clash (or music) generated when the carriers of different identities come together. The noun directs us inward, toward the experience of identity and its sources.

What do these two directions entail in analysis? The outward direction pushes us to acknowledge context, the inward to grasp content. As social forces, identities are part of realpolitik, in Bismarck's sense; yet to comprehend each identity, we must practice *Verstehen*, in Weber's sense. Inquiries in either direction inform each other. You cannot fully understand how the threat of large neighbors shapes Singaporean identity, and how that identity affects those neighbors, without understanding the nature of Chinese, Indian, or Malay identity within Singapore and without asking similar questions about Malaysia, Indonesia, Thailand, the Philippines, China, and the social groups within them.

Together, then, the verb and the noun direct us to get down to cases. Generalizations about conflict are important as guides, but to assess how identities matter, we must analyze the particulars of each situation. One learns by doing, and our cases can serve as surrogates for experience. Pilots learn to fly aircraft today in simulations, making their mistakes in virtual reality rather than risking lives while learning. This volume serves a similar purpose: it provides practice cases for analysis as a step toward working in real situations. By analyzing cases, one can begin to fathom how, when, and where identity matters and what those matters entail.

This is not merely an academic exercise. The forces of identity can fuel commerce or chaos, creativity or destruction anywhere in the world. We all need to learn to understand the moral frameworks of those around us and assess how they relate to our own, asking if a fruitful alliance is possible or if a separate peace is achievable or if imminent, violent conflict must be averted, avoided, or accepted. To attempt this understanding is to run a risk, because cultural contact inevitably brings some change with it. That risk is unavoidable. In a globalizing world, maintaining any identity's purity through isolation is less and less possible.

Notes

1. As it happens, both authors are products of North American cultures similar to Taylor's—children of white, nominally Christian families, born and raised in the racially segregated US South, recipients of liberal educations, descendants of immigrants (religious refugees and Scotch-Irish overseers) and of millers, teachers, soldiers, engineers, tobacco farmers, both conservative and liberal newspaper editors, novelists, and healers. We find Taylor's terminology adequate to the task at hand because it seems to account for the variety of identities we have known at home, have observed while living in Europe and Asia, and have encountered in scholarship and in literature.

2. We endorse Weber's method but not all the particular findings of *The Protestant Ethic* ([1930] 1992). Numerous scholars, most recently summarized by Hamilton (1996: chap. 3), have pointed out that Weber misread the statistics he used to suggest a relationship between Protestantism and entrepreneurship, used sources selectively, and,

quite simply, succeeded only in suggesting a link between ideas and practices that may have emerged in the religious life of certain sects in the sixteenth through eighteenth centuries and the "steel-hard cage" of a work ethic that persists today. Economic historians, Hamilton shows, no longer cite Weber when they attempt to explain the rise of capitalism. Weber does not provide evidence that testifies to the juxtaposition, in the hearts of Protestant business owners, of the inner states of "unprecedented inner loneliness," anxiety for salvation, and determination to fulfill one's calling. What Weber *does* provide, however, is a vision of how overarching values and a worldview, as illustrated by Protestant Puritanism, could transform societies and psychologies. His insight can help us understand human motivation not only in early America and industrializing Britain and Germany but in today's world, when neo-Calvinistic analogues propel globalization in Asia and elsewhere. Our goal here is to suggest how social scientists can help facilitate communication between identities. *Verstehen* imputes a meaningful purpose to the behavior of the other and attempts to make those purposes and meanings explicit. Weber may not have lived up to his intentions—*The Protestant Ethic* can be read as evidence of the disdain of an ivory tower scholar for the dirty world of moneymaking—but *Verstehen* requires respect, the acknowledgment that the other's motives may make as much sense as one's own, and the acceptance that there are ideas and principles in each of our lives that have the power we attribute to religion, clan loyalty, racism, utopianism.

3. The society's defenders may attempt to isolate the infiltrators, labeling them "outside agitators." Examples drawn from the history of the US South include Christians, opponents of slavery, carpetbaggers, union organizers, and proponents of racial equality.

4. For those unfamiliar with Shakespeare, Romeo and Juliet are two teenagers whose families are at odds. Mercutio is Romeo's best friend. The Nurse and Friar are inadequate guides to the couple as they meet and marry in secret.

5. Hobbes's preference was for a Christian monarch, but his purpose in writing, his friend John Aubrey ([ca. 1680] 1951) tells us, was to justify the submission of the Royalists to Parliament once the latter's victory was assured.

6. Samuel Huntington's thesis (1996) is at once prescient, controversial, and unavoidable in discussion of ethnic and sectarian conflict. Much commentary, including that of several authors in this book, is critical, faulting Huntington for exaggerating both unities within "civilizations" and differences among them, resulting in a picture of Islam, the West, and Asia as divided absolutely ("never the twain shall meet" as Kipling once said, famously, of East and West) and on a collision course. Critics, such as Waseem, emphasize instead that so-called civilizations such as Islam and the West, in fact, overlap greatly owing to histories of interaction, and that many situations and persons exemplify cross-overs and mixing among cultures rather than sharp and absolute boundaries.

We recognize both the power and the problems in Huntington's analysis. A comparison with it may clarify our own alternative but related approach. Huntington argues that after the end of the Cold War between communism and capitalism, represented by coalitions of nations allied with the US and the USSR, cultural identities, which he calls "civilizations," emerged as the colliding forces in international affairs. He injects cultural anthropology into political science, finding the root values and motivations of contending parties in their cultural heritages and identities, but he does not abandon political science; he analyzes how these identities are mobilized in political and military conflict.

We share with Huntington this thesis that "identities matter" in international relations. We differ in our level of analysis; his is macro, ours more micro. He gives a big picture, emphasizing a few major identities in the world that clash, while we dig into smaller domains—a particular nation, a particular rebellion—to analyze how, in such locales, certain identities (including the civilizational ones) are constituted and how they clash or co-exist. The two approaches, his and ours, are complementary; both are needed, and to criticize Huntington, as many do, because he ignores microcomplexity is to fail to credit him with mapping major forces, identities, and conflicts that, in fact, are shaping our world today.

A close reading of Huntington shows that he does recognize complexities within and interactions among cultures to an extent. However, he distills the complex variations into a small number of so-called civilizations, most prominent of which are the three noted—Islam, the West, and the East—and he emphasizes the "fault lines" that divide them. Academic analysts might term these major identities or civilizations "ideal types," abstractions from the complexities of life, but Huntington, who states at the outset that his book "is not intended to be a work of social science" but rather to be a "meaningful and useful lens through which to view international developments" (1996: 13–14), presents civilizations as a dramatist would characters in a play performed on a world stage. No playwright would deny that characters are fictionalized and compressed representations, simplified to fit into a plot. That is Huntington's technique. Like the dramatist, he avoids taking his audience backstage, boring them by explicating his method, i.e., abstraction. Instead, he performs the play. He presents the abstracted characters and their logically implied, historically unfolding interactions.

The result is informed, insightful, compelling, and provocative. Yet it is often misunderstood or even reviled. Because it depicts differences, *The Clash of Civilizations and the Remaking of World Order* is thought to encourage and exacerbate them, and because it describes conflict, it is blamed for igniting it. Any attempt to epitomize world cultures must sacrifice some detail and nuance. Charles Tilly (2002: chap. 6), writing about the macro-micro problem, once noted that writers and readers want a story with characters and a plot, but lamented that social phenomena do not unfold that way. Huntington, with a keen ear to audiences, as well as brilliant insights into social forces, presents a fable that often, regrettably, comes true. (Remember that he wrote long before 9/11.)

Our own approach is both similar and different. We say up front that our types are "ideal," i.e., abstracted, simplified. The purpose of our types is different from Huntington's. He wants to define the key actors on the world stage; we want to define key dimensions (ethnic and sectarian) that can illuminate actors on many stages and in many situations, whether global or localized. He highlights the dynamics of world conflict; we highlight some features that apply to many conflicts. He treats one big case, the world; we offer an aid to thinking about many cases, many situations. In a word, his is a substantive theory, a singular vision of what is happening in the world; ours is an analytical scheme that can be used to make sense of actual and potential conflicts and may inform many interpretations.

7. As we write this, this seems even more true in France.

8. In fact, while generalizing from the cases during the Fulbright discussions, twenty-two such "bullets" or aphorisms were suggested, many of which are researched and applied frequently. Among them is the "contact hypothesis," which postulates that contact between groups with different identities tends, on the whole, to dampen conflict—a postulate as obvious as it is debatable, but supported by some 2,500 studies, according to Pettigrew.

References

Aubrey, John. [ca. 1680] 1951. "The Life of Mr Thomas Hobbes of Malmesburie." In *English Biography in the Seventeenth Century: Selected Short Lives*, ed. Vivian de Sola Pinto, 168–189. London: George G. Harrap.

Baggett, John. 2005. "Seeing Through the Eyes of Jesus." Unpublished manuscript.

Burger, Thomas. 1987. *Max Weber's Theory of Concept Formation: History, Laws, and Ideal Types*. Expanded ed. Durham, NC: Duke University Press.

Collier, Paul, V. L. Elliott, Håvard Hegre, Anke Hoeffler, Marta Reynal-Querol, and Nicholas Sambanis. 2003. *Breaking the Conflict Trap: Civil War and Development Policy: A World Bank Policy Research Report*. Washington, DC: The World Bank.

Craig, Gordon A. 1978. *Germany 1866–1945*. London and New York: Oxford University Press.

Douglas, Mary. [1970] 2003. *Natural Symbols: Explorations in Cosmology*. 2nd ed. London and New York: Routledge Classics.

Ellis, Richard J., and Michael Thompson. 1997. *Culture Matters: Essays in Honor of Aaron Wildavsky*. Boulder, CO: Westview Press.

Elshtain, Jean Bethke. 1995. *Democracy on Trial*. New York: Basic Books.

Gilmore, David D., ed. 1987. *Honor and Shame and the Unity of the Mediterranean*. Washington, DC: American Anthropological Association.

Ginzburg, Carlo. 1989. "Clues: Roots of an Evidential Paradigm." In *Clues, Myths, and the Historical Method*, trans. John and Anne C. Tedeschi, 96–125, 200–214. Baltimore, MD: Johns Hopkins University Press.

Hamilton, Richard F. 1996. *The Social Misconstruction of Reality: Validity and Verification in the Scholarly Community*. New Haven, CT: Yale University Press.

Harff, Barbara. 2003. "No Lessons Learned from the Holocaust? Assessing Risks of Genocide and Political Mass Murder since 1955." *American Political Science Review* 97, no. 1: 57–73.

Herzfeld, Michael. 1992. *The Social Production of Indifference: Exploring the Symbolic Roots of Western Bureaucracy*. Chicago: University of Chicago Press.

Hirschman, Albert O. 1970. *Exit, Voice, and Loyalty: Responses to Decline in Firms, Organizations, and States*. Cambridge, MA: Harvard University Press.

_____. 1977. *The Passions and the Interests: Political Arguments for Capitalism before Its Triumph*. Princeton, NJ: Princeton University Press.

Hobbes, Thomas. [1651] 1998. *Leviathan, or The Matter, Forme, & Power of a Commonwealth Ecclesiasticall and Civill*. Ed. J. C. A. Gaskin. Oxford: Oxford University Press.

Huntington, Samuel. 1996. *The Clash of Civilizations and the Remaking of World Order*. New York: Touchstone.

Jacob, Margaret C., and Matthew Kadane. 2003. "Missing, Now Found in the Eighteenth Century: Weber's Protestant Capitalist." *American Historical Review* 108, no. 1: 20–49.

Kittay, Eva Feder. 1999. *Love's Labor: Essays on Women, Equality, and Dependency*. New York: Routledge.

Kuhn, Thomas S. [1962] 1996. *The Structure of Scientific Revolutions*. 3rd ed. Chicago: University of Chicago Press.

Leach, Edmund. 1954. *Political Systems of Highland Burma: A Study of Kachin Social Structure*. Cambridge, MA: Harvard University Press.

McLemore, Lelan. 1984. "Max Weber's Defense of Historical Inquiry." *History and Theory* 23, no. 3: 277–295.

Pateman, Carole. [1979] 1985. *The Problem of Political Obligation: A Critique of Liberal Theory*. Reprint. Berkeley: University of California Press.

_____. 1989. "Sublimation and Reification: Locke, Wolin, and the Liberal-Democratic Conception of the Political." In *The Disorder of Women: Democracy, Feminism, and Political Theory*, 90–117. Stanford, CA: Stanford University Press.

Peristiany, J. G., ed. 1966. *Honour and Shame: The Values of Mediterranean Society*. Chicago: University of Chicago Press.

Scott, James C. 1998. *Seeing Like a State: How Certain Schemes to Improve the Human Condition Have Failed*. New Haven, CT: Yale University Press.

Smith, Anthony D. 1998. *Nationalism and Modernism: A Critical Survey of Recent Theories of Nations and Nationalism*. New York: Routledge.

Szelényi, Balázs. Forthcoming. "The German Diaspora of Hungary, Slovakia, and Romania." *Past and Present*.

Taylor, Charles. 1989. *Sources of the Self: The Making of the Modern Identity*. Cambridge, MA: Harvard University Press.

Thompson, Michael, Richard Ellis, and Aaron Wildavsky. 1990. *Cultural Theory*. Boulder, CO: Westview Press.

Thompson, Michael, Gunnar Grendstad, and Per Selle. 1999. *Cultural Theory as Political Science*. London and New York: Routledge.

Tilly, Charles. 2002. *Stories, Identities, and Political Change*. New York: Rowan and Littlefield.

Tronto, Joan C. 1993. *Moral Boundaries: A Political Argument for an Ethic of Care*. New York: Routledge.

Volkan, Vamik. 1997. *Bloodlines: From Ethnic Pride to Ethnic Terrorism*. Boulder, CO: Westview Press.

Weber, Marianne. 1975. *Max Weber: A Biography*. Trans. and ed. Harry Zohn. New York: John Wiley and Sons.

Weber, Max. [1930] 1992. *The Protestant Ethic and the Spirit of Capitalism*. Trans. Talcott Parsons. New York: Routledge.

_____. 1952. "The Protestant Sects and the Spirit of Capitalism." In *From Max Weber*, trans. and ed. H. H. Gerth and C. Wright Mills. London: Routledge and Kegan Paul.

_____. 1962. *Basic Concepts in Sociology*. Trans. H. P. Secher. London: Peter Owen.

_____. 1978. *Economy and Society: An Outline of Interpretive Sociology*. Ed. Guenther Roth and Claus Wittich. 2 vols. Berkeley: University of California Press.

Wikan, Unni. 2002. *Generous Betrayal: Politics of Culture in the New Europe*. Chicago: University of Chicago Press.

Winnicott, D. W. 1971. *Playing and Reality*. New York: Tavistock Publications.

Wolin, Sheldon S. 1996. "Fugitive Democracy." In *Democracy and Difference: Contesting the Boundaries of the Political*, ed. Seyla Benhabib, 31–45. Princeton, NJ: Princeton University Press.

Yoshino, Kenji. 2006. *Covering: The Hidden Assault on Our Civil Rights*. New York: Random House.

INDEX

Page numbers in italics refer to figures and tables.